# THE SERMON
## ON THE MOUNT

# THE SERMON ON THE MOUNT

## *The* CHARACTER *of a* DISCIPLE

DANIEL M. DORIANI

P&R
PUBLISHING

P.O. BOX 817 • PHILLIPSBURG • NEW JERSEY 08865-0817

*Page design and typesetting by Lakeside Design Plus*

Printed in the United States of America

**Library of Congress Cataloging-in-Publication Data**
Doriani, Daniel M., 1953–
    The Sermon on the mount : the character of a disciple / Daniel M. Doriani.
        p. cm.
    Includes bibliographical references and index.
    ISBN-13: 978-1-59638-003-5 (paper)
    ISBN-10: 1-59638-003-9 (paper)
    1. Sermon on the mount. I. Title.
BT380.3.D67  2006
226.9'06—dc22
                                                                2006043176

# CONTENTS

# 1

# Reading and Interpreting the Sermon on the Mount

Among Jesus' teachings, the Sermon on the Mount is perhaps the most beloved, the best known, the least understood, and the hardest to obey. Its attraction is obvious.

## The Appeal of the Sermon

The Sermon on the Mount opens with sweet promises: "Blessed are those who mourn, for they will be comforted. . . . Blessed are the peacemakers, for they will be called sons of God" (Matt. 5:4, 9). It describes disciples in stirring terms: "You are the salt of the earth. . . . You are the light of the world. . . . Let your light shine before men, that they may see your good deeds and praise your Father in heaven" (5:13–14, 16).

Jesus' sermon presents noble values in appealing terms. He promotes peace when he commands estranged brothers to seek reconciliation (5:23–24). He defends the sanctity of marriage when he forbids lust and divorce (5:27–32). He advocates truth-telling when he says, "Let your 'Yes' be 'Yes,' and your 'No,' 'No'" (5:37).

The sermon often presents ideas that secular society admires. Society respects sincerity and integrity, and Jesus warns against practicing righteousness before an audience (6:1). Society is skeptical of materialism, and Jesus says that we should never treat money as a god (6:19–24). Society dislikes a judgmental spirit, and Jesus says, "Do not judge, or you too will be judged" (7:1). It is no wonder, then, that the Sermon on the Mount is loved by Christians and admired by secular people.

## THE RIGOR OF THE SERMON

The Sermon on the Mount is as daunting as it is appealing. We may be the light of the world, but we still fail to meet God's standards. Jesus says that anyone who is angry with his brother is subject to judgment (5:22). Anyone who looks at a woman lustfully has committed adultery in his heart (5:28–29). Anyone who receives a blow to the right cheek from an evil person must "turn to him the other also" (5:39). The demands rise to a crescendo when Jesus says, "Love your enemies and pray for those who persecute you" (5:44), and, "Be perfect, therefore, as your heavenly Father is perfect" (5:48).

No one can meet such standards. The rigor of Jesus' precepts is both exciting and demoralizing. His sermon is penetrating, almost *too* penetrating, as he analyzes our motives. He knows that when we perform a good deed, we secretly hope that someone will notice it and recognize us for it: "Be careful not to do your 'acts of righteousness' before men, to be seen by them" (6:1). Instead, we must give in secret, pray in secret, and fast in secret, so that our Father will see and reward in secret (6:3–6, 16–18).

These commands provoke self-examination. Do I practice righteousness to be seen by men? If so, does that prove that God is not my Father? Further, if I hide my deeds from men, so only God will see them, but then think much of God's reward and little of God himself, is that another sin?

The Sermon on the Mount shows how easily pride and self-interest become false gods, even when religious people are performing religious duties. But then, lest anyone think that Jesus singles out the religious, he shifts to worldly folk who fix their thoughts on wealth: "No one can serve two masters. . . . You cannot serve both God and Money" (6:24).

## THE AUTHORITY OF THE SERMON

Confronted with this challenging ethic, a critical reader will step back and evaluate it. Even if he admires Jesus' clarity and consistency, he may muse, "I'm a thinking person. I cannot submit to a moral code grounded in a worldview that features angels in heaven, demons in hell, and miracles on earth. Jesus was a wise sage, but also a premodern peasant. I cannot surrender my autonomy to him." A gentler agnostic may wish to enter into a dialogue with Jesus. She may be open to his words, even willing to let them change her, but she will remain the final arbiter of her truth.

Yet disciples know that Jesus has the right to expect submission to his word, for Matthew reveals that Jesus is the son of Abraham and the son of David, anointed to save people from their sins. He is Immanuel, "God with us" (Matt. 1:1, 16, 21, 23). He is greater than Moses. Like Moses, Jesus ascends a mountain to deliver law to his people (Ex. 19:20, 25; Matt. 5:1). As the Decalogue begins, the Lord declares that he brought Israel out of Egypt and made them a nation (Ex. 20:2). Shortly before the sermon begins, Jesus announces his kingdom (Matt. 4:17). Moses speaks directly to his people, saying "You shall not" or "You shall" (Ex. 20:3–17). Jesus directly addresses his disciples, saying "You are . . ." or "When you . . ." and uttering dozens of commandments.

When I was a professor, I learned to accept two awkward questions from students. The first arose when I spoke too fast: "You said there were four reasons for your conclusion, but I only have three; could you please repeat all four?" Too often I had to say, "Sorry, I had three in my notes; the last one came to me spontaneously and I've already forgotten it." The second arose on those rare occasions when a student detected a change in my thinking: "I heard you address this two years ago and I believe you took a different position then." There are escape clauses for such moments: "Yes, but I have now superseded that stage in my intellectual development." Witticisms aside, if a teacher changes his view, then either the previous opinion is wrong or the current opinion is wrong—or both. Jesus never faced that problem. He never changed his mind, never forgot what he had said.

There is always a gap between our words and our thoughts, but Jesus' words perfectly represent his thinking. He never had to correct himself or explain what he "meant" to say. Whoever hears Jesus' words hears *him*. His words perfectly express his convictions; they also represent his character. His thought, his character, and his actions are wholly consistent. If we follow his word, we become more like him, and that

3

is a blessed thing (Matt. 5:3–12).[1] That is another reason to accept the authority of his every word (7:28).

The clarity and power of Jesus' teaching is stirring, yet alarming, because honest people know that they cannot obey it. Some believe that it is also impractical, since it calls disciples to turn the other cheek and to give to all who ask, and these are hardly strategies calibrated for survival in a rough world. Taking the beauty, the authority, and the rigor together, it is no wonder that the church struggles to interpret the Sermon on the Mount.

## THE INTERPRETATION OF THE SERMON[2]

Some verses in the Sermon on the Mount are difficult to grasp, but overall the parts are easier to follow than the whole. Above all, Jesus seems to preach an ethic that no one can obey. Why does Jesus imply that only the obedient can enter his kingdom? He says, "Not everyone who says to me, 'Lord, Lord,' will enter the kingdom of heaven, but only he who does the will of my Father who is in heaven" (7:21). In isolation, that statement seems to contradict the gospel itself.

At times, the sermon reads like a string of commandments. But if it is simply a series of commands, its beauty is a burden and its commands condemn. Since Jesus did not come to condemn, theologians have interpreted the sermon in ways that retain Jesus' authority, yet reduce his demands.

Thomas Aquinas, a medieval theologian, suggested that ordinary Christians need not observe the sermon's hardest laws. He thought that the Bible presents a two-tiered ethic: the first tier applies to every Christian, but the second tier (the "counsels of perfection") is expedient, not mandatory. On this view, Jesus' most stringent laws are optional, given especially to those who seek Christlike perfection.[3] This idea coheres with the distinction that medieval Christians drew between clergy and laity. The clergy followed a higher calling and had higher duties, such as chastity (no marriage), poverty (no possessions), and obedience to the clerical hierarchy. Theologians appealed to Matthew 19, where Jesus seems to present celibacy as an option for disciples: "Let the one who is able to receive this receive it" (19:12 ESV). But Matthew 19 merely says that people have different callings, and that thought cannot support

4

Aquinas's two-tiered paradigm. And while the two-tiered ethic does remove some of the burden of the sermon, Jesus never hinted that any of his commands was optional.

Some early Protestants favored a simple, literal reading of the sermon. They saw Jesus as the supreme teacher who presents laws that we should strive to obey, whatever the cost. Since Jesus forbids violence (5:38–39), they said that no Christian could be a soldier, judge, or magistrate. And since Jesus forbids vows (5:33–37), a disciple cannot take a vow for any purpose—even to become a citizen, let alone to hold public office. Eventually, literal obedience led these people to withdraw from mainstream society. But literalism prompts questions. First, how can disciples be the light of the world if they withdraw from it? Second, if we read the sermon as law, have we obscured God's grace and gospel?

Lutheran theologians had a ready answer for the latter question. They argued that honest readers have to conclude that no one can obey all of Jesus' precepts. Therefore, Jesus' law, like Moses' law, is a tutor that leads people to Christ. As Jesus intensifies Moses' law and then adds his own laws, he drives sensitive readers to despair of their ability to obey. That despair prepares them to receive the gospel. Thus, Lutherans turn to Paul to decipher the Sermon on the Mount. Paul says that the law presents its standards and the principle "Do this and you will live" (see Gal. 3:10–12; Luke 10:28). Since people cannot "do this," they fall under God's curse. Fearing that curse, they turn to Christ. Luther said that the law only brings us to "the knowledge that by our own ability we cannot properly fulfill an iota of it . . . but must always creep to Christ."[4]

There are other views of the Sermon on the Mount. Classic liberals say that it presents the fatherhood of God and the brotherhood of man. Existential theologians say that the sermon is Jesus' guide to authentic living. However they put it, most of these interpretations read the sermon as law—law that tells us what to do and how to cope after we fail.

The sermon certainly contains a great number of commands; the original Greek has fifty imperatives. But a high number of commands does not prove that the sermon is *essentially* legal. Indeed, if we consider the sermon's audience and theme, we will see that it describes more than it commands. Specifically, it does not command people to do this or that in order to enter the kingdom or remain in it. Rather, it *describes* life in the kingdom.

## THE AUDIENCE FOR THE SERMON

The context shows that the Sermon on the Mount is primarily for those who are already disciples. Jesus has been proclaiming the coming of his kingdom (Matt. 4:17, 23), and now he needs to describe life in it. Jesus has started to gather disciples (4:18–22) and must explain what it means to follow him. He is attracting great throngs, largely because of the miracles and the spectacle (4:23–25). He needs to ensure that people follow him for the right reasons. Above all, we know that the sermon is for disciples because Matthew says that Jesus called his disciples out of the crowds and taught them: "Now when he saw the crowds, he went up on a mountainside and sat down. His *disciples* came to him, and he began to teach *them*" (5:1–2).

Jesus fills his sermon with indications that he is addressing disciples, men and women who have already entered the kingdom of God.

1. Jesus begins by blessing those who know their need for God's grace. The Beatitudes begin: "Blessed are the poor in spirit" (5:3).
2. Jesus tells his hearers to expect persecution for his sake (5:11–12).
3. Jesus tells them that they already share in kingdom life and benefits. When he blesses the poor in spirit and the persecuted, he adds, "For theirs is the kingdom of heaven" (5:3, 10).
4. Jesus' hearers know God as their Father (5:16, 48; 6:1).
5. They already practice spiritual disciplines. He does not tell them that they ought to give, pray, and fast. Rather, he assumes that they do these things: "When you give . . . When you pray . . . When you fast" (6:2, 5, 16).

When Jesus forbids anger and lust, he assumes that his audience has an interest in God's will that extends from external deeds to internal attitudes. As the sermon probes the meaning of Moses' law, it presupposes an interest in that law. Such an interest is a mark of belonging to the family of God. Thus, Jesus' sermon primarily speaks to disciples. We listen to Jesus and strive to obey him, not in order to gain entry into the kingdom, but to live faithfully within it.

Although the disciples are Jesus' primary audience, the crowds listen in, as people often do when they sit within earshot of an interesting conversation. The crowds will not suffer persecution for Jesus' sake, and they cannot embrace the worldview or the ethic of the sermon, unless they repent. But they can learn what the Christian worldview and ethic are; they can discover the meaning of discipleship. After Jesus called his disciples to himself (5:1–2), members of "the crowds" filtered in behind them. Therefore, as he concluded his message, Jesus invited the crowds to follow him, call on him, obey him, and bear fruit for him (7:13–27). When he finished teaching, "the crowds were amazed," because he taught with such authority (7:28–29).

## THE TOPIC OF THE SERMON: LIFE IN THE KINGDOM

It is mistaken to view the Sermon on the Mount as an essentially legal message. It is mistaken to think that Jesus propounds laws that one must keep in order to enter the kingdom or to obtain God's favor.

Matthew carefully locates the *words* of Christ *to* the disciples in the context of the *work* of Christ *for* the disciples. To make that clear, Matthew places accounts of Jesus' miracles immediately before and immediately after the sermon (4:21–25; 8:1–9:34). In Matthew 4, Jesus says, "Repent, for the kingdom of heaven is near." A few verses later, he recounts miracles that demonstrate that the kingdom has dawned (4:17, 21–25). Matthew highlights the unity of Jesus' words and works by using a specific summary of Jesus' ministry. Using virtually identical language, Matthew 4:23 and 9:35 both say that Jesus went through Galilee "teaching in their synagogues, preaching the good news of the kingdom, and healing every disease and sickness." The repetition of 4:23 in 9:35 marks these summary passages as bookends that unify all of Jesus' works and words in Matthew 4–9. In the sermon, in chapters 5–7, Jesus' teaching makes infinite demands. In his signs, in chapters 4 and 8–9, Jesus manifests infinite, loving power to bless his people.

Clearly, Matthew invites his readers to see the *demands* of Christ in the context of the *gifts* of Christ. He heals his people (4:23–25), then teaches them (5:1–7:29), and then heals them again (8:1–9:34). His instruction of mankind carries the same power as his "instruction" of nature, for he speaks with authority in both cases. The people marvel at the authority of Jesus' word as he teaches (7:29); they also marvel at the authority of his word as he heals (9:6–8; cf. Luke 4:31–37, which also links his authoritative teaching and his authoritative healing). Jesus commands people and commands nature and expects both to obey. Indeed, Jesus frequently performs a miracle by speaking a command to nature, so that nature is more obedient than mankind. A perceptive centurion recognizes Jesus' authority over nature. He says, "Just say the word, and my servant will be healed" (Matt. 8:8). Jesus drives out evil spirits "with a word" (8:16). By his word, he stills the raging sea (8:26), expels demons (8:32), and forgives sins (9:6).

We see, therefore, that the Sermon on the Mount is the word of King Jesus to his people. But Jesus' main goal in the sermon is not to declare laws, even laws for disciples. Above all, he describes the disciples' way of life under his authority. With about fifty imperatives in roughly one hundred sentences, we certainly hear Jesus' commands.[5] Since the King has arrived and begun to reign, Jesus' commands explain how disciples ought to live under his authority. It is true that Jesus delivers one command after another—the sermon does have fifty imperatives. But it also has about 320 verbs that are not commands.[6]

If we simply count verbs, the sermon describes more than it commands.[7] Of course, it is better to consider the tenor of the sermon, paragraph by paragraph, and that leads to the same conclusion. The Beatitudes describe the character of a disciple and the rewards that God promises them (5:3–12). The "salt and light" passage presents the effect that a disciple has upon this world (5:13–16). The next section describes Jesus' devotion to the law and righteousness (5:17–20).

Even a command-laden section like 5:21–48 features illustrations, metaphors, and graphic images that appeal to the imagination—the way we see the world. In these paragraphs, angry people leave gifts at the altar and warring people make peace at the courtroom door. Men throw away eyes to avoid lust. They turn their cheeks to violent men and give their coats to people who sue them for their shirts. Jesus commands all this, but is literal obedience his sole concern? If it is, why are churches not filled with one-eyed Christians? With all of these images (and many more), Jesus both propounds laws and promotes a mind-set. The topics are murder, adultery, lying, and revenge, but the gripping imagery invites the mind to hear more than law. Once we see the world as Jesus does, we can apply his principles to new situations. Images abound in the final section (7:13–27), too: people choose roads, wolves dress like sheep, trees bear fruit, and storms lash houses. Throughout, Jesus teaches us how to see more than a set of specific, literal commands. And he always maintains a keen interest in a disciple's heart and motives.

Even in passages that are filled with imperatives, Jesus does not simply tell us what to do; he invites us to see the world as he does. Matthew 6 has its share of commands, but Jesus' main focus is on a series of heart issues: pride, worry, the misguided interest in reputation and the misguided interest in wealth, our loyalty to God, and our trust in him.

The sermon also has quite a few questions: Can tasteless salt restore its saltiness? Do tax collectors love each other? What does worrying accomplish? Can it lengthen life? Do fathers dole out stones when their hungry children ask for food? Do grapes grow on thornbushes? Each question invites us to ponder a life issue. The last chapter also poses implicit questions: What kind of fruit will you bear? What kind of confession will you make? What road will you take? Upon what foundation will you build (7:13–27)?

The Sermon on the Mount is also highly theological. It mentions God over twenty times. It tells us that he dwells in heaven and sees all things, that he does good to all people, but rewards good and punishes evil. He knows us and our needs, hears our prayers, and forgives our sins. As the sovereign Lord, he counts our hairs, clothes the grass, and feeds the birds. He also makes promises, which are God's declarations of how he acts. Six beatitudes end with a promise. He comforts those who mourn, ensures that the meek inherit the earth, and guarantees that the pure will see God (5:3–9). He promises to meet our needs and to give us what we ask for (6:31–33; 7:7–8).

Finally, the sermon describes the aspirations of God's people. We pray that God's kingdom will come (6:10, 33) and that we will possess a righteousness that suits us for it (5:19–20; cf. 7:21). The sermon also instills hope in blessings to be received on the last day. Then we will inherit the earth, see God, and become righteous (5:5–8). So then, the Sermon on the Mount is law, but much more than law. It tells us what we should do, but it also describes who we are and should be. It probes our character and invites us to see the world in a new way, as Jesus sees it.

## THE GOSPEL IN THE SERMON

We have seen that the Sermon on the Mount is more than the law of Christ, but does it lead us to the gospel of Christ? There is a path from the sermon to the gospel if we turn to Paul's letters. Jesus blesses those who hunger and thirst for righteousness, and Paul tells us how God ultimately satisfies that desire. When we repent of our sin and turn to Christ, God grants us his righteousness. This answer is true and important, yet it does not come from Matthew. Can we find grace, mercy, and gospel in the Sermon on the Mount itself? We can—in four ways.

First, Jesus' disciples are his primary audience, and they already know about grace. Jesus begins his sermon with the words "Blessed are the poor in spirit." To be poor in spirit is to know our spiritual neediness (see the next chapter). The poor in spirit know that we cannot behave as we should, that we cannot deliver ourselves from our weaknesses or sins. By the end of the sermon, we can feel overwhelmed by its breadth and depth. If we feel that burden and cannot obey all the words of Christ, then we can return to the beginning. From the beginning, Jesus blesses all those who know their need for grace.

An unbeliever will respond to the Sermon on the Mount either with foolish optimism: "I can do this!"—or with hopeless despair: "I can never do this." Only a believer, a child of God, can rightly respond to its high standards. As John Stott says, we cannot achieve that status by reaching Christ's standards. Rather, by approximating them, "we give evidence of what, by God's free grace and gift, we already are."[8]

Jesus makes a similar point later in the sermon. As Matthew 6 ends, he has presented his essential ethic. Soon he will issue his call to discipleship (7:13–27). But first, the famous "Judge not" section (7:1–5) leads us to grace. Drawing on the context, we can paraphrase Jesus this way:

> After hearing my teaching, you will be tempted to use it to judge others. Don't do it. Don't listen and then think of friends who *really* need the message. Don't find specks in others' eyes, while logs hang out of yours. If you judge others, the same standard will be used on you, for you will have shown that you know the rules. When you violate your own standards, you have no excuse. Instead of criticizing others, examine yourself first, and then perhaps you can instruct others.

Instead of using his law to condemn others, Jesus says, evaluate yourself. Then, when you see the depth of your need, ask for grace. To put it another way, while the command to ask, seek, and knock in Matthew 7:7 does invite disciples to take their desires to God, the context suggests something more specific. Since Jesus has just described his high standards for discipleship, we should ask for the ability to obey and for mercy when we fall short. This point suggests the second path from the sermon's ethic to the gospel.

Second, therefore, the sermon can prepare one for the gospel. It teaches listeners to turn to Jesus for grace when they see their inability to obey him. An unbeliever who hears the sermon and feels its weight may feel guilt, even despair. If the Holy Spirit is at work, that unbeliever will seek a remedy. Thus, the Lutheran perspective (discussed above) has a point. The commands of Jesus do set us thinking: Can my poor deeds shine so brightly that they bring glory to God (5:16)? Can my righteousness—my external observance of the law—exceed that of the scribes and the Pharisees (5:20)? Can I avoid all anger and lust (5:22–28)? Can I be perfect, as God is perfect (5:48)? Since we cannot, Jesus bids us to ask for grace. He says, "Ask and it will be given to you"—that is, God will give you grace.[9] By pointing out our sin and inability, the sermon leads us to the cross of Christ, where we find the grace that forgives our sin.

Third, as Jesus ends his message, he invites people to come to God. He sets four choices before them.

There are two roads (7:13–14). One is easy now, but leads to destruction. The other is narrow now, but leads to life. Which road will you take?

Two trees bear two kinds of fruit (7:15–20). As a fruitless tree deceives people from a distance, so a wicked person can deceive others for a time. But eventually our words and deeds reveal our hearts. What fruit do you bear? What does it reveal?

People call on Jesus in two ways (7:21–23). Do you call on his name sincerely or superficially? Do your actions confirm or invalidate your claim of faith?

Two builders construct houses on different foundations (7:24–27). In dry weather, both look sound, but when the rain comes and the rivers rise, they reveal the quality of the builders' work. Just so, many creeds seem valid when life is easy. But when storms come, only the house built on Christ will stand. Upon what foundation do you build?

Jesus says that the wise man builds his house upon "the rock." Since we expect him to say "a rock," we wonder if he has a particular rock in mind. The Bible often compares God to a rock. He is the foundation on which his people build. He is the rock or shelter in storms and in the wilderness (Pss. 31:2–3; 42:9; 62:1–7; 78:35; 92:15; 94:22; 95:1). Later, when Peter confesses that Jesus is the Christ, the Son of the living God, Jesus replies, "On this rock I will build my church" (Matt. 16:18). Jesus is "the rock," the foundation that we seek.

Fourth, the Sermon on the Mount leads us to Christ and his gospel by virtue of its location in Matthew's gospel. After Jesus teaches, he accomplishes our salvation, dying on the cross and rising on the third day. The Jesus who gave the law also gave his life as a ransom for those who do follow his law (20:28). Matthew shows that Jesus was willing to pay for the sins of both moral and immoral people, people who work hard at obedience and people who do not work at all. He gave himself for disciples who could not even pray with him for an hour, even his hour of greatest need. Thus, the sermon is not a self-contained legal unit. It stands within a narrative that presents the person and work of Jesus Christ.

Once we see how the Sermon on the Mount leads us to the gospel, its beauty and authority remain intact, but its burden is lifted. Jesus' words reveal his will, his character, and his grace. His will we cannot perfectly follow, and his character we will never perfectly attain, but his grace is sufficient for those (in the language of 7:21–23) who call on his name with a sincere desire to know him and be known by him.

# 2

# A Blessed Character

As an exercise, I sometimes invite a group to list traits they admire, traits they wish they, their spouses, the children, or their friends possessed. People list certain traits over and over: loyalty, faithfulness, trustworthiness, kindness. We admire people who are agreeable, energetic, and funny; intelligent, sensitive, and wise. Most of these lists are solid, but it is also interesting to notice what is missing. They usually fail to mention the classic virtues of courage, wisdom, temperance, justice, and endurance, even though they received the imprimatur of Greek, Roman, and medieval culture. Occasionally, someone lists humility, but no one has yet said that they aspire to meekness or poverty of spirit, even though Jesus starts there.

Perhaps, therefore, we should not view the Beatitudes as a list of ordinary virtues. The first three beatitudes describe weakness and neediness, rather than strength. In the abstract, almost no one will declare a desire to be poor in sprit, mournful, or meek. Of course, Jesus' teaching is not abstract. He has just been proclaiming the good news of the kingdom and verifying his claim to power with his public healings (Matt. 4:23–24).

The miracles made Jesus popular. But Jesus wanted *disciples*, not crowds, so he called a few men to himself. To do so, he separated them from the crowds, for the crowds did not necessarily follow him for the best reasons. They were curious and eager for healing. But mere popularity and miracle working could not fulfill the purpose of the incarnation.

13

Jesus never intended to heal all the sick in Israel. He sought to raise up true disciples.

So Jesus called his disciples to himself, sat down, and began to teach them (5:1–2). The crowds were free to listen in (7:28), but the Sermon on the Mount was given primarily to Jesus' disciples. It describes the heart, mind, outlook, and values of a disciple.

## THE NATURE OF A BLESSED CHARACTER

As we know, each beatitude begins with the words "Blessed are." The Greek term translated "blessed" is *makarios*. It can mean "happy" or even "carefree." But since Jesus goes on to say, "Blessed are those who mourn," we know he does not have ordinary happiness, the happiness that comes from food or entertainment, in mind. Jesus' "happy" disciples are poor and hungry; they mourn and suffer persecution. For disciples, happiness means wholeness and integrity even in the darkest hour.

We ought to be interested in Jesus' concept of happiness. We certainly pursue happiness. We seek it in better food, funnier jokes, and more exciting vacations or movies. Consider the amusement park. There we lay down substantial sums of money for the privilege of standing in long lines on ninety-degree pavement to sit in a short ride that promises to put our heart in our throat and threatens to put our lunch in our lap. A trip to an amusement park often turns into a chore, teaching us that happiness, like friendship, is best found when we are not necessarily looking for it, when we are busy at something else.

Jesus says that real happiness—blessedness—comes from mature character. Physical pleasures are fragile. If we take pleasure in food, by the time we can afford finer foods and wines, they are probably bad for the heart or the waistline. If we take pleasure in our bodies, strength erodes and sensations fade. If we take pleasure in nature, we contend with crowds and pollution.

It is precarious to seek happiness in external things, for they can always be alienated from us. But outside forces cannot deprive us of our character. A model once said, "If I weren't so beautiful, maybe I would have more character." That was twenty years ago, when she was thirty. Perhaps she has found time to work on character since then. So from a selfish standpoint, we should strive to develop character. But disciples principally care about character because the Lord cares. Jesus says that mature character is blessed by God.

## THE UNITY OF A BLESSED CHARACTER

Even dedicated Christians, sitting in Bible studies, rarely say that they aspire to the blessed traits that Jesus mentions in the Beatitudes. They are not the traits that we would first choose for ourselves. The classic virtues of the past and the fashionable virtues of the present—toughness, independence—are missing. Instead, the first three beatitudes describe weakness and neediness. Why does Jesus bless poverty of sprit, mourning, and meekness?

First, these are kingdom virtues; we *expect* them to differ from the virtues of this age. More importantly, we must see the Beatitudes as a multifaceted description of a whole person. They are not seven or eight random statements about virtue. Rather, they are a holistic portrait of a kingdom citizen. More than that, they portray the heart of the King.

The Beatitudes do more than describe a disciple; they also describe Jesus, the master. Matthew implicitly asks disciples to pattern their lives after Jesus. In Matthew 10:24–25, Jesus says, "A student is not above his teacher, nor a servant above his master. It is enough for the student to be like his teacher, and the servant like his master." The goal of becoming like the master is evident in almost all of the beatitudes:

1. Jesus says, "Blessed are those who mourn," and he mourned when he saw that the people were like sheep without a shepherd (9:36; cf. 23:37).
2. Jesus says, "Blessed are the meek," and Jesus is meek and humble (11:28–30). He lays a gentle, easy yoke on his people.
3. Jesus says, "Blessed are those who hunger and thirst for righteousness," and he hungered for righteousness. He fulfilled all righteousness (3:15). No one could convict him of any sin (John 8:46).
4. Jesus says, "Blessed are the merciful," and he is merciful. What most often moved Jesus to perform his miracles? He had compassion on the sick and needy. When he saw people in need, he empathized and healed them (Matt. 14:14–21; 20:34; 9:36).

5. Jesus says, "Blessed are the pure in heart," and he was so pure that no one could find a legitimate charge against him at his trial (26:59–60).
6. Jesus says, "Blessed are the peacemakers," and he often offered peace in healing and salvation to the people he met (Mark 5:34; Luke 8:48; John 14:27). Jesus offers peace, though not at any price (Matt. 10:13, 34).
7. Jesus says, "Blessed are those who are persecuted because of righteousness," and he was persecuted constantly, even to the point of death.

The only beatitude that Jesus did not claim for himself is "Blessed are the poor in spirit." But to be poor in spirit is to know one's spiritual neediness—especially our sinful nature. Jesus certainly needed the Spirit's sustaining strength for his ministry, but he was not poor in spirit in the ways that we are. This reminds us of an important point: we can progress toward Jesus, but a gap always remains between the Creator and his creatures. Jesus does not *share* that gap with us; he *bridges* it. Jesus reaches out to the poor in spirit, to teach and heal them—to teach and heal *us*.

Incidentally, Paul also says we should aspire to be like Christ. For Paul, maturity means reaching "the fullness of Christ" (Eph. 4:13). Believers know Christ and therefore should put on the new self, "created to be like God in true righteousness and holiness" (4:20–24). We are "imitators of God," loving one another and forgiving each other as Christ did (4:32–5:2). So we are transformed into the likeness of Christ.

There is no higher privilege than this, to become like the Son of God. A student who discipled my youngest daughter illustrated this for me when she described the first time she met my daughter: "She was ten years old and she used *non sequitur* correctly. I could tell that she loves words—just like you, Dr. Doriani." It warms a father's heart to hear that a child resembles him in positive ways. Much more, our heavenly Father takes pleasure in us when we resemble his excellent character.

It is God's design that we should aspire to a character that is ever more like the character of Jesus. God permits us to pursue that goal; more importantly, he gives us grace for the journey, making it a privilege rather than a burden. By grace, God sent his Son. By grace, Jesus came to seek and save the lost. By grace, he atoned for our sins. By grace, the Father raised Jesus from the tomb and sent the Spirit to testify to him. By grace, God completes his work by changing our hearts, so that we love him and believe in him. This is how we become like Christ, from heart to toe.

Grace also holds the Beatitudes together. The first three beatitudes describe a disciple's knowledge of his spiritual need. The fourth states God's promise to meet that need. The fifth through seventh describe the results of the fourth beatitude (see fig. 1).

**Figure 1. Progression among the Beatitudes**

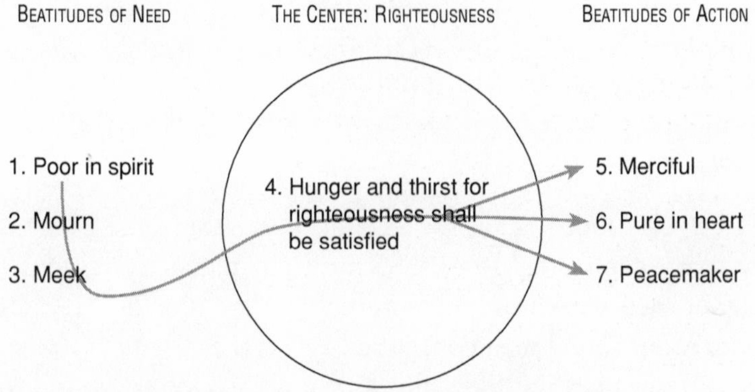

BEATITUDES OF NEED  THE CENTER: RIGHTEOUSNESS  BEATITUDES OF ACTION

1. Poor in spirit

2. Mourn

3. Meek

4. Hunger and thirst for righteousness shall be satisfied

5. Merciful

6. Pure in heart

7. Peacemaker

## BLESSINGS FOR THE NEEDY

### *The Poor in Spirit (5:3)*

Jesus said, "Blessed are the poor in spirit, for theirs is the kingdom of heaven" (Matt. 5:3). To understand who this refers to, we must distinguish between character and personality. "The poor" are not those who have a poor personality, as if God favored the shy, the nervous, and the cowardly. He blesses the spiritual character trait we can call *self-acknowledged weakness*. Disciples can be virile and tough, yet "poor in spirit." However strong or forceful their personality may be, disciples know their spiritual needs, their sin, their inability to reform themselves. Whatever our strengths, we know that we need God's grace and mercy.

Human society admires self-reliance and self-confidence. We admire the self-made businessman. We admire children who refuse to receive help when they eat their food or tie their shoelaces. Picture the household scene where a father watches his daughter struggling mightily to tie her shoelaces. Her immature fingers fumble with the strings. Her face, steely with determination during the first attempts, begins to don the mask of frustration. The kindly father offers to help, but the girl looks up with rugged resolve and declares, "No Daddy, I can do it myself!" That kind of tenacity and confidence fills a typical father with pride.

But is the child right? Can we do it ourselves? Jesus' disciples admit they cannot. We lay pride aside. We pray, "Whatever my strengths, I am poor in your sight, Lord. I need your grace to live, now and forever." When disciples take their poverty to God, he makes them rich, giving them the grace they seek. The Lord also grants an inheritance: "Theirs is the kingdom." Membership in the kingdom is a gift the Lord bestows upon all who take their spiritual poverty to him.

### Those Who Mourn (5:4)

The first beatitude leads to the second: "Blessed are those who mourn, for they will be comforted" (5:4). This means that Jesus blesses those who mourn over their weakness and sinfulness. Taken literally, "Blessed are those who mourn" is almost contradictory. How can Jesus say *mourners* are happy? Jesus does not bless all mourning; he blesses the mourning that coheres with kingdom values. There are kinds of mourning that God does not bless: criminals mourn their arrest; corrupt politicians mourn their loss of power. God does not promise to comfort everyone who mourns for every reason.

But God does promise to bless those who mourn over the right things. There is godly mourning over sin. After Paul rebuked the Corinthians for certain sins, he said that he regretted hurting them, "yet now I am happy . . . because your sorrow led you to repentance. . . . Godly sorrow brings repentance that leads to salvation and leaves no regret, but worldly sorrow brings death" (2 Cor. 7:9–10). This suggests the types of mourning that the Lord does bless:

1. He blesses when disciples mourn over their own sins.
2. He blesses when disciples mourn over the sins of their brothers in the church.

3. He blesses when disciples mourn over sins that pervade society. Amos mourned over injustice and oppression. God will not avert his wrath against the sin of Israel, he said, for "they trample on the heads of the poor . . . and deny justice to the oppressed" (Amos 2:6–7).
4. He blesses when disciples mourn indifference to the gospel. Jesus mourned, "O Jerusalem, Jerusalem, . . . how often I have longed to gather your children together, as a hen gathers her chicks under her wings, but you were not willing. Look, your house is left to you desolate" (Matt. 23:37–38; cf. Rom. 9:1–5).

Steve Garvey, a former baseball star for the Los Angeles Dodgers and the San Diego Padres, unintentionally showed how important it is to mourn. When he was a player, the media called him "Mr. Clean." But his teammates called him "Mr. Phony," and eventually all Los Angeles knew why. Garvey divorced his wife (with whom he had two children) and became engaged to a second woman, who claimed to be pregnant by him. Just before the wedding day, however, Garvey married a third woman. When that became public, a fourth woman asserted that Garvey had fathered a child recently born to her. One commentator reported the conclusion this way:

> Surprisingly, Garvey did not deny either woman's claim. (He acted, shall we say, more like a padre than a dodger.) Indeed, he said, "If the children are mine, I'll live up to my moral obligations, which I feel strongly about because I am a Christian." In a television interview, when asked why he did not seem embarrassed or disturbed by all these affairs, Garvey said that God has a purpose in everything that happens to us.[1]

Garvey's fatalistic shrug toward his sin shows that he knew not how to mourn. Both his sin and his indifference brought shame to the name of Christ.

David, by contrast, knew how to mourn. He said, "Streams of tears flow from my eyes, for your law is not obeyed" (Ps. 119:136). James also knows that sinners need to mourn: "Wash your hands, you sinners, and purify your hearts, you double-minded. Grieve, mourn and wail.

Change your laughter to mourning and your joy to gloom. Humble yourselves before the Lord, and he will lift you up" (James 4:8–10). Such mourning *is* a blessing, for it leads disciples away from sin. It is far better to mourn over sin than to be indifferent to it.

Jesus says mourners will be comforted. That is, *God* will comfort those who mourn correctly. First, he forgives our personal sins, if we repent of them. Second, he cleanses us from sin. He begins now, and he finishes when we meet him. Finally, he will cleanse his world at Christ's return, and we will rejoice with him.

### The Meek (5:5)

When Jesus moves from "Blessed are those who mourn" to "Blessed are the meek" (Matt. 5:5), the connection should be clear. Those who truly mourn over their sins will be meek. As with "poor in spirit," we must not think of meekness as a personality trait. The meek personality suffers indignities without complaint, always aims to please, and never asserts itself.

But for Jesus, meekness is a character trait, not a disposition. As a character trait, it is the opposite of ambition and envy. It is the gentle, humble, unassuming approach of one who knows his spiritual poverty and lets it guide his behavior.

Jesus could be bold, forceful, and confrontational, yet meek, and so can we. When I was a young pastor, there was a CEO in my little church. His bass voice, steely eyes, powerful physique, and assured carriage were so intimidating that I consciously leaned toward him when he spoke, so that the force of his person wouldn't blow me into the wall. Yet he was meek, because he used his powerful personality, not to assert himself, but to assert the rights of others.

The mark of meekness is not the absence of assertiveness. It is the absence of self-assertion. Successful and forceful people must learn how to use their strength for others, not themselves. We wound people if we use our strength selfishly.

Further, if we love the gospel, if we know our spiritual poverty and sin, we know that we have no right to exalt ourselves. People may naturally defer to a forceful person. He or she may naturally give commands and gather followers. But the forceful person is still meek if he uses his powers for God and neighbor. That is the way of Christ.

The meek admit that their sins disqualify them from grasping privileges for themselves. In prayer, they may say, "Lord, I am a wretched sinner and have no right to ask anything for myself." This is a sensible prayer. The difficulty comes when we talk to others. Then we are not so quick to admit that we are wretched sinners who have no rights. If someone tells us, "You are a wretched sinner and have no rights," we might retort, "You're a wretched sinner yourself!" It is easy to tell God that we merit no favor, but it is much harder to lay aside self-assertion with others.

Of course, everyone has certain rights as a human being. But the meek do not ask for special treatment or demand special rights. We trust God to protect and provide, and he promises to do so. The meek "inherit the earth." As we said before, we may get a taste of this now, but Jesus looks primarily to his return. He will give the earth to his children when he renews all things. The first beatitude offers the kingdom as a present possession. The second and third beatitudes promise a future blessing. This reminds us that we live between the times. We enjoy some of the privileges of redemption, but we wait for the fullness.

## THE PIVOTAL BLESSING: HUNGER AND THIRST FOR RIGHTEOUSNESS (5:6)

When Jesus blesses "those who hunger and thirst for righteousness" (5:6), he declares the spiritual consequence of the first three beatitudes. If we know our sin and spiritual poverty, if we mourn over it and live meekly because of it, we will hunger and thirst for righteousness. That is, we will seek it, yearn for it, and ask God to help us attain it. The language of hunger and thirst is well known in Scripture. The psalmist says that the hungry and thirsty cry out to the Lord in their distress and he delivers them. He satisfies them with good things (Ps. 107:5–9). God also says:

> Come, all you who are thirsty,
>     come to the waters;
> and you who have no money,
>     come, buy and eat!

21

Come, buy wine and milk
    without money and without cost. . . .
      . . . your soul will delight in the richest of fare. . . .
  . . . come to me;
    hear me, that your soul may live. (Isa. 55:1–3)

Jesus declares, "Whoever comes to me shall not hunger, and whoever believes in me shall never thirst" (John 6:35 ESV).

To "hunger and thirst for righteousness" means to seek it as fervently and regularly as we seek food and water. This hunger is a yearning for God's rule in our life. It is a thirst for his kingdom (Matt. 6:33). It is a longing for God:

As the deer pants for streams of water,
    so my soul pants for you, O God.
My soul thirsts for . . . the living God. (Ps. 42:1–2)

This hunger longs for God's word and its life-changing effects. The blessed man gets hungry when he is separated from the word of God, when good teaching and preaching are scarce. Amos threatens this punishment for unrepentant Israel: "'The days are coming,' declares the Sovereign LORD, 'when I will send a famine through the land—not a famine of food or a thirst for water, but a famine of hearing the words of the LORD'" (Amos 8:11).

In the Bible, hunger for righteousness has at least four aspects. First, there is *personal righteousness*, which we have stressed so far. This hunger leads us to uproot our sin and become more like Jesus. It leads us to pray that God's Spirit will make us more holy. The Bible calls this *sanctification*.

Since we know that our quest for righteousness will always fall short, we think, in the second place, of something very different from our personal righteousness—what theologians call an *alien righteousness*. That is the righteousness of Christ, bestowed upon us when we believe in him. The Bible calls this *justification*. Justification confers legal righteousness on us in God's courtroom, so that we can stand before God, the judge of mankind, on the last day. Justification wipes away all our sin and guilt, whether we have progressed much toward personal righteousness or not.

Third, disciples long for *social righteousness*, for a God-led cleansing of society. The Lord's people are not individualists. We do not withdraw from the world and hope to be left alone. We are willing to engage in social action, to promote God's cause in such spheres as business, education, politics, and the arts.

Fourth and finally, while disciples see the world as it is, they also anticipate something that is barely on the horizon—something that is not, but will be. In theological terms, our hunger has an eschatological dimension. We hunger for the day when the Lord will return and set the cosmos right. Then our great foe will be cast down, and God's righteousness will cover the earth—indeed, all creation. Matthew is most interested in personal and social righteousness, but disciples must seek God's righteousness in all its forms.

One problem we have when we hear this teaching is that we are so well fed and well watered that the metaphors of hunger and thirst have lost their potency. We can always grab something to eat, so we rarely get really hungry. A while ago I endured a series of travel fiascos en route to a conference, so that I ended up going an entire day without food. At 10 p.m., the last meeting ended and my only hope was a short van ride from the conference to our lodgings, where I already knew there was no food. Theologians in the van were discoursing on fascinating subjects, but my long-deprived stomach, threatened by an additional night of privation, let me think of nothing but food. I polled my fellow passengers and found that several were as hungry as I. In view of the time, and seeing some signs just ahead, we settled on fast food. But the driver seemed more intent on getting home than on pleasing his clients. Ignoring my pleas to stop, he passed by three famous franchises. Growing desperate, I saw that only one more fast-food restaurant lay between us and a night of starvation. "Turn into the left lane," I insisted, acting as if I would grab the wheel. "Turn into the left lane now!" A hamburger, fries, and milkshake never tasted so good, because I was truly hungry, as Americans rarely are, and it drove me to action.

Disciples must ask themselves: does our hunger for righteousness ever impel us to action? If we know our spiritual poverty, if we mourn over our sin, then our hunger for righteousness should lead us to do something to pursue holiness. Perhaps you can think of such an area in your life—a place where you need to do battle with sin. Or perhaps you see a social evil that you can help remove.

We are often satisfied with a nibble or a snack of righteousness. A taste, one small act of goodness, will satisfy us. On other days, we are not hungry at all. We live dutiful, dull, passionless, routine lives. We fit in, hang on, hold out, drift along. The years pass like a lazy summer afternoon, without a passion for anything, let alone righteousness.

Disciples, on the other hand, mourn over sin, yearn for God's righteousness, and seriously pursue it. The next three beatitudes, which we will examine in the next chapter, suggest that our pursuit of godliness accomplishes something and produces change. As we will see, the disciples' knowledge of their spiritual poverty leads them to be merciful to others, and their lack of self-assertion lets them become peacemakers. In all this, we grow toward the character of Jesus.

# 3

# CHARACTER AND ITS
# CONSEQUENCES
## *Matthew 5:1–10*

GOALS HAVE CONSEQUENCES, and consequences are often unforeseen. It was the goal of legendary track coach William Bowerman to see his runners excel. He gave them every possible advantage, from their training regimens to their running gear. To that end, Bowerman designed supportive shoes and light running gear in his home after practices ended. He even cut out prototypes of new shoes on his wife's waffle iron and gave them to his runners. Bowerman took his shoes and running gear to Phil Knight, a businessman, and as a consequence Nike, Inc. was born.

The goal of taking the gospel to every nation had a wider consequence: it brought literacy to millions. Christianity is a religion with an authoritative book. The prophets and the apostles wrote down the acts of God so that the truth would be preserved after the witnesses died. Books can go anywhere, but when missionaries stepped outside the Roman Empire, they often met peoples who had no written language. The missionaries adapted their own alphabets and grammars to the spoken languages they encountered and created written languages so that pagans could read the Bible in their native tongue. Thus the desire to transmit The Book introduced literacy to millions.

Before that, Jesus made a similar point about goals and their consequences. He said that the quest for righteousness leads to godly results: "Blessed are those who hunger and thirst for righteousness, for they shall be satisfied" (Matt. 5:6 ESV). Jesus promised that if his disciples had this hunger, the consequence would be the satisfaction of their hunger.

Similarly, the merciful will receive mercy, the pure in heart will see God, and peacemakers will be called sons of God.

## THE ASPIRATION FOR CHARACTER

It is generally agreed that our temperament and bearing are to a large extent given at birth. *Personality* changes little through life. A cheerful boy will probably be a cheerful man, and sunny girl, a sunny woman, but a sour child will probably be a sour adult. We tend to play out the dispositions that are present from the early stages of life.

Character is more changeable. People sometimes gain and sometimes lose their moral compass. Liars and thieves can become honest. Good politicians, policemen, and businessmen can become dishonest. The great question is, How does moral change occur? What is the source of noble character?

Aristotle said, "We become just by doing just acts; temperate by doing temperate acts; brave by doing brave acts."[1] In his view, character is a role we play until we gradually become that role. Character begins with a choice to behave in a certain way. An action repeated often enough becomes a habit, and habit, once sufficiently ingrained, becomes a virtue or a vice.[2] Aristotle's approach accents the outer life rather than the inner life of character. It emphasizes public virtues, such as civility and self-control.

Political leaders can be drawn to this concept. They adopt the practices that suggest a dignified and honorable persona. The concept is that they *are* what they *do*, at least in public. Private thoughts and traits matter little; the public's perception of character counts most. Character, then, is the role that one chooses to play.[3] If we play a role well, we gain honor before our peers and a pride in our status. If we leave God out of the picture, the move from character to status—and pride in it—is complete.

This interest in the public projection of character is not entirely misguided. Aside from hypocrites, our public behavior at least roughly reflects our true character. Furthermore, a good reputation is valuable. The book of Proverbs says that a good name is precious, more valuable than riches (Prov. 22:1). Still, the strong interest in presentation and reputation does lead to pride and hypocrisy. Besides, as John Piper says, humility, which is a biblical virtue, "can only survive in the presence of

God." It has to be nurtured in private.[4] Scripture certainly looks to the heart, the inner life, far more than it looks to the public presentation of character. Public presentations certainly did not motivate Jesus. His pursuit of righteousness led people to call him a glutton, a drunkard, and a sinner (e.g., John 9:24; Matt. 11:18–19). Thus, a noble character may reap public dishonor.

## THE PRESENCE OF GOD IN THE BEATITUDES

At first, God seems all but invisible in the Beatitudes, appearing but once: "Blessed are the pure in heart, for they will see God" (Matt. 5:8). In fact, God's hand is hidden in several of Jesus' promises. In the original Greek, there are passive verbs in four of the promises: those who mourn shall be comforted, the hungry shall be satisfied, peacemakers shall be called sons of God, and the merciful shall (literally) "be mercied" (Matt. 5:4–9). In these sentences, we are not told who will fulfill these promises. By whom will those who mourn be comforted? The comforting agent is never stated. In biblical times, the Israelites were so zealous to avoid taking God's name in vain, that some tried to avoid its use altogether. One way to avoid his name was to use a "divine passive," that is, a passive verb having God as its unstated agent. The sense, therefore, is that God comforts those who mourn and fills those who hunger for righteousness.

The Bible teaches both that God grants us a new heart or character (Ps. 51:10) and that we must pursue a righteous character. Paul says that the man of God must "pursue righteousness, godliness, faith, love, steadfastness, gentleness" (1 Tim. 6:11 ESV, cf. 2 Tim. 2:22; Prov. 15:9). The Beatitudes also make both points. When Jesus blesses the disciples who hunger and thirst for righteousness, he blesses those who make righteousness their goal. But the divine passives remind us that he is also present in our quest. He will comfort, satisfy, and show mercy to his sons and daughters as they pursue their goal.

## THE PIVOTAL BEATITUDE REVISITED:
## HUNGER AND THIRST FOR RIGHTEOUSNESS (5:6)

To hunger and thirst for righteousness is to long for God. If we seek first the kingdom, then we also seek the King. We long for his rule and his presence. As David said, "My soul thirsts for God, for the living God" (Ps. 42:2). Jesus said, "Whoever comes to me shall not hunger, and whoever believes in me shall never thirst"(John 6:35 ESV). To hunger for righteousness is also to long for God's word.

This hunger and thirst is personal, but it is more than personal. We long for God to change us, but we also long for him to transform society, so that his reign will be more visible. Disciples are not individualists. We do not achieve holiness by withdrawing from the world. We yearn for social transformation and social influence.

Some time ago, I was getting a haircut. I ordinarily read a book through the waiting and the scissor-work. This day the cutter and the client next to me were spouting truly spectacular foolishness on the topic of child rearing. I kept telling myself, "You are not their pastor. You are not their teacher. This is not your conversation." But eventually I could stand it no longer. As gently as possible, I interjected, "Actually, what you are saying is not quite correct. The operative principle for that situation is . . . and it applies as follows . . ." To my astonishment, the two people next to me, and then gradually everyone in the shop, fell silent and listened. It was an unusual moment, but many of us rightly yearn to speak up, gently but confidently, to offer guidance and models that could bless others.

Of course, not everyone is open to advice. But if we manifest even a semblance of the character that Jesus outlines in the Beatitudes, people just might listen. Perhaps too, our lives are just messy enough, just far enough from our own counsel, to keep us humble. And a humble awareness of our failings is endearing when we give advice to others. The larger point is that our quest for righteousness leads us to help others, not just to seek self-improvement.

No one lives up to his or her aspirations. Our reach exceeds our grasp. But that does not lead to despair; it increases our hunger for righteousness. It makes us long for the day when "we shall be like him, for we shall see him as he is" (1 John 3:2), the day when we "shall hunger no more, neither thirst anymore," for God's righteousness will cover the earth (Rev. 7:15–17).

Mature Christians can settle into a dull, passionless life, guided by routine and duty. We fit in, hang on, and drift along. The years pass like lazy clouds on a summer afternoon. Either we have no passions, or we have a misdirected passion for possessions, prestige, pleasure, and power. Jesus bids us to nurture the right passion, the hunger for righteousness, and to satisfy it.

Ultimately, of course, God satisfies our desire for righteousness. When he does, we change. The next three beatitudes describe that change. Each of these beatitudes of action corresponds to an earlier beatitude of need. The poor in spirit are merciful, mourners become pure, and the meek make peace. Growth in these character traits ought to be the consequence of the right hunger, the right spiritual goals (see fig. 2).

**Figure 2. Corresponding Beatitudes**

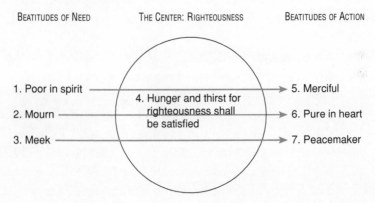

FORMS OF BLESSED RIGHTEOUSNESS

*Mercy (5:7)*

When Jesus says, "Blessed are the merciful, for they will be shown mercy" (Matt. 5:7), it is no isolated remark. It flows both from the fourth beatitude, describing our hunger, and the first. When Jesus blesses the poor in spirit, he promotes mercy, for the poor in spirit are merciful. When we recognize our spiritual poverty, our weakness and sin, we see the weakness and sin of others differently. If we are poor in spirit, we come to understand our own failings and develop a certain patience with them. As a result, we learn to be tender, empathetic, patient, and compassionate with the failings of others. Then we no longer condescend, asking, "What's wrong with him?" or "How could she ever do that?" We know that we could do (or have done) the same thing. When we see a troubled friend, we empathize. We ask, "How can I help?" not "How did he ever get into that ridiculous situation?"

The feeling of compassion also leads to action. The poor in spirit are merciful. We offer help to others, whether they have a claim on us or not. Mercy is a gift to mankind, yet a demand from God. He says, "I desire mercy" (Matt. 9:13; 12:7). Jesus says that mercy is one of the "weightier matters of the law" (23:23 ESV; cf. 25:31–46).

But, as we saw in the last chapter, the Beatitudes are also a portrait of Jesus. His demand is also his gift. The Father bids us to conform to the Son. As Augustine said, "Demand what you will, and give what you demand." We show mercy because we have received his mercy (Matt. 18:21–35). God promises to give his mercy to those who live by his mercy.

The miracles of Jesus show how mercy breaks into action. Compassion moved him to heal crowds (Matt. 9:36; 14:14), to feed four thousand hungry followers (15:32), to restore sight to the blind (20:34), and to bring a widow's only son to life (Luke 7:11–15).

We cannot perform miracles, but we can say what Peter once said to a needy man: "I have no silver and gold, but what I do have I give to you" (Acts 3:5 ESV). So let us ask, when we see the needy: How can I help? What can I give? Need takes many forms. We may meet it with a meal or a bed, with our time or with our counsel. Whatever the need may be, if we are hungry for righteousness, we will show mercy.

### *Purity of Heart (5:8)*

Purity of heart has two distinct but related senses in Scripture. First, it is that inner moral holiness that is the opposite of external piety. Old Testament prophets contrasted ritual observance of the law (especially laws of sacrifice and circumcision) with covenant obedience that flowed from love and sincerity of heart. Moses called on Israel to circumcise their hearts, not simply their flesh (Deut. 10:16; 30:6). Samuel said, "To obey is better than sacrifice" (1 Sam. 15:22). In a psalm of worship, David asked:

Who shall ascend the hill of the LORD? . . .
He who has clean hands and a pure heart. . . .

30

He will receive blessing from the LORD
and righteousness from the God of his salvation. (Ps. 24:3–5 ESV)

Jeremiah heaped scorn on Israelites who claimed refuge in the temple of the Lord while they oppressed the weak and chased after other gods (Jer. 7:2–10; cf. Isa. 1:10–17).

Second, purity can mean simplicity and freedom from double-mindedness. The pure, on this view, are those who show mercy because they love mercy, not to gain a reward. The pure show kindness to children who cannot thank us, to strangers whom we will never see again.

In Matthew's gospel, Jesus promotes purity in both senses. As for the first, Jesus expects our internal purity to match our external purity. For example, we must shun adultery in thoughts and deeds (5:27–30). We should pray in public, but should be more intent on praying in private (6:5–6).

Jesus flays the scribes and Pharisees for their merely external religion: "You tithe mint and dill and cumin, and have neglected the weightier matters of the law: justice and mercy and faithfulness" (23:23). They look righteous on the outside, but are full of hypocrisy and lawlessness (6:1–18).

As for the second sense of purity, Jesus blesses the eye that is set on one thing, the will that determines to serve one master (6:22–24).

Purity of motivation is essential to discipleship. I once received an invitation to speak at a high-profile event. I felt honored, but there was a problem. Besides the demands of extensive preparation, I doubted that I was the best person for the assignment. I told a friend and colleague, "I'm afraid that if I did it, half the motive would be vainglory." He replied, "Of course you would be motivated by vainglory. What decision do we make that is not?" It was a salutary bit of exaggeration. We hope to make a difference in this world, but we also hope to gain recognition for it. As D. A. Carson says:

We human beings are a strange lot. We hear high moral injunctions and glimpse just a little the genuine beauty of perfect holiness, and then prostitute the vision by dreaming about the way others would hold us in high esteem if we were like that. The demand for genuine perfection loses itself in the lesser goal of external piety; the goal of pleasing the Father is traded for its pygmy cousin, the goal of pleasing men.[5]

The second and sixth beatitudes form a pair. The disciple who mourns over sin will desire to be pure in heart. If we recognize our sins, both sinful deeds and sinful thoughts, and if we hate those sins, then we will try to rip them out, like so many noxious weeds. We will become pure in heart; we will see God.

We may find ourselves at a party where we do not belong. Inebriated guests may tell lewd or racist jokes and embarrass themselves with clumsy dancing. Or we may be with society mavens eating cucumber sandwiches and waxing eloquent about Hungarian linens. God also has a party, a feast for the redeemed. The party is grand and happy for all who feel at home at God's kind of party. That sense of belonging comes not from our race, gender, social class, or musical tastes, but from a desire to see the pure God and to share his holiness.

To be pure in heart means to live without compromise. Studies of World War II have shown that some American industries did a profitable business with Nazi Germany until the final stages of the war. *IBM and the Holocaust,* by Edwin Black, shows that Hitler's regime used American technology to organize slave labor and to manage death camps. IBM facilities operated in Germany throughout the war. Indeed, IBM's chairman, Thomas Watson, received Germany's Merit Cross for his contributions to German industry during wartime.[6] Other researchers have shown that IBM was hardly alone. ITT sold components for V-1 "buzz bombs." Ford and General Motors sold trucks; Standard Oil sold oil. RCA, Chase Manhattan, and others did the same, selling what they could. William R. Hawkins says that when national security and profits collide, expect businessmen to be businessmen.[7]

Not so with you, Jesus says. In Jesus' house, men and women seek purity and single-mindedness. We shun dual loyalties. We do not serve two masters, God and mammon. To pursue the Lord is to pursue his purity.

## Peacemaking (5:9)

Finally, Jesus says, "Blessed are the peacemakers, for they will be called sons of God" (Matt. 5:9).

We readily see how the third beatitude leads to the seventh. The meek become peacemakers for two reasons. First, the meek know that they are without merit. The meek stop promoting themselves, stop grasping for privileges and recognition. When they stop demanding, peace tends to emerge, for most strife stems from self-assertion.

Second, warring tribes trust the meek to make peace between them. The meek aren't seeking an advantage. They aren't asking, "Whose favor can I gain?" They are impartial, honest brokers. People trust the meek because they are not angling for future favors. For two of my years as a college professor of biblical studies, I was the tennis coach. It was a very small program, but we won enough matches to place third in our district. At the district playoffs, the coaches of the two dominant teams erupted in an altercation about a semifinal match. The programs had such small budgets that there were no officials on hand. Players made their own line calls, and coaches settled problems. But when the leading coaches had a problem, they turned to me and said, "Look, you have a good team, but you're coming in third, and besides you're a prof more than a coach. So you can be honest. You decide . . . "

True disciples have peace with God. Anyone who shares the gospel of Christ is a peacemaker. This peace is not the obliviousness that lets someone go to Europe on a one-way ticket with $700 in his pocket. This peace is the logical result of a healthy relationship with the Lord through faith in Jesus, God's Son.

Of course, peace with God will not lead to temporal peace. Peacemaking is a process that requires several *willing* people. Thus, Paul says, "As far as it depends on you, live at peace with everyone" (Rom. 12:18).

Peace is more than absence of conflict. It is maturity and well-being, as God defines them. We may need constructive conflict to achieve real peace. Jesus certainly made peace through conflict. He said, "I have come to bring fire on the earth, and how I wish it were already kindled!" (Luke 12:49).

Peacemaking also has internal, subjective aspects. Insecurities and worries destroy peace. Discontentment disrupts peace. Envy disrupts peace. When we try to read other people's thoughts, it disrupts peace. The pastor of a healthy, small-town church recently learned that lesson afresh. The church and the pastor loved and admired each other, but there was some resistance when he lengthened morning worship by fifteen minutes. No one got upset, he said, but then he began the story of one man:

> Church used to end at 10:30; now it goes to 10:45. One man sits near the back. Each week, he stands up at precisely 10:30, straightens his jacket and pants, and walks out. He never *said* anything, but I could feel his displeasure over the longer services. Indeed, sometimes I had to labor to stifle my anger at the weekly display. Then one week, I changed the order of worship and put the sermon first. The man still left at 10:30, but later that day his wife called.
>
> "Pastor," she said, "you can't imagine how happy my husband was today. You see, he has to report to work at 10:45 on Sundays. He waits until the last possible minute each week, but it grieves him that he can never stay until the end of your message. Today he heard your whole sermon and he is so pleased. I just had to tell you."

Guessing other people's motives is a prime way to subvert our peace, especially since, by some perverse impulse, we tend to make the most negative, self-damaging guesses. Instead, let us remember that if we have peace with God, we can free ourselves of worry about lesser things.

## CONCLUSION

As we have seen, the Beatitudes are not a list of isolated virtues, not a list comparable to classic virtue lists. Any review of the Beatitudes is daunting, for it reveals our inability to attain the qualities that Jesus outlines. Yet, if we take that burden to Christ, admitting our weakness, the blessing has already begun. After all, the first beatitude says, "Blessed are the poor in spirit." We are blessed when we take our poverty to Jesus. The Beatitudes enumerate seven facets of a character grounded in the desire to share Jesus' righteousness. Our desires have consequences. The desire for a better shoe led to the creation of Nike, Inc. A desire for evangelism led to the creation of written languages, Bible translations, and teaching illiterate people to read. The desire for righteousness leads us to hunger and thirst for righteousness. That hunger leads us to the gospel, and the gospel leads us to the godly character that Jesus both has and inspires.

# 4

# FOUR RESULTS
# OF A BLESSED LIFE

*Matthew 5:10–16*

I KNOW A MAN who is a candidate for nomination to a United States circuit court, just one level below the Supreme Court. He is a man of character, intelligent, hardworking, and a dedicated Christian. Yet the very people who may nominate him have told him: "Think hard before you accept the nomination. Your opponents may attack you, distort your record, and slander your name." In the past, hard decisions and long hours made political and judicial candidates pause before taking office. Today's contentious political atmosphere creates a potential for insults and slander that stop many candidates. With all these negatives, why would this good man seek judicial office? Because he hopes to bring justice to the land.

Our passage says that Jesus' disciples are in much the same position as this judicial candidate. We may suffer persecution for following our master. Yet disciples may also gain influence, even acclaim. To be precise, in Matthew 5:10–16 Jesus lists four possible results when his disciples interact with secular culture. He moves from the most negative to the most positive:

- We may suffer *persecution*. Persecution was certainly common for Jesus and his first disciples.
- We may be *salt*. In antiquity, salt served as a preservative to retard the decay of food. So the presence of disciples can rein in the evils of society.

- Better yet, we may be *light* for a darkened world. The light may illumine individuals or society as a whole.
- Finally, the good deeds of a disciple may lead people to *praise* God.

We begin with the first possible result, persecution.

## PERSECUTION (5:10–12)

As we have seen, the Beatitudes are full of surprises. We have learned to expect the unexpected from Jesus, and he has already blessed the poor in spirit and those who mourn. But how can he possibly call persecution a blessing? Yet he does: "Blessed are those who are persecuted because of righteousness, for theirs is the kingdom of God" (Matt. 5:10).

This blessing does follow logically from the previous one. Jesus blesses peacemakers, but not everyone agrees. Some people prefer war to peace. Certain Egyptians assassinated Anwar Sadat, their own prime minister, for seeking peace with Israel. Later, an Israeli assassinated his prime minister, Yitzhak Rabin, for seeking peace with Palestinians and Arabs.

More importantly, we remember that Jesus, our master, suffered persecution. Jesus says that we will walk a path much like his. Alongside great influence, we will encounter great opposition. He said that a servant is not above his master. If opponents slander the master, they will also slander his disciples (10:24–25). Jesus is never one to hide bad news. Therefore, he says:

> If the world hates you, keep in mind that it hated me first. If you belonged to the world, it would love you as its own. As it is, you do not belong to the world. . . . That is why the world hates you. . . . "No servant is greater than his master." If they persecuted me, they will persecute you also. (John 15:18–20)

Let us pause to be sure that we heard Jesus aright. He does not mean that is it pleasant to experience suffering (Heb. 12:11). It is never pleasant to be put to flight, driven off, and pursued with violent intent. It is never pleasant to suffer insults and slander because those who hold power dislike our beliefs. Further, Jesus does not bless all who suffer. He says, "Blessed are those who are persecuted *for righteousness' sake*" (Matt. 5:10 ESV).

### Persecution versus Troubles Caused by Folly

Jesus blesses all who suffer persecution for living by kingdom standards, but he does not bless those who are punished for their sin, their tactlessness, or their folly, even if they can somehow connect their follies to their faith.

- He does not bless a male college student who fails a test because he was comforting a beautiful but sad classmate the night before that test.
- He does not bless those who lose their job because what they call "witnessing" looks to the boss like socializing and failure to perform.
- He does not bless those who defend their faith in obnoxious ways and suffer rejection for it.

Peter says, "It is commendable if a man bears up under the pain of unjust suffering because he is conscious of God. But how is it to your credit if you receive a beating for doing wrong and endure it?" (1 Peter 2:19–20). Ordinarily, we will suffer no harm if we do what is good (3:13). "But if you suffer for doing good and you endure it, this is commendable before God" (2:20).

### Suffering with Christ

Jesus blesses those who suffer for righteousness and for him. The next two verses (Matt. 5:11–12) repeat and expand the beatitude of 5:10, adding several points and nuances. First, after mentioning persecution in general in 5:10, he enumerates the forms it takes: insults, violent pursuit, and slander (5:11).

Second, Jesus personalizes the blessing he gives sufferers. He no longer says, "Blessed are those . . ." Rather, he says, "Blessed are *you* when people insult you, persecute you and falsely say all kinds of evil against you because of me" (5:11). Character assassination is a real tragedy, and no one wants to suffer physical persecution. Yet we do want to be like Jesus, who loved us and gave himself for us and became the supreme case of an innocent man suffering unjustly. Like Jesus, we neither *seek* persecution nor *retreat* from it. We know suffering is not inherently meritorious, but we accept it if it comes, for we give our allegiance to the suffering Christ.[1] Paul says, "I want to know Christ and the power of his resurrection and the fellowship of sharing in his sufferings" (Phil. 3:10). Disciples are united to Christ. If we believe in him, we share in his life and in his victory over death; we also share in the suffering that preceded his death.

Third, while Jesus says in Matthew 5:10 that we are blessed if we suffer evil "because of righteousness," in verse 11 he says that we are blessed if we suffer evil "because of me." The prime point remains: Jesus blesses us if we suffer innocently. Yet, while verse 10 says we may suffer for our allegiance to kingdom values, verse 11 says we may suffer for our allegiance to the King. The first statement says we may suffer opposition just for being good. The second says we may suffer just for believing in Jesus. This statement contains an implicit claim of deity: The prophets were persecuted for their allegiance to *God, the Father*. Disciples will be persecuted for their allegiance to *Jesus, the Son*. Both prophets and disciples are willing to suffer for their supreme loyalty to God.

Fourth, verse 11 says *that* we should rejoice in persecution, while verse 12 explains *why*: "Rejoice and be glad, because great is your reward in heaven, for in the same way they persecuted the prophets who were before you." First, we rejoice because our persecution links us with the prophets, who suffered the same thing. If we suffer for Jesus' sake, we are in good company. The prophets illustrate how righteousness leads to persecution. Because Israel was prone to rebellion and sin, the prophets often had to rebuke Israel. Alas, Israel often despised their God-given message. Indeed, the Lord told Isaiah that Israel would be ill disposed to listen—"ever hearing, but never understanding; . . . ever seeing, but never perceiving." Therefore, Isaiah's prophecy served to make hearts calloused, to make ears dull, and to close eyes (Isa. 6:9–10). Therefore, the people told the prophets, "Give us no more visions of what is right! Tell us pleasant things, prophesy illusions" (Isa. 30:10). The prophets frequently endured hostility from the kings' courts too. But they continued to prophesy. Today, we count them blessed because they had the privilege of hearing and declaring God's very words.

The prophets suffered, but stayed engaged with their age. Likewise, Christians do not withdraw from their age. Our convictions lead to action. When we see pain, we show mercy (Matt. 5:7). When we see conflict, we try to make peace (5:9). Jesus blesses such actions. Yet, when we engage the world, conflicts of values, whether sharp or benign, will inevitably arise.

The movie *Family Man* is a Christmas-season comedy/morality tale that illustrates benign conflict. In one scene, the two main characters, Jack and Kate, must decide if they will leave their modest, family-friendly life in New Jersey's suburbs for a life of wealth in New York City. When Kate hesitates, Jack argues, "Kate, we can have a life that others *envy*." We might guess that the writers wanted viewers to see a flaw there, until Kate replies, "They already do, they already do." Parts of society define the good life as "one that others envy." We will inevitably have a "soft" conflict with that view.

We have sharp conflict with others, such as Friedrich Nietzsche. In the last book he wrote before descending into insanity, Nietzsche declared that "the good" is whatever heightens power and the will to power in man. Further, he said, weakness is evil and the greatest vice is sympathy for the weak. Since Jesus blesses children and blesses those who show mercy, Nietzsche inevitably condemned Christianity. Whether we consider the sharp conflict with philosophies that are antithetical to Christianity or the softer conflicts with popular culture, there will be conflict between Christianity and the world.

- The world blesses the rich; Jesus blesses the poor.
- The world blesses the carefree; Jesus blesses those who mourn over evil.
- The world blesses the assertive and aggressive; Jesus blesses the meek and the gentle.
- The world blesses those who can get what they want; Jesus blesses those who are hungry and thirsty for righteousness.
- The world prizes the trouble-free life; Jesus tells disciples to rejoice in persecution.

### Rejoicing in Persecution

Next, Jesus gives us a second and greater reason to rejoice in persecution: "Your reward is great in heaven" (5:12 ESV). He does not say that we *gain* a reward because we suffer; rather, he says that our reward *is* great. The term "reward" here almost needs quotation marks, because the English term implies that we earned something. But, of course, the chief reward for believers is eternal life, and Jesus earned that for us. We might avoid misconceptions if we called eternal life a sign or recognition that we are on God's team. We can never truly earn anything from God, so that he would become our debtor. But God does bless our faithfulness to him.

The matter of rewards is important, but more important is the matter of rejoicing. Some years ago, two missionaries to Columbia were kidnapped by Marxist guerrillas and kept as pawns in their political game. Both had been teaching at a missionary school. How could they rejoice at their separation from their wives, children, and students? And then, after eighteen months, their captors executed them for no apparent reason. How could their wives, children, and friends rejoice in that?

The call to rejoice in persecution demands that we reappraise our values. Jesus asks us to detach ourselves from this age and to recalibrate our ideas about time. We should tell ourselves, "Our time on earth is short; eternity is long. If we endure insults or privation in this life, they are short-lived in comparison to eternity. If we should die because of persecution, then we meet the Lord and taste his goodness earlier than we anticipated."

Jesus summons us to compare this life with eternity. The Bible affirms the value of this life. It teaches us what we need to know to live well on earth. It enables us to lead a morally upright and personally satisfying life. God tells us that he gives us his commands and decrees "for your good" (Deut. 10:13 ESV).

But Jesus also states a vital qualifier. Sometimes our "reward" for living well is persecution. Sometimes warriors scorn peacemakers. They are angry and want to stay that way, so they despise peacemakers. Jesus warns us that we may do almost everything right, and yet the only payoff may be opposition or persecution.

One of my longtime friends has a son and a daughter. He and his wife are dedicated Christians. They are patient and loving; they strive to be good parents. Their daughter is a paragon of virtue—sweet, multitalented, self-disciplined, and a dedicated Christian. Their son has similar abilities, but he squanders them. He has experimented with drugs and alcohol. He has disappeared for days at a time. He wastes money and wrecks cars. He has been in jail. His parents have been firm, patient, and loving through it all. Sometimes he loves them for it, but at other times he tells them, "I hate you; I wish you were dead."

My friends know their responsibility. They pray, they continue to be the best parents they can, and they tell themselves, "Our efforts may be rewarded here, but we may have to wait for heaven." Jesus never guarantees positive results in this life.

Of course, Christians still seek good results. When we go to a nice restaurant, we expect a result—a good meal. When we invest our money, we expect a result—a return on the investment. But Jesus never guarantees us positive results in this life. Our labors may yield a fistful of dollars; they may yield a fistful of dust. Our good deeds may garner praise or persecution.

Scripture says, "God rewards those who earnestly seek him" (Heb. 11:6). But it does not specify when that will happen. If we never taste it on earth, we will taste it in heaven. This thought can be either troubling or liberating. It is troubling to know that we may suffer undeservedly, like Job or Jesus. But it is liberating to admit that we cannot control results. We should seek good results, but leave them to God. He will set things right on the last day. He will reward us in heaven. Let us therefore work hard and live well, and trust our careers, our relationships, and our health to God.

When life is good, when we are successful, it is possible to get so engrossed in temporal blessings that we forget about God's eternal blessings. Jesus asks us to see things in the light of eternity.

There is a strange feature in the way we speak about time. We speak of long hours, long days, and long weeks, yet we often say a month or a year is short. We say, "That month flew by," or "Spring seemed so short this year." Life seems short, but eternity is long.

As the hymn says, "When we've been there ten thousand years," we will not be one second closer to the end of eternity. After ten million years, the fabric of heaven will not show the first signs of wear. After ten billion years, we will not exhaust the range of activities that God has prepared for us.

When our bodies die, either our life ends at once or it never ends. The Bible says that our life never ends. Therefore, we should be willing to await our reward in heaven. When we go to law school, medical school, or seminary, we labor several years to gain the qualifications that lead to professional and perhaps material rewards that last a few decades. So why not wait seventy years for a reward that will last forever?

Churches rightly proclaim God's guidance on practical matters, such as marriage, parenting, and the use of money. But before we take up the practical matters that promise to make this life better, let us ensure that we are ready for eternity by knowing Christ and trusting him for life eternal.

## SALT (5:13)

Jesus' band of disciples may be persecuted, but the results of faithfulness are often happier. Disciples can change the world. We may become its salt and light. Today, we use salt as a condiment to enhance the flavor of meat and vegetables. But in the days before refrigeration and chemical preservatives, people used salt primarily to prevent the decay of meat. Similarly, the presence of a morally strong disciple can retard moral decay in society. For example, someone may refrain from telling a lewd or demeaning joke in the presence of a disciple. Our reputation for moral probity lets us function like bank auditors. Bank employees who might be inclined to embezzle money rarely attempt to do so, because they know that the auditors will catch them. Similarly, men with evil plans may abandon them simply because they know that a righteous disciple will resist them. We live in a pragmatic society. Its moral standards are low and changeable and subject to improvisation. But a salty disciple doesn't improvise. Like salt, we are stable and unchanging.

Sodium chloride, common table salt, is a stable chemical compound, so we may wonder what Jesus means when he speaks of salt losing its saltiness (Matt. 5:13). To grasp his point, we need to understand that in ancient times "salt" was a piece of rock dug from the ground and containing many impurities. Water could wash through it, dissolving the sodium chloride and leaving a residue that looked like a salt rock and even retained its original shape, yet lacked the flavor of salt.[2]

Jesus says, "Have salt in yourselves" (Mark 9:50), which means that we must retain our distinctive flavor. We must preserve the distinction between disciples and the world. The church is alien, so that it suffers persecution, and it is influential, so that it retards decay. The more we sense and accept our difference from the world, the greater our influence will be. The more we allow the secular society to affect us, morally and spiritually, the more we lose our saltiness.

If the only visible difference between Christians and secular people is that we go to church on Sunday and give money away more regularly, why would they want to join us? If we divorce, alienate our children, tell lies, and make dirty deals like everyone else, why not play golf on Sunday and spend our money on exotic vacations?

## LIGHT AND PRAISE (5:14–16)

Jesus says, "I am the light of the world" (John 8:12). He is "a light for the nations," to bring God's salvation to the end of the earth (Isa. 49:6 ESV). Here Jesus tells his followers, "You are the light of the world" (Matt. 5:14). A disciple hopes to become like his master, to bless the world. As we "walk in the light, as he is in the light" (1 John 1:7 ESV), we are the light of the world.

As with salt, Jesus warns us about losing our efficacy as light. Just as "a city on a hill cannot be hidden" (Matt. 5:14), so the light of a disciple cannot and should not be hidden. In the days before electric lights, it would have been absurd to light an oil lamp and then cover it up (5:15).

After warning us against losing our influence, Jesus tells us how to retain it: "Let your light shine before men, that they may see your good deeds" (5:16). "Good deeds" are practical acts of kindness and neighborly love. A virtuous life gives light to all around us.

It is impossible to gaze directly at the sun, high in the sky; it is painful even to try. But we gaze happily at a full moon. On a clear night, many will admire its beauty, We often forget that the moon only reflects the greater light of the sun. Somewhat similarly, many people find it difficult to gaze directly at God. Prayer, Bible reading, and meditation are too much for them. But they will observe Christians as they reflect the greater light of Jesus.

Then sometimes God sends the grace—call it epistemological grace—to see things as they truly are. Then men and women manifest the fourth and best response to a righteous disciple. They "see your good deeds" as the result of God's work, and so they "praise your Father in heaven" (5:16). When they see our light, they will realize that there must be a source for our goodness, and conclude that God is that source. They will praise God for his work in us.

## CONCLUSION

So then, there are four possible responses to a disciple's faithful life. At the extremes are persecution and praise of God. Between them, we can serve as salt and light. Jesus says we *are* different, and therefore we are accountable to act like it. Let us accept the responsibility to *be* the light of the world. Let us not fail due to laziness, compromise, or fear. Let us act boldly and speak freely, leaving the results to God.

We all live under a common curse, because of sin. We all live under common grace from God. The common curse means that Christians do foolish things, like everyone else, and so we face opposition, for our folly as well as to our faith. But there is also common grace, so that unbelievers will listen to what we say, watch how we live, and sometimes even admire it. That grace may become uncommon, if people look beyond our goodness to its source, the goodness of God. May our light and God's grace so shine that we will not fear opposition. May many praise God for the good that they see in us and so turn to the Lord and gain eternal life in him.

The first sixteen verses of Matthew 5 constitute the overture to the Sermon on the Mount. In these verses, Jesus describes the character of a disciple and the results that we can expect when a disciple enters a world that operates by different standards. The Sermon on the Mount is not essentially a body of laws, yet in the next section, and in our next chapter, Jesus does describe the laws and principles that guide the behavior of a disciple, so that we can be the salt and light that this world needs.

# 5

# Be Still, O Angry Heart

*Matthew 5:17–26*

It was my birthday, but four problems met me before 8 a.m. It started small—I left my lunch on the kitchen counter—but soon escalated. Rain soaked the roads and caused a series of accidents and traffic jams on the way to work, so I arrived late. I needed to print some documents before I flew, at noon, to a small city to speak at a Bible conference. But when I started up my computer, it told me that our printing network was down and that my computer was out of memory, even though it had gigabytes to spare the night before. Next, my airline called to say that my flight had been canceled. They would switch me to another airline, which would fly me to a nearby city, where I could rent a car, then drive to my original destination, almost arriving on time. When I got to that other city, an additional delay placed me in a construction project at rush hour. Amazingly, I arrived only an hour late for the conference, which actually went well. On the way home, however, one last thing went wrong. When I checked in, the airline agent smiled and told me, "We cannot let you on this flight because you did not arrive on your scheduled flight."

"That is true," I replied, "but I did not fly down on my scheduled flight because you canceled it and put me on another airline."

The agent, still smiling, was unmoved. "Well, maybe, but you came here on the wrong flight. We cannot let you on this plane."

Dumbfounded, I prayed for a calm heart as I tried to reason with the agent. "I'm sure your system will show that your plane was grounded, so you canceled my flight here." The grinning agent repeated, "Our records say you did not board the proper flight to get here, so I can't let you on this plane." Twenty minutes of futile conversation later, the flight was about to depart, my patience was exhausted, and I was struggling mightily to control the anger I felt at the smiling incompetent, the buffoon who would not let me go home.

Perhaps you empathize with my plight, but Jesus has something to say about the anger that rises in us and causes us to label people "incompetents" and "buffoons" and worse. His message about anger is austere; to follow it, we must step back and set the context, from Matthew 5:17–20.

## THE CONTEXT: JESUS AND THE LAW (5:17–20)

Do not think that I have come to abolish the Law or the Prophets; I have not come to abolish them but to fulfill them. I tell you the truth, until heaven and earth disappear, not the smallest letter, not the least stroke of a pen, will by any means disappear from the Law until everything is accomplished. Anyone who breaks one of the least of these commandments and teaches others to do the same will be called least in the kingdom of heaven, but whoever practices and teaches these commands will be called great in the kingdom of heaven. For I tell you that unless your righteousness surpasses that of the Pharisees and the teachers of the law, you will certainly not enter the kingdom of heaven. (Matt. 5:17–20)

Christians know that Jesus was perfectly righteous, but he baffled his contemporaries. He was obviously a rabbi, since he gathered disciples and taught the meaning of the law. But there was something about Jesus that made it seem that he was setting aside the law. His lifestyle certainly contradicted traditional Jewish interpretations of the law. For example, he spent too much time with women, disregarding what the great rabbis said: "He that talks much with womankind brings evil upon himself and neglects the study of the law and at the last will inherit Gehenna." He spent too much time with sinners and even shared table fellowship with them. This signified that he accepted them and considered them friends, although the great rabbis said, "Keep thee far from an evil neighbour and consort not with the wicked." Holy men were not supposed to dine with sinners or talk much with women, but Jesus did both.[1]

Jesus also seemed to repeal parts of the law. He said that all foods were now clean (Mark 7:14–19; Matt. 15:17–20). He healed on the Sabbath, he limited the freedom of men to divorce their wives, and he declared people forgiven on his own authority, without a glance at priests or the temple. He cast recognized businessmen out of the temple precincts for performing approved money-changing services. At each of these points, Jesus disregarded traditional Jewish understandings of the law.

In our passage, he quotes the Old Testament six times, but then appears to correct it. Six times he says, "You have heard that it was said . . ."—only to add, "But I say to you . . . ," as if his word were the final authority. Did Jesus oppose the law or think that he needed to correct it?

### Jesus, the Law Keeper (5:17)

When we look closely at our passage, we see that Jesus violated traditional Jewish understandings of the law, but not the law itself. He declares, "I have not come to abolish them [i.e., the Law and the Prophets] but to fulfill them" (5:17). Jesus understood the law perfectly, and because he did, he explained and obeyed it perfectly.

Jesus declares that it would be easier for heaven and earth to pass away than for "the smallest letter" to disappear from the law. "The smallest letter" is a Hebrew letter that is the size of a comma and can sometimes be omitted without loss of meaning, somewhat like our silent *e*. When he says "not the least stroke of a pen" will disappear, he refers to a small shift of the pen that differentiates two similar letters, much as our *c* and *e* differ in only one crossing stroke.

The word of God expresses God's very attributes and shares many of his traits. His word can fail no more than God can fail. Furthermore, no one who violates or disregards even the smallest commandments in the law can be great in the kingdom of heaven (5:19). Jesus' commitment to the law and its righteous standards is complete. Therefore, he tells his disciples that "unless your righteousness exceeds that of the scribes and Pharisees, you will never enter the kingdom of heaven" (5:20 ESV).

## *Exceeding the Righteousness of Scribes and Pharisees (5:20)*

The idea that our righteousness must surpass that of the scribes and Pharisees requires some clarification. We tend to think that it is a simple matter to exceed the scribes and Pharisees, since they were misdirected and hypocritical. But Jesus' initial audience considered scribes to be the most accurate interpreters of scripture and Pharisees to be the most devout practitioners of scripture. Today, Jesus might say, "Unless your righteousness is greater than that of pastors, missionaries, and seminary professors . . ."

As the sermon progresses, we realize that Jesus did not expect his disciples to surpass the scribes and Pharisees at their own game; rather, he redefined righteousness. The scribes and Pharisees sought to codify righteousness, prescribing proper behavior in minute detail for every foreseeable situation. For example, they specified proper Sabbath rest by setting precise limits on work. They codified how far one might walk (one thousand yards), how much one might write (one word), and how much food one could take out of storage (one gulp) without breaking the Sabbath.

Jesus protested this view of righteousness, which was legalistic. To be clear, we should distinguish three senses of legalism. The first and most pernicious form of legalism attempts to attain (or retain) salvation by works. The legalist in this sense performs good works to gain the favor of God, who becomes the patron of achievers. The second form of legalism fabricates new laws, based on tradition or misinterpretation of Scripture, and then grants these laws the force of Scripture itself. This kind of legalist may forbid what is permissible, such as playing cards, or he may require what is advisable, such as morning devotions. Third, "legalism" can mean an exceptional concentration on law and obedience, to the exclusion of other facets of the life of faith. Many scribes and Pharisees suffered from all three forms of legalism.

Jesus' disciples cannot exceed the scribes and Pharisees in achieving such forms of "righteousness," and they must not attempt to do so. Jesus refused to offer minute prescriptions of behavior that make righteousness a relationship to the law, rather than to God. He knew that no moral net is fine enough to catch every moral question that swims. Therefore, he addressed the heart and mind, the motives of obedience.

Jesus demands much of his disciples, but his demands are not essentially legal. They specify goals and attitudes more than particular deeds for particular situations. No law is comprehensive enough to cordon off all sin; regulations cannot control the sinful heart. Jesus' instructions are far too brief to form a legal code. Rather, they illustrate the ways of an obedient heart. We surpass the scribes and Pharisees by having a heart for God.

This true righteousness shows itself when disciples do the right things for the right reasons. For example, some men boast of their fidelity to their wives. But when we get to know them, we realize they are faithful only because they cannot find a willing partner or are afraid of getting caught. Some men handle large sums of money faithfully, but only because they know competent auditors visit regularly. The world is full of people who never did anything really bad, but only because they never had a chance. Jesus expects his disciples to do the right things for the right reasons—not out of fear or calculation, but out of love for God and man.

Since motivation is as vital as external obedience, the actual instructions in Matthew 5–7 are quite brief, compared to the volumes of Jewish religious commentary on the law. Jesus does not propound exhaustive specifications of moral behavior. He illustrates the thoughts and deeds that characterize a disciple. Ideally, these disciples find a perfect harmony between behavior and thought. Too many people perform good deeds from craven fear, resentful duty, or selfish calculation. Jesus wants his disciples to obey from the heart.

## MURDER, ANGER, AND CONTEMPT (5:21–22)

### *Murder (5:21)*

Jesus begins by restating the law against murder: "You have heard that it was said to the people long ago, 'Do not murder, and anyone who murders will be subject to judgment'" (5:21). The law has long forbidden murder. Further, murderers are liable to judgment in the courts of God and mankind.

The prohibition of murder is well liked. Very few people commit murder, and the law against it offers a certain protection. But Jesus probes the depths of our affinity for this law by exploring the pre-murderous dispositions that lie behind the act.

People do not murder at random. Whether they have white-hot rage or cool hatred, and whether they hate one person, a race, or all mankind, murderers are angry. If hatred leads to murder, then hatred is culpable too, even if it never leads to action. Therefore Jesus says, "Anyone who is angry with his brother will be subject to judgment" (5:22).

### Anger (5:22a)

Someone will ask, "Is anger always wrong, then? Surely there is a place for righteous moral indignation." Indeed, there is. Jesus himself showed righteous anger. He threw money changers out of the temple, since their trade made it impossible for Gentiles to pray and their rates made it a den of thieves (21:12–13). He became angry at hypocrites (Mark 3:1–5) and even grew exasperated with his disciples (Mark 7:18; 9:19).

But mark the nature of Jesus' anger. He was "slow to anger" (Ex. 34:6; James 1:19). His anger was mingled with grief over such sins as hypocrisy, willful misunderstanding, fruitlessness, and unbelief. Unlike us, he did not become angry at personal mistreatment. When arrested, mocked, beaten, and crucified, he was as quiet as a lamb led to the slaughter. He did not rebuke them or offer a self-defense. Jesus was silent, except to say, "Father, forgive them, for they do not know what they are doing" (Luke 23:34). Peter says, "When they hurled their insults at him, he did not retaliate; when he suffered, he made no threats. Instead, he entrusted himself to him who judges justly" (1 Peter 2:23).

Jesus became angry for the sake of others. There is an anger that is loving, that wishes no one any evil. It loves the sinner while it hates the sin. Our anger is typically just the opposite. We burn with anger at petty offenses to our honor. We scream at referees whose whistles harm our favorite team. We become offended at minor snubs, minor acts of disrespect. We rage at people who cut us off in traffic or squeeze yellow lights until they run red. We are quick to anger at personal offenses, but slow to anger over sins that offend God and mankind. When someone else is upset, we urge calm. When someone offends God, perhaps by taking his name in vain, we say, "What do you expect of sinners?" Of course, it is good to stay calm. But there is a place for righteous anger, for grief over sin (see Pss. 11:4–6; 119:36; 139:21–22).

### Contempt (5:22b)

Besides anger, Jesus also prohibits casual insults and contempt: "Anyone who says to his brother, 'Raca,' is answerable to the Sanhedrin. But anyone who says, 'You fool!' will be in danger of the fire of hell" (Matt. 5:22). The terms *raca* and *fool* are not quite identical. *Raca* expresses contempt for someone's mind. It means "Stupid idiot! Dummy! Moron!" *Fool* expresses contempt for someone's heart and character. It means, "Scoundrel!" If *raca* insults the brains, *fool* insults the heart. Together, they imply that someone is worthless, good for nothing. At a literal level, we should avoid contemptuous words, but we should shun every whiff of condescension. We should treat no one, whether young or old, whether weak in mind or weak in body, as if he has no value.

Whoever violates this principle, Jesus says, is liable to judgment before the Sanhedrin. The Sanhedrin was the highest court in Israel. More than that, contempt makes us liable to the very court of God and the fires of hell. The Greek literally reads "the Gehenna of fire." Gehenna was a smoldering rubbish heap in a valley outside Jerusalem. So the contemptuous are liable to God's fiery judgment.

Jesus does not mean that one insult gets one level of punishment and another earns a more severe penalty. Rather, he says that anger and contempt are interior states that can lead to murder. Indeed, they are forms of murder, and deserve murder's punishment. As John says, "Anyone who hates his brother is a murderer" (1 John 3:15). Behind murder lies the judgment that someone who has failed us or wronged us deserves to die.

If *raca* means "idiot," and *fool* means "good for nothing," then most of us are murderers, for almost everyone has judged someone to be a fool or an idiot. We say things like: "He's worthless. He doesn't deserve to live. I wish he were dead. I'd shed no tears if he were dead." Therefore, let us guard our speech. When someone ruins our plans, we mutter, "I could kill him!" When a disobedient child runs away, frustrated parents utter dire threats: "Just wait till I get my hands on you! I'm going to . . ."

My mother is a paragon of patience and compassion, yet as a child I was mischievous enough to drive my mother occasionally to say, "Wait till I get my hands on you! I'm going to wring your neck!" At the age of five, I imagined that this meant she would pick me up by my feet and swung my head back and forth like a bell; it hardly sounded unpleasant. Then one day it was time to slaughter some chickens on Grandpa's farm. A discussion ensued: shall we use an ax or wring their necks? I listened intently until I realized, in an unsettling flash, the difference between "ring" and "wring." My mother had threatened to twist my neck until . . .

I now know that there was more laughter than wrath in my mother's threats. Still, quite a few parents are guilty of murder in God's eyes. Even in Christian homes, children hear their parents say they are worthless, good for nothing, untalented, and unwanted, and that their parents are going to kill them. Such language murders the soul.

Some of us heard such words as children. Some of us may still be trying to prove our mother or father wrong, trying to prove that we will amount to something. If so, know that God has spoken another word. He has called us his beloved, his children. Good for nothing? Hardly. God valued us enough to give his only Son for us, while we were still sinners.

So far, we have followed Jesus in stressing the harm of a contemptuous heart and tongue. But we must add that a murderous spirit can lead to action as well. Abortion occurs because people judge that an unborn human being is worthless. They decide they will be—what? happier?—if this unborn child were dead. Euthanasia for the ill and the aged is similar. There is no virtue in prolonging the process of dying, and there is no benefit in machines that keep the heart pumping and the lungs inflating after the brain has ceased to function. But we must take utmost care in evaluating such cases, lest we make an evil judgment that a life has no value and is not worth the cost of preserving it.[2]

Because the thought "He is worthless" can lead to murder, it is liable to judgment, even if the action never follows. Neglect of the hungry, the homeless, and the chronically poor can be similar. Yes, there are dangers in endless, unqualified giving; it causes dependency and fails to instill responsibility. But sometimes we neglect the poor because we judge them worthless.

## MAKING PEACE (5:23–26)

So far, Jesus has forbidden murder itself and the hatred and contempt that both kill the spirit of others and potentially lead to murder, abortion, and euthanasia. Next, he says, we must not simply refrain from violence ourselves, but must make peace with others, so as to assuage *their* anger and contempt. Consider the structure of Matthew 5:21–26 and the lesson becomes clear:

1. First, Jesus approves the ancient command and forbids the act of murder (5:21).
2. He adds that anger and contempt amount to murder, too (5:22).
3. Further, a disciple is responsible to prevent murderous acts or attitudes by a brother in the faith (5:23–24).
4. Finally, Jesus says that disciples must even strive to prevent anger in their enemies (5:25–26).

### *Making Peace with a Brother (5:23–24)*

It is so easy to misread Matthew 5:23–24 that it is worthwhile to reread the text:

> Therefore, if you are offering your gift at the altar and there remember that your brother has something against you, leave your gift there in front of the altar. First go and be reconciled to your brother; then come and offer your gift.

Christians sometimes say, "I know that if I have a problem with my brother, I must go to him and work it out." True enough, but what Jesus says *here* is not, "If you have something against your brother, go," but, "If your brother has something against *you*, go."

The word "therefore" indicates that verse 23 draws a conclusion from verses 21–22. The reasoning goes this way: If it is good *for us* to refrain from murder and murderous attitudes, then it is also good to prevent murderous attitudes *in others*, if possible. That is, we should love our brothers enough to act to remove their murderous dispositions toward us.

Jesus says that this duty is so important that a worshiper should interrupt the sacred duty of presenting an offering to God on the altar in order to make peace. Today, it is more important to be reconciled to a brother than to go to church, since worship is a sham if anyone hates his brother and fellow worshiper.

Notice that Jesus does not even say that the brother is right to be offended. The anger may be just or reasonable, or it may not. We may have offended him, or he may have taken offense when none was given. But even if we believe ourselves innocent or consider the problem trivial, if enough tension exists that we remember it and it troubles us, we should stop and seek reconciliation.

### Making Peace with an Adversary (5:25–26)

The final verses take us to the apex of Jesus' teaching. First, Jesus forbids the *act* of murder (v. 21). Second, he prohibits the *attitudes* that lead us to murder a brother (v. 22). Third, he commands us to seek peace with an angry *brother* (vv. 23–24). The "brother" includes relatives, siblings, parents, and other family members, as well as fellow believers—fellow Jews then, fellow Christians now. Finally, he commands us to remove anger in an *adversary*. We are responsible even to prevent murder in our enemies.

In his illustration, in 5:25–26, Jesus envisions a foe taking a disciple to court over a monetary problem. There is an unpaid debt, or at least the adversary thinks so. As angry as two people usually are when they invoke legal authorities against one another, disciples must try to make peace, even on the steps of the courthouse at the last minute. Make peace, Jesus says, lest greater grief come.

This is something our litigious society needs to hear. We ought to be careful about the way we insist on our rights. We must watch ourselves, to see if we are harboring anger, licking our wounds, or plotting revenge. This applies to everyone we meet, whether a beloved brother or a sworn foe. Make peace if you can, Jesus says, if you offended someone or if he foolishly took offense. Of course, one party cannot make peace alone. Paul says, "If it is possible, as far as it depends on you, live at peace with everyone" (Rom. 12:18). He concedes that it may be impossible, if someone refuses your plea for peace. But we must try.

In order to make peace, we must know how to take responsibility for mistakes. In a conflict, we can always take responsibility for our part of the problem. If most of the fault lies with others, our confession may free them to confess their faults. Even if another party refuses to join our quest for peace, we can still apologize and make amends for our part. As a practical matter, peacemaking usually works best face-to-face. Written correspondence is easily misunderstood. In person, face and voice can convey love, hope, and sincerity.

## THE HEART OF THE MATTER

The command "Do not murder" seems so simple. It is familiar, it protects us, and, externally at least, it is easy to observe. But Jesus comes to fulfill the law, to disclose its complete meaning, which is this: We must give up rage and contempt. We must be peaceful and make peace, with both brothers and enemies, with those whom we offend and with those who wrongly take offense.

By now, Jesus' will is quite clear. Indeed, his clarity becomes a problem because we cannot follow his will. We do grow angry; we are reluctant to heal broken relationships. In short, Jesus' word exceeds our capacity. But there is good news. The same Jesus who issues these commands also blesses the poor in spirit—those who know they cannot obey. The same Jesus who issues these commands gave his life as a ransom for disciples who cannot obey them. Jesus also gives empowering grace; he sends his Spirit to give us the capacity to begin, at least, to obey him. Yes, our obedience is always imperfect, but we can make progress.

I experienced this at the airport on the day I described earlier. With minutes to spare before the plane departed, a supervisor arrived and quickly resolved our difficulties. As events fell out, the smiling "You can't get on the plane" agent was at the ramp to take my ticket. For a moment, no one else was near. I walked toward her hesitantly. The smile was still on her face, but it was sweeter, as if she was glad that our tense conversation was over.

"Hello again," she said brightly. "By the way, what was your business here?"

My heart sank. I had tried to stay calm, but had I done well enough to tell her the truth? I tried a dodge: "I was at a conference."

"Really? What kind of conference was it? What did you do there?"

It was hopeless now. I felt miserable, but had no choice but to tell her the truth. "It was at a church. I was speaking at a Bible conference."

Her face brightened again. "Oh, I *thought* you were a Christian," she exclaimed. "I am a Christian, too."

I was dumbfounded. Either God had given me more calm outside than I felt inside, or this was a woman who really knew how to see the good in people. Yet as I look back on our encounter, it makes sense. She never stopped smiling, never stopped being polite, however negative her message was. Perhaps I had done better than I knew; and I wondered what kind of verbal abuse she had suffered from other passengers in similar circumstances. It reminds us that our progress may be slow, but Jesus does work in our hearts. By his grace, we may attain more of his righteousness than we see.

To be sure, we must trust in God's grace, for the next teaching of Jesus is just as important, just as daunting as this one. In the next chapter, we turn from life and death, war and peace, to lust, adultery, and divorce.

# 6

## BE STILL, O WANDERING EYE

*Matthew 5:27–32*

ONE SUMMER, while I was attending seminary, I worked on a construction crew. The worst rumors about the language of construction workers were true of my coworkers. Day after day, they unleashed torrents of the most crude, perverse language imaginable, especially when they spied an attractive woman. At first I thought it was a joke, something they put on to tease their seminary student. But when it persisted week after week, I realized it was genuine.

I tried to interrupt their streams of obscenities a few times, but to no avail. Finally, one day I tried a different approach with the foreman. "You have so much to say about women," I began. "Why don't you tell us about some of your adventures and conquests?" This shocked the man, who protested that I was badly mistaken. Using his "colorful" vocabulary, he said that he had always been faithful to his wife. This puzzled me, but later some members of the crew explained why the foreman was so faithful. His wife, they said, was bigger than he, and a fierce woman besides. He was afraid that she would clobber him if he fooled around.

The crew chief boasted of his fidelity to his wife, but his loyalty probably did not impress God, for even if his behavior met the legal standards, he did the right thing for the wrong reasons. Given his mindset, we might wonder how long he would remain faithful if he met a certain kind of woman. It is not our purpose here to judge construction workers, but we do need to recognize that Jesus does not want his people merely to obey the law. He wants his children to do the right things for the right reasons.

## THE HEART OF THE MATTER

In the previous passage, Matthew 5:21–26, Jesus told his disciples that they not only must not murder, but must not harbor the anger and contempt that lead to murder. Instead, we should be reconciled to our brothers when something stands between us. Indeed, we should even strive to make peace with our enemies.

Jesus pushed beyond external deeds to probe the motives that lead to murder. Now he does the same thing with adultery. He briefly addresses our physical deeds, but he chiefly explores the heart issues behind adultery.

While Jesus probes the heart of the matter, our public discourse becomes ever more superficial. Our comedies treat adultery and fornication as jokes. Our commercials and clothing styles promote lust. Our public policies assume that everyone over the age of eighteen is sexually active. And we deride the concept of absolute standards. But then we fret over the consequences of sexual immorality, such as teenage pregnancy and the host of sexually transmitted diseases, starting with AIDS. The solution, society proposes, is not fidelity within marriage and abstinence outside of marriage, but "safe sex" and condom distribution.

## THE MORAL STANDARD (5:27–28)

Jesus begins by restating the seventh commandment, "Do not commit adultery." Perhaps everyone agrees that murder is wrong (Matt. 5:21), and perhaps a solid majority still affirms that adultery is immoral. But the gap grows wider in practice. A large church probably has no murderers in attendance, but it probably has many who have either committed adultery or suffered it.

If someone has committed a sexual sin, God offers forgiveness if he or she repents. Whatever the sin may be, Scripture says, "If we confess our sins, he is faithful and just and will forgive us our sins and purify us from all unrighteousness" (1 John 1:9). Once someone is forgiven, he seeks each day to be faithful and obedient. Further, if God is willing to forgive all those who genuinely repent, then those who suffer adultery should also forgive them, forgo vengeful anger, and, if possible, trust their spouse again.

Adultery is Jesus' principal concern, for two reasons. First, it is the most grievous sexual sin, for it betrays the promise of lifelong, exclusive loyalty. Second, almost all Jews were married before the age of twenty, so that the leading sexual temptation was adultery, not fornication. But today, in nations where people reach sexual maturity earlier than ever and the time of marriage is often later than ever, the leading temptation is fornication.

Yet whether adultery or fornication is the greater issue, Jesus presses deeper. Just as Jesus forbids the anger that leads to murder, so also he forbids the lust that leads to adultery. He cares about more than physical acts and superficial definitions of purity. He cares about the heart, about the motives.

Therefore he says, "Anyone who looks at a woman lustfully has already committed adultery with her in his heart" (Matt. 5:28 NIV). The ESV translates this verse as "Everyone who looks at a woman with lustful intent has already committed adultery with her in his heart." The ESV hints at a small riddle in the text. The original Greek may be translated "anyone who looks at a woman *in order to* lust after her" (cf. KJV, NASB) commits adultery. That is, Jesus forbids the leering looks that are intended to stir up lustful thoughts. But the Greek may also be translated, "anyone who looks at a woman so as to cause her to lust" commits adultery. In this case, Jesus opposes the man who looks at a woman and wonders how he can cause her to desire him, so he may seduce her.[1]

Jesus warns men against such sins, but surely women should neither lust nor attempt to stir up lust in others, either. Wise women know that it is one thing to make themselves attractive and another to make themselves look seductive.[2]

Beyond this, Jesus forbids all sexual acts outside of marriage, not just adultery *per se* (Matt. 15:19; 19:9).[3] Premarital sex is not compounded by the betrayal of a promise of lifelong, exclusive loyalty. But it is still sin before God, against others, and against oneself.

Homosexual unions also constitute an intimate relationship outside the bounds of marriage, so they also violate God's will. Sexual expression belongs inside the love, the commitment, and the safety of marriage. We should have compassion for those who struggle with same-sex attraction, but we cannot bless homosexual unions without doing violence to Scripture (Gen. 19:4–11; Lev. 18:22; 20:13; Judg. 19:22–25; Rom. 1:24–27; 1 Cor. 6:9; 1 Tim. 1:10).[4]

## IS JESUS TOO STRICT? REASONS FOR HIS STANDARDS

Lust is the problem Jesus addresses in Matthew 5:28, but before we consider that, we should address those who question the idea that physical intimacy belongs only in marriage. In high schools and colleges, and among single adults, many question the biblical teaching. The argument goes like this:

> The laws against adultery may have been necessary long ago, for social reasons: to prevent birth outside of marriage. They also protected women, who were so dependent on men. But now we can solve the problem of unwanted pregnancy. And today's women, so liberated, so educated, need not depend on men any longer. So the rationale for prohibiting these acts is outdated. People should be free to choose their own lifestyle.

Instead of answering this directly, let us consider the way too many Christians respond to such challenges. Lewis Smedes, a Christian ethicist, says that Christians defend the biblical teaching in three somewhat inadequate ways. He calls them the morality of caution, the morality of concern, and the morality of personal relationship.[5]

The *morality of caution* asks "Can I get hurt?" and answers "Yes." According to this approach, we should avoid extramarital sex because it is dangerous and painful. It leads to serious and even deadly diseases. It causes guilt and unwanted pregnancies, emotional pain and self-corruption. These points are generally valid, but they operate on the basis of a cost-benefit analysis, and a cost-benefit analysis cannot support an absolute veto on extramarital sex. After all, people persuade themselves that the cost is worth it, or that they can control the consequences.

The *morality of concern* asks, "Can I hurt others? What if I cause a pregnancy or a disease? What if I bring guilt or sorrow to another?" This reasoning seems less selfish than the first. But again, it rests on a cost-benefit analysis, and passions can lead people to think that the benefits are clear and the costs are controllable.

The *morality of personal relationship* asks, "Can this hurt our relationship? Will one of us exploit the other sexually? Will the move toward sexual gratification hurt other aspects of our relationship? Will the tender, gradual process of self-disclosure be cut short by the quick charge of sexual gratification?" As Smedes says, in sexual intimacy, there is "such explosive self-giving, such personal exposure, that few people can feel the same toward each other afterward." One partner may yearn for a commitment that the other is unwilling to make. Then one feels needy and the other feels trapped and looks to escape.[6]

Pastoral experience leads me to agree with Smedes. The "morality of personal relationship" still has a whiff of self-interest and cost-benefit analysis, but it takes us closer to the divine plan that places sexual expression inside marriage. In God's design, three things go together. As God told Adam and Eve, "A man will leave his father and mother and be united to his wife, and they will become one flesh." Then we read, "The man and his wife were both naked, and they felt no shame." This is the God-given trio:

1. Exclusive loyalty. Father, mother, and the dearest friends take second place.
2. Lifelong loyalty. Husband and wife are united to one another.
3. Bodily loyalty. Husband and wife become one flesh. They express and seal the union of their hearts and minds with the union of their bodies.

By its very nature, physical love is a life-uniting act. God intended it to be a sign and a seal of the union of two lives. "Casual sex" is a misnomer. Sex is no mere bodily function. Our bodies are us. To quote Smedes again, "When two bodies are united, two *persons* are united. Nobody can go to bed with someone and leave his soul parked outside. The soul is in the act."

Therefore, the trouble with extramarital sex is that it is "a life-uniting act committed without life-uniting intent." It is not just adultery. It is a thieving lie. Intimacy is a sign and a seal of the union of two lives.

But outside of marriage, the act and the intent clash.[7] Intimacy of body and intimacy of soul go together. That is why adultery—as well as other sexual relations outside of marriage—is wrong.

## LUST: THE MIND FOR ADULTERY

After Jesus forbids adultery, he warns against lustful eyes, against adultery in the heart. Jesus cautions men about lustful eyes, for men are more oriented to seeing than feeling. But our culture is trying hard to teach women to lust after "eye candy" too, so Jesus' warning applies to them as well.

We must understand what Jesus forbids. It is harmless and natural to notice that a woman is beautiful or that a man is handsome. But it is one thing to make an aesthetic observation, another to turn it over to the imagination and entertain immoral fantasies. Likewise, it is good to dress attractively, but not to dress seductively.

The fashion industry is not necessarily the friend of chastity. At the moment, social critic David Brooks observes, "the average square yardage of boys' fashions grows and grows while the square inches in the girls' outfits shrink and shrink, so that while the boys look like tent-wearing skateboarders, the girls look like preppy prostitutes."[8] That is today's problem. In five years, the problem will change, but the essence remains the same. The clothing industry rarely promotes modesty.

Jesus says adultery begins in both the heart and the eye. The heart moves the eye, and the eye inflames the sinful heart. Adultery doesn't just happen. Adultery with the body follows adultery with the heart and the eye. Knowing this, righteous Job said, "I made a covenant with my eyes not to look lustfully at a girl. . . . If my heart has been led by my eyes . . . [or] my heart has been enticed by a woman," may the Lord punish me (Job 31:1, 7, 9).

We understand that it is not sinful to *be* tempted. Temptations assail us all—even Jesus was tempted. Jesus was "tempted in every way, just as we are—yet was without sin" (Heb. 4:15). So then, Jesus faced the temptation to entertain lustful thoughts, but he resisted. He refused to envision or plan or taste sin, even with his mind.

We cannot prevent certain thoughts from entering our minds. But once they enter, we may either entertain them or cast them aside and

64

*Matthew 5:27–32*

turn our minds elsewhere. Martin Luther said that we cannot stop birds from flying over our heads, but we can keep them from building nests in our hair. We cannot keep impure thoughts from flitting into our minds, but we can refuse to let them roost and find a home there.

*don't look to observe — observe & let in go*

## THE GOODNESS OF SEXUALITY AND IMAGINATION

While we affirm that Jesus wants his disciples to resist certain sexual thoughts, we must remember that sexuality is good. Like all of God's creations, sexuality is good in itself. Since sexuality is part of human nature, sexual desire is proper and natural. Yet, like all good things, it must be used the right way, in the right place and time. Similarly, food is good, but there are times when it is wrong to eat. Sleep is good, but there are times when it would be immoral to take a nap (a physician, during surgery, for example). So too, sex is good in the right place and time and wrong in others. The right place is the commitment and safety of marriage. God blesses sexuality when it is surrounded by loving faithfulness between a man and a woman (Prov. 5:15–19).

God wants to bless our use of his gifts, as we use them the right way. A vivid imagination is also a gift from God.[9] Almost all of the world's literature depends upon it. For us to witness the torment of Hamlet or the courage of Henry V, Shakespeare had to imagine it first. Great leaders must first imagine a better future. Inventors must imagine better ways to live and conceive of means to achieve them. God blesses such uses of the imagination. But if we turn the imagination toward taking what does not belong to us, it corrupts the mind and can lead to actual misdeeds. Therefore, Jesus warns against lust.

## RECOILING FROM LUST (5:29–30)

Lust is a form of coveting, and coveting is the gateway to many sins, including adultery. Jesus shows how serious lust is when he says, "If your right eye causes you to sin, gouge it out and throw it away" (5:29). This is hyperbole, of course. In all of church history, no group of Christian leaders ever endorsed literal mutilations or amputations. Indeed, the Council of Nicaea formally forbade it. Besides, if Jesus thought mutilations and amputations could actually cure evil, he would have ordered

65

his disciples to put out both eyes, for a one-eyed man can still lust, and to cut off both hands, for a one-armed man can do terrible evil. Indeed, even the removal of both eyes would not suffice, for the memory can still "see." The root of sin lies in the heart, not in sense organs or limbs.

The point, then, is that it is better to suffer bodily pain in the present than to suffer spiritual pain for eternity.[10] So we can be sure that Jesus does not want us to take this sentence literally. Still, we have to decipher Jesus' figure of speech.

First, Jesus used repugnant, grotesque images to show how repugnant and grotesque sin is in his sight. Few things are more horrible than the thought of maiming. Yet Jesus says, "It is better for you to lose one part of your body than for your whole body to be thrown into hell. And if your right hand causes you to sin, cut it off and throw it away" (5:29–30). If Jesus says it is better to go through life maimed than to enter hell whole, then sin should seem horrible to us. We should shudder at the thought of it, as we shudder at the thought of losing a limb.

Second, if our eye tempts us to sin, we should strive to *act as if* we had no eye, and refuse to look at the tempting object. If a hand or foot tempts us to sin, we should act as if we had none, by refusing to walk toward that which tempts us and by refusing to touch the source of temptation.

This teaching applies to pornography, which is so accessible today. Pornography is wrong in many ways. It degrades women and teaches them to degrade themselves. It inflames lust. It is unfair to spouses, present or future, who cannot compete with models who polish their bodies for a living while photographers delete all defects.

When we come across pornography, we should strive to live as if we have no eyes. Yet we do have eyes, and pornography gains a strange grip on some people, almost like an addiction. Let me suggest three things to those who may be tempted by it:

- Keep yourself away from temptation. Avoid the books, movies, websites, and magazines that lead you into temptation.
- If self-control is difficult, if the sin is getting a hold on you, tell someone who will have the right to ask you about your progress against this sin. Out of the blue, a friend once told me that he had found a stash of pornographic magazines by accident and,

66

to his surprise, spent thirty minutes looking through them. Apparently I looked a bit nonplussed by his confession, so he explained himself: "I'm telling you this because I *don't* want this to be my secret."

• If such a sin gains a grip on you, seek a Christian counselor.

In our verses, Jesus connects sexual sins with Gehenna, the place of punishment. That does not mean that everyone who commits sexual sins goes to hell. By God's grace, every sin is forgivable. But if we love the thought of sin, and indulge it instead of resisting it, we are rejecting God's ways. Deliberate rebellion does lead to death. But if we take our struggles to the Lord, seeking mercy, he will forgive us and renew us.

## CONTENTMENT: THE ANTIDOTE TO LUST

Contentment is the antithesis of lust. The Bible often commands believers to be contented with their possessions and with their life situation (e.g., Eccl. 4:8; Luke 3:14; Phil. 4:11–12; 1 Tim. 6:6–8; Heb. 13:5). Paul says, "Godliness with contentment is great gain" (1 Tim. 6:6)—not material gain, but spiritual gain. The general command to be content means we should be content with our singleness, if that is God's gift. If we are married, it means that we should be content with the spouse that God has given us.

Our culture encourages us to be discontented with many things, including our spouses. It presents images of fitness and beauty that few people can match. Movies imply that singles who lack a partner are missing the best thing in life. Television comedies show us how entertaining it is to mock and ridicule a spouse who lacks a scintillating wit and endless talents. Some self-improvement gurus tell us that we are right to be discontent if our spouse simply isn't keeping up with us.

Of course, every husband or wife has failings. My wife eats the big strawberry at the top of my ice-cream sundae, and I drink the orange juice she pours for herself the next morning. We fail to listen, leave messes, and hog the covers. It is no sin to notice these flaws, but it is a sin to become discontent with the spouse that God has given us.

Discontentment with a spouse drives out love and respect for her. Discontentment is prideful, for the discontented think they deserve better. Discontent is distrust in God's providence, for it accuses God of providing the wrong spouse.

The culture says, "Get the best partner you can." But we should say, "God has given me this man, this woman." Then we should ask not what our spouse can do for us, but what we can do for our spouse. Contentment is the partner of love and the scourge of the roving eye. Contentment breeds faithfulness.

## THE HEART ISSUE

Wherever they begin, marital problems end with the heart. "Success" in marriage depends on our response to events more than it does on the events themselves. The cause of lust is not attractive women, but an improper response to attractive women. The cause of marital discontentment is less "my spouse's flaws" than it is a hard-hearted response to those flaws.

There is no ideal man or woman. Every one of us is flawed from head to heart to hands. The unmarried seek a compatible partner, but in an important way the quest is vain. Every potential partner is a sinner, and no two sinners are perfectly compatible. No two sinners, rubbing elbows day by day, can keep their wedding vows perfectly.

People love to ask questions like "What are the two biggest causes of trouble in marriage?" There are many potential answers: money, children, sex, children, in-laws, communication. But the two biggest causes of marital strife are the husband and the wife.

## DIVORCE: A CONSEQUENCE OF LUST AND DISCONTENT (5:31–32)

If lust begins with a wandering eye, perhaps divorce begins with a wandering mind. Lust can start with sexual dissatisfaction. Divorce can begin as marital dissatisfaction. It may begin with a discontented thought: "My spouse is not so interesting, not so attractive, not so interested in pleasing me these days." Today, wherever no fault divorce is the law, mere dissatisfaction is a sufficient legal basis for a divorce. In Jesus' day, women had few rights, but men could get a divorce as easily as today.

In our passage, Jesus prohibits cavalier divorce. According to Jewish tradition, a man could legally divorce his wife if he simply gave her a certificate that declared her a free woman. Jesus rightly notes, "It has been said, 'Anyone who divorces his wife must give her a certificate of divorce'" (Matt. 5:31). Conservative rabbis said a woman had to do something shameful before a husband could divorce her. But others said that a man could obtain a divorce for any reason at all. Some rabbis judged it a sufficient cause for divorce if a woman spoiled her husband's food or even if he "found another fairer than she."[11] The book of Ecclesiasticus, found in the Apocrypha and dated to roughly 150 B.C., says, "If she will not do as you tell her, get rid of her" (25:26).

Jesus calls cavalier divorce "adultery" in Matthew 5:31–32. Further, he says that such divorce can drive the divorced woman into adultery: "Anyone who divorces his wife, except for marital unfaithfulness, causes her to become an adulteress, and anyone who marries the divorced woman commits adultery." This is not the place for a full discussion of divorce, but we will make a few observations about Scripture and the contemporary scene.

The biblical regulation of divorce began with Moses at a time when hard-hearted men divorced their wives all too easily. Because their hearts were hard, they were not ready to hear God's plan for lifelong fidelity. So Moses did not insist on God's perfect standard, but permitted men to divorce their wives for significant offenses, provided that they gave their wives a certificate that freed them to marry another man. If she did remarry, her first husband could never touch her again (Deut. 24:1–4).

This legislation accomplished two things. First, it protected divorced women by giving them a clear right to remarry. Second, it slowed men down, for it forced them to think twice before acting. If a man divorced his wife and she remarried, he could never regain her. Thus, Moses' law permitted divorce, but also restricted it.

Jesus effectively says that such laws had their purposes, but that lifelong faithfulness is the goal, except in the case of adultery. (Scripture elsewhere makes it clear that desertion is a legitimate ground for divorce, and a strong case can be made that physical violence is as well.) Jesus says that those who divorce simply because they are tired of their spouse are guilty of adultery.

In Jesus' day, the rabbis debated how readily a man gained the right to divorce his wife. Today, people wonder how fast they can get a divorce and still be considered respectable. But later, in Matthew 19, Jesus says that our standard should be God's plan for marriage, not social respectability. There he cites Genesis 1 and 2, which present three principles. First, God has blessed marriage from the beginning, when he created one man and one woman and married them (1:27–28; 2:18–25). Second, marriage was Adam and Eve's central human relationship. They were married before they were parents and stayed married after their children matured. Marriage is stronger and more enduring than the bond between parent and child: "A man will leave his father and mother and be united to his wife" (2:24). Third, the union of their hearts, with God as their witness, leads a man and a woman to become "one flesh" (2:24).

"One flesh" certainly includes physical intimacy, but it is broader than that. It means hearing both the words and the silences of the beloved. It means dreaming great dreams, but also cleaning up the kitchen. It means sharing the deep concerns of the heart and the little bumps on the toe.

Jesus says that only the radical betrayal of adultery can sever all this. Is that because adultery is so much worse than other sins? Not necessarily. But physical adultery usually occurs after much mental adultery. To commit adultery, one must think it, plan it, and persuade oneself that it is justified. The adulterer must decide that his spouse no longer deserves his loyalty. To act on this thought is a profound betrayal of the essence of marriage, which is the pledge of exclusive, lifelong faithfulness. That is why lust leads to adultery, and adultery leads to divorce.

## THE WORD OF GRACE

The greatest source of healing in a marriage is the grace of God poured into our hearts. That grace has two facets. First, God is patient and faithful toward us, despite our sins and flaws. As we behold our Lord and live in union with him, we participate more and more in his character. Then we grow into his patience and faithfulness.

Second, God graciously forgives our sins and flaws. Drinking deep at the fountain of his mercy, we have mercy for others. Some days our spouse's failures loom large. Sometimes the virtues of a friendly and attractive person of the opposite sex loom even larger. Just as we cannot control our angry hearts, so we cannot repeal the heart's tendency to become discontent, to wish for a better spouse.

What then? Remember God's grace and providence. The church is the bride of Christ, and we are hardly the perfect spouse to him. Yet God tells us,

> I will betroth you to me forever;
>> I will betroth you in righteousness and justice,
>> in love and compassion.
> I will betroth you in faithfulness,
>> and you will acknowledge the LORD. (Hos. 2:19–20)

So God's faithfulness inspires us. More than that, the Lord gives grace to forgive our sins and to make us new. With this grace, he can build a strong marriage, with all the faithfulness and contentment that two sinners can know. Amen

# 7

# To Tell the Truth

*Matthew 5:33–37*

In this section of the Sermon on the Mount, Jesus' teaching moves from one challenging topic to the next. After addressing anger, he moves on to lust, to marriage and divorce, and now to speech, especially careless and deceptive speech. As always, his interests go through our deeds to our hearts.

## The Need for Jesus' Teaching

Truthfulness is Jesus' central concern in this passage, and he knows that we struggle with veracity. "Talk is cheap," we say, for we are careless with our words—even with our promises. Politicians are renowned for breaking promises. A presidential candidate once won election, in part, on his bold promise, "Read my lips: no new taxes." Two years later, he signed a large tax increase.

Ordinary folk do the same thing. Businessmen call home and say, "It's been a busy day, but I will still be home by 6:00, 6:15 at the latest, 6:30 at the very latest. I'll call if I'm delayed." Almost half the time, we even violate the sacred promise: "I promise to take you as my lawful, wedded wife till death do us part." Clearly, we need Jesus' word about our words, from Matthew 5:33–37:

> Again, you have heard that it was said to the people long ago, "Do not break your oath, but keep the oaths you have made to the Lord." But I

73

tell you, Do not swear at all: either by heaven, for it is God's throne; or by the earth, for it is his footstool; or by Jerusalem, for it is the city of the Great King. And do not swear by your head, for you cannot make even one hair white or black. Simply let your "Yes" be "Yes," and your "No," "No"; anything beyond this comes from the evil one.

## Jesus' Teaching on Oaths in Context

In Matthew 5, Jesus tells his disciples, "I tell you that unless your righteousness surpasses that of the Pharisees and teachers of the law, you will certainly not enter the kingdom of heaven" (v. 17). The scribes and Pharisees were famed for their impeccable observance of the law's external regulations, as they understood them, so the disciples must have wondered how they could surpass them. But Jesus does not ask his disciples to surpass the Pharisees by obeying more regulations. A disciple's surpassing righteousness is not essentially a matter of legal observance. Remember, Jesus points beyond the act of murder to the problem of anger. He points beyond adultery to lust. Here he points beyond oaths to truth-telling.

Jesus does not urge us to redouble our efforts to observe the law. Nonetheless, we must let his moral teaching have its weight. If God's commands are difficult, we need to face that squarely, confess it to ourselves and to God, and ask for mercy.

Many people prefer less candor. They deny that God's will is so clear. Or they redefine the law so it is easier to obey. In Jesus' day, the Pharisees tended to do that. When they faced a difficult law, they whittled it down to something manageable. We are prone to do the same sort of thing, redefining Jesus' commands to make them more manageable.

When the rabbis heard "Love your neighbor as yourself," they defined "neighbor" narrowly, so that only a small percentage of people counted as neighbors. If most people did not count as neighbors, then perhaps they could love the few that were left. When the rabbis read "You shall not commit adultery," they refrained from literal adultery, but reserved the right to divorce their wife and take another woman at any time. Thus, they removed much of the temptation to commit adultery by making it legal to divorce one woman and take another whenever they pleased. They did much the same thing with oaths and truthfulness. Jesus corrects these abuses by expounding the true meaning of the law. Therefore he argues, "You have heard that it was said . . . but I tell you . . ."

## THE NATURE AND USE OF OATHS (5:33)

At the most basic level, Jesus tells his disciples that they must tell the truth, but Jesus reaches that principle by discussing the matter of oaths. Oaths are a convention designed to restrain lies and false promises. We rarely use oaths or vows today. We reserve them for formal situations. We take oaths when we join the church or become an officer, when we get married, and when we are called to testify in court. While we rarely take oaths today, we use similar conventions with the same goal. We make promises to friends and family, and we sign contracts in business dealings. Oaths, promises, and contracts all have the same goal—to induce people to tell the truth and be true to their word, especially when there are temptations to lie or to break a commitment.

In biblical times, oaths and vows were more prominent. Long ago, Israel learned to guarantee their veracity by swearing, in God's presence and in his name, to tell the truth (1 Sam. 12:3; Prov. 29:24). They invoked God as witness, and they invoked him as judge if they lied. If someone swore that something was true, it had to be true. If someone vowed to perform a deed, it had to be done.

Jesus summarizes the Old Testament lesson when he says, "You have heard that it was said . . . 'Do not break your oath, but keep the oaths you have made to the Lord'" (Matt. 5:33). Jesus understood that several Old Testament laws blessed and regulated the use of oaths and vows:

- "When a man makes a vow to the LORD . . . he must not break his word" (Num. 30:2).
- "If you make a vow to the LORD your God, do not be slow to pay it" (Deut. 23:21).
- "You shall not swear by my name falsely, and so profane the name of your God" (Lev. 19:12 ESV).

It is still God's will that we do what we say, especially in solemn settings, when others depend on our words. Even if circumstances change,

75

even if we get a better offer, even if faithfulness becomes difficult, even if the temptation to break a vow seems unbearable, even if keeping the vow brings real loss, even if no one but God will know if we break our vow, we should still do what we say. We should disregard a vow only if keeping it requires us to sin.

## THE ABUSE OF OATHS (5:33–36)

The teaching on vows seems helpful; why then does Jesus want to amend it? First, in Jesus' day, rabbis concocted a convoluted system that defeated the very purpose of oaths. They said that oaths might or might not be binding, depending on what one swore by. They said that if you swear *by* Jerusalem, it is not binding, but if you swear *toward* Jerusalem, it is. If you swear by the temple, it is not binding, but if you swear by the temple's gold, it is. If you swear by the altar of sacrifice, it is not binding, but if you swear by the gift on the altar, it is.[1]

These strange rulings perverted the purpose of oaths. Instead of calling on God to assure their honesty, they phrased their oaths so as to avoid God's punishment when they spoke dishonestly. Perhaps no one planned to corrupt the law, but the rabbis spoiled the goal of verifying truthfulness and substituted the goal of getting away with deceitfulness.

Since the system was corrupt, since oaths no longer guaranteed anything, Jesus said, "Do not swear at all" (Matt. 5:34a). He removed the artificial distinction between vows that invoke God's name (and so are binding) and those that do not (and so are not binding). Whatever we swear by, Jesus said, it refers to God, for he created heaven and earth. If someone swears by heaven, he invokes God, for heaven is his throne (5:34b). If someone swears by the earth, he invokes God, for it is his footstool (5:35a). If someone swears by Jerusalem, he invokes God, for it is the city of the King (5:35b). If someone swears by the hair of her head, she invokes God, for he rules our heads (5:36).

Jesus says, "Do not swear by your head, for you cannot make even one hair white or black" (5:36). Of course, we can change our hair color by applying certain chemicals at the salon. But we cannot change the natural color of even one hair. Whatever we swear by is related to God in some way. All oaths call God as our witness, for he created and sustains all things, even our hair and its color.

## WHAT GOD'S OATHS REVEAL

Jesus' disciples should simply tell the truth. The Essenes said, "He who cannot be believed without [swearing by] God, is already condemned."[2] Jesus said that we should be so true to our words that the need for oaths disappears, that a simple "Yes" or "No" is enough. The word of a disciple should be so reliable that no one asks for more.

This leads to an important question. If Jesus wants disciples to take no oaths, why does God take oaths, apparently violating his own ideal? For God does takes oaths:

- He said to Abraham, "By myself I have sworn . . . I will surely bless you" (Gen. 22:16–17 ESV).
- God confirmed his promises to Israel "with an oath" (Heb. 6:17).
- God swore to mankind that he would never send another flood (Gen. 9:8–11).
- He swore to send a Redeemer (Luke 1:68, 73) and to raise him from the dead (Ps. 16:10; Acts 2:27–31).
- God took oaths to guarantee his covenants (Pss. 132:11; 95:11; 119:106).

Why does God do something that he tells us not to do? John Stott replies, "Not to increase his credibility but to elicit and confirm our faith."[3] God does not take oaths because his credibility is in doubt, but because we, having told and heard so many lies, have learned to be doubters. We are accustomed to breaking our word and having others break their word to us. Therefore, God knows that we need assurance of his reliability. He knows that our standards are so low that we expect falsehood from everyone, even him. So for our sake he takes an oath to guarantee his word.

## WHAT OUR OATHS REVEAL

If God's oaths reveal that we are accustomed to hearing lies, what do our oaths reveal? Let us answer by considering something similar—the promise. Consider why we make promises. Suppose it is Thursday evening. A father tells his children, "If you help me clean up the yard today, I will take you out for ice cream on Saturday." A wary child may reply, "Do you promise?"

The request for a promise is a testimony against us. It shows that a child has learned she cannot entirely trust her father's word. In the past, she cleaned up the yard, but never received the ice cream. When the child pointed this out, her father said, "I forgot," or "Something came up," or "You should have reminded me." So the child learned to seek a guarantee. When she asks, "Do you promise?" she means, "Do you mean it? Can I count on you?"

The very request for a promise testifies that we are not reliable. When a child asks, "Do you promise?" he testifies that our "Yes" has not always been "Yes." Ideally, a parent's word should be so reliable that it never occurs to a child to request a guarantee. Our word should be so reliable that our "Yes" does mean "Yes" (not "Probably"), and our "No" does mean "No." Then the need for oaths and promises should wither away.

The very existence of customs such as oaths and promises reveals that human life is tainted by deception. Jesus says that the family of God should be an exception to this. In the kingdom, we should be so truthful that we need neither promises nor vows.

## THE USE OF OATHS TODAY

This leads to a practical question: may disciples take oaths today? I believe we may, although a few Christians disagree. They say we must take Jesus' words literally and take no vows. To take any military or civic position, we must swear an oath of loyalty to the nation and its laws. Therefore, this position entails a willingness to forgo all public service.

Most Christians take a different approach. Following Luther and Calvin, among others, we distinguish between public and private speech. In private, among friends and brothers, we should simply tell the truth, so that the need for oaths disappears. Yet, since God himself sometimes swears oaths for the sake of his doubting listeners, we can take oaths for the sake of our doubting listeners.

Oaths are never ideal, but the law permits and regulates them (as we saw earlier) because oaths can make us think twice before we speak, thereby encouraging us to be truthful. Much of the law—both God's law and civil law—has the same goal of regulating and mitigating the effects of sin. Laws about such things as divorce, oaths, and property, not to mention the entire penal code, do not describe God's perfect will, but rein in the effects of sin.

Here then are standards for disciples. First, let us be so truthful that someone who knows us well would never solicit a vow from us. On the other hand, we may take a vow to grant assurances to someone who does not know us. God took vows to aid those who did not know how reliable he is.[4] For the same reason, Jesus spoke under oath at his trial (Matt. 26:63–64). Paul also took vows, calling God as his witness (Rom. 1:9; 2 Cor. 1:23; 1 Thess. 2:10). Therefore, for the sake of people who do not know that we are reliable, we may take vows.

Second, for the same reason, we may take oaths and vows in the courtroom, or before entering military or political service. The alternative is that Christians would forfeit most of their influence on public life. They would also have to rethink many commercial transactions, since contracts resemble oaths.

There is a third, broader lesson. By permitting and regulating oaths, God permits us to get involved in the dirt and the mess of public life. He does not say, "Withdraw, lest your hands be touched by evil." We have already been touched by evil. Now we are the light of the world. In a "crooked and depraved generation" we "shine like stars in the universe" (Phil. 2:15). To take an oath is to get involved in the world of liars. We bring the transforming power of God to that world, but we may get a little dirty there. In the Old Testament, Joseph, Daniel, Ezra, and Nehemiah got involved and got dirty, but also accomplished great things.

Christians do not spend all their time in the ideal world. The disciple's goal is that his words be so reliable that people do not even think to ask, "Do you promise?" Then we will never need oaths. But when people do not know us, when the habit of lying is old and the pressure to lie is strong, we may take an oath to guarantee our word.

## WHY TELLING THE TRUTH IS A CHALLENGE

So Jesus wants us to tell the truth; we probably want to, too. Why then do we fail? Consider two reasons: carelessness with our words and fear of telling hard truths. Cowardice in speech refuses to bring bad news to someone face to face.

Cowardice is telling people what you think they want to hear, whether it is true or not. Cowardice is bringing good news in person, but sending bad news in memos. Cowardice is criticizing someone at lunch and hoping it gets back to them. Courage is telling the truth as plainly and purely as possible, whether it is pleasant or not.

Years ago, I worked for a man who hated to tell the hard truths. He was a pleasant and empathetic man, and he wanted everyone to like him. For that reason, he promised people things that answered their deepest longings. Sadly, those who worked for him learned that he made promises that he could not keep. He meant well; he was a compassionate man. But he failed the test of courage and caused bitter disappointment to many people.

Many of us are like that. We want people to like us, so we want to bring good news. We think we are being nice when we do. But in the end it is cruel, not kind, to refuse to bear news that is bad, but necessary.

Imagine that a woman awakens one day with a severe headache. It persists, so she visits her physician. Her doctor performs tests that reveal cancer. But the physician is a sensitive man. He hates to see people shattered by such diagnoses. So he calls the woman in and says, "Ma'am, I can see why you might be having these headaches, but I want to assure you that within a few months you won't be feeling a thing." When we fail to tell a hard truth, we are cruel, not kind.

People who have worked both for a truth-teller and for a people-pleaser ordinarily prefer the leader who brings bad news promptly (yet tenderly) and keeps small promises rather than merely making big promises. It is good to know where we stand and what to expect. It is the way of Christ, who never withheld the bad news about sin and who kept every promise he made, no matter what the cost.

Our culture encourages careless speech. We take words lightly today. Older businessmen lament the end of the era when a man's word was his bond. We live in a world of print and computer screens, a culture of text. We say, "Talk is cheap," and "I want to see it in black and white." If it's in print, we think it counts more. We need to revalue the word *spoken*, so that it has the same value as the word *written*.

Some of us talk so much that we hardly pay attention to ourselves. The church must regain God's view of the sanctity of words. As James says, we should be "slow to speak," careful to weigh our own words. Most of us rarely tell a direct, deliberate lie. Months may go by without anything worse than exaggeration or the omission of a key detail. But we do squeeze the truth and evade it and exaggerate it to our benefit.

We also redefine the truth to our advantage. In *The Diary of Anne Frank*, there is a scene where eight Jews are hiding in a small, hidden room in a large house. There is not enough space, and the fear of getting caught leads to enormous stress. A married couple adds to everyone's anxiety by bickering constantly. At length, an exasperated member of the group asks them to stop quarreling. They immediately reply, "This isn't a quarrel, it's a discussion."[5] Just so, we try to change reality by redefining it.

## To the Heart of the Matter

The standards for oaths and promises are now clear enough. We know it is our duty to prove so faithful to our word that the use of oaths and promises withers away. But a problem remains. Although we know that we should keep our word, we bend or break the truth anyway. Why? Why do we make promises that we scarcely intend to keep? Is it a shallow desire to please others? Is it a device that we use to escape difficult conversations, so that when someone presses us, we finally say we will do something just to get rid of them?

Sometimes we falter through folly more than sin. We fail to keep our word because we fail to anticipate readily foreseeable obstacles to keeping it. We could have kept our word if no problems had arisen. But obstacles do arise. Thus, our failure is due to folly more than malice.

But other failures are not so innocent. Consider when we are most prone to break a promise. We violate words spoken to the powerless—such as a child—much more than we break promises spoken to the powerful—such as a boss. We break less visible commitments, such as nursery duty, and keep more highly visible ones, such as leading a meeting.

Then there is the problem of exaggeration. We heighten our sorrows to gain sympathy. We exaggerate the hours spent at work. We puff up statistics to make an impression. We may not tell many big fat lies. We rarely take a blunderbuss and blast a hole through the truth. But we do slay the truth with a thousand paper cuts. However we try, flawed humans cannot always tell the truth just as it needs to be told. It is like trying to drink coffee with a fork. It can't be done.

## THE FINAL GOAL: PERFECTION

I believe that Jesus wanted us to draw the conclusion that we are unable to keep his demands. For the longer his sermon goes on, the more demanding it gets. Watch how the challenge of Jesus' teaching grows progressively more difficult:

- Matthew 5:31–32. Jesus' first word is about marriage; he tells us how to treat one who is nearest and dearest to us.
- Matthew 5:33–37. The second command deals with the truth, which we must tell our neighbors.
- Matthew 5:38–42. Third, he declares that we owe mercy, not vengeance, to someone who harms us. This may be feasible in some cases, since some harm is accidental.
- Matthew 5:43–47. Finally, Jesus tells us to love our enemies, to love those who harm us by design.

Jesus' last word is harder still: "Be perfect, therefore, as your heavenly Father is perfect" (5:48). The standards of Jesus' sermon are too high for us. We have neither the pure heart nor the character that it demands. In this way, Jesus' teaching drives us to the gospel. We must try, and we do try, to lay aside anger and lust and falsehood. But as we try, we see that sin is like kudzu. The root is so deep. No one can kill it. We are incapable of following our Lord's standards. Therefore, we need our Lord's grace.

We need the gospel. It teaches us to ask the one who gives the standard to forgive us for breaking it. We ask the one who kept the standard in perfect righteousness to give us his righteousness and clothe us with it. And the Lord does it. He accepts us as his children and grants us the family resemblance that he requires. For the hardest command is also stated in a way that gives hope. Translated literally, Matthew 5:48 states, "You shall be perfect as your Father in heaven is perfect." We rightly read the words "You shall be perfect" as a command, yet, reading it again, we notice that it hides a promise: you *shall* be perfect.

In Christ, we *are* a new creation, yet we await a wholly new creation. There is a future for the disciple, and that future draws us forward. We lean toward that future, and it both beckons us and spurs us onward. In fact, the Sermon on the Mount has many promises about the future of a disciple: We shall inherit the earth (5:5). We shall receive mercy (5:7). We shall see God (5:8). We shall be called sons of God (5:9). We shall be perfect (5:48). God is in heaven, so his moral excellence vastly exceeds our pitiful attempts at holiness. Yet he is our Father. He has come near to love us and to bring us to maturity.

So let us hear Jesus' call to truthfulness. Let us measure our words and speak carefully, so that "Yes" means "Yes." Let us describe events, without the distortions, theatrics, embellishments, and exaggerations that mislead our neighbors. Let us not claim to know what we do not know. Let us measure each promise so that we mean what we say. Our families, our churches, our society, will be stronger for it.

Yet let us also admit that, strive as we will, we will never master the tongue. The tongue is too loose, the heart is too wild. So after we hear the law of Christ, let us plead for the grace of Christ. May he forgive our sins.

In our house, we often exaggerate for fun, but everyone knows that dishonesty and deception are the great social sins. If a child tells a lie, it does not go unpunished, for lies destroy trust. If a child tells the truth when it is hard to do so, it does not go unnoticed. In the home, trust is the coin of the realm. By telling the truth, we build trust.

Each Christian is also part of a larger family. That family is founded on perfect truth-telling. God the Father tells us the painful truth about ourselves: we are sinners, we fall short of God's holy standards, and we are unable to reform ourselves so we can meet those standards.

The Father also made a sweet promise to send a Redeemer, to deliver us from sin. He kept that promise, though it was painful to him. If God is your Father, you now belong to a family that tells the truth in love. He is building a new society, where we tell hard truths in love, so we can fix problems. We tell happy truths without adding flattery to gain a favor. As a result, we trust each other's words. Truth-telling works, of course. But we have another reason to tell the truth: we are children of the Father, who tells us the truth about himself, about us, and about our relationship with him.

# 8

# Do Not Resist Evil

THERE ARE FEW commands in the Bible that clash more with our natural inclination to protect our person and our honor than the commands found in Matthew 5:38–42:

> You have heard that it was said, "Eye for eye, and tooth for tooth." But I tell you, Do not resist an evil person. If someone strikes you on the right cheek, turn to him the other also. And if someone wants to sue you and take your tunic, let him have your cloak as well. If someone forces you to go one mile, go with him two miles. Give to the one who asks you, and do not turn away from the one who wants to borrow from you.

Turn the other cheek? We would rather clench our fist. This teaching is so hard to accept that an old Scottish preacher once expounded it this way: "Jesus said, 'If someone strikes you on the right cheek, turn to him the other also.' But the third lick, the third lick I say, belongs to you!"

The old preacher explained our text away. Our goal is to explain what Jesus really meant. It does require explanation, as Jesus' teachings often do. The challenge is to hear his message and to determine when he does and when he does not want literal obedience.

Remember, Jesus also said, "If your right eye causes you to sin, gouge it out and throw it away" (Matt. 5:29). But Jesus did not expect literal obedience there, as if he wanted to see battalions of one-eyed Christians. Jesus was using hyperbole; he often used hyperbole to get our attention, to make a point. It is our task to discover his true intent. We must neither take a false burden on ourselves by interpreting Jesus in a hyperliteral way, nor explain away the rigorous demands of discipleship.

## An Eye for an Eye (5:38)

When Jesus says, "You have heard that it was said, 'Eye for eye, and tooth for tooth.' But I tell you . . . ," he seems to be criticizing the law of Moses, where the rule of "an eye for an eye" is found three times in Israel's penal code (Ex. 21:23–25; Lev. 24:19–20; Deut. 19:21). To modern Western observers, this rule, known as the *lex talionis*, seems cruel and vindictive. It conjures up images of gruesome maiming and grim executioners.

However, the *lex talionis* did two things. First, it gave judges a clear and just formula for punishment. Second, it forbade vendettas and excessive retribution. It restrained men like Lamech, who boasted, "I have killed a man for wounding me" (Gen. 4:23). It reined in the vindictiveness of the proud man who exacted whatever vengeance he could get. "An eye for an eye" sounds harsh, but originally it restrained anger. It forbade the vengeful mind that thinks, "If you knock out my tooth, I will knock out six of yours." It stopped the spiral of violence. It said, "One tooth for one tooth—and no more."

In Israel's penal code, "an eye for an eye" is a fundamental principle. It teaches that punishment must be proportional to the crime and suited to it. It governs property violations (Ex. 22:4–6), personal injury (Lev. 24:19–20), and manslaughter (Lev. 24:17, 21). For example, if a man steals his neighbor's ox or sheep, he must pay back two oxen or sheep, restoring the one he stole and adding one of his own. Thus, the thief loses precisely what his neighbor would have lost. Again, in the case of perjury, a convicted perjurer must suffer the same punishment that his lie would have inflicted on his victim (Deut. 19:16–21).[1]

There is great wisdom in the principle of an eye for an eye. It is part of God's law, and neither Jesus nor any apostle says that the principle is wrong. Jesus affirms it when he says, "Whoever denies me before men, I also will deny before my Father who is in heaven" (Matt. 10:33 ESV;

cf. Mark 8:38). Paul affirms it too: "If anyone destroys God's temple, God will destroy him" (1 Cor. 3:17).

In itself, "an eye for an eye" ensures that criminals are treated justly and are protected from malice and vengefulness. Thus, theft is punished by restitution, not by maiming or incarceration. The law protects society, too, for just laws deter crime. Just laws purge evil from the land and instill fear of the Lord (Deut. 19:20–21).[2]

In these ways, especially in the public sphere, the *lex talionis* is holy, righteous, and good (Rom. 7:12). Yet, as Jesus, Paul, and the prophets knew, we tend to distort the law. We twist it to our advantage or evade it, so we can do as we please. In public, the *lex talionis* is necessary justice. But in private, it can cover a vindictive spirit. Society needs justice, but we do not need to exact justice with our own hand. As individuals, we can entrust justice to God and the state, and act in mercy.

In the law of Moses, public leaders enforced "an eye for an eye" in the land of Israel. But the church has no territory or public magistrates. Jesus addresses that borderless nation, the church, in its private life. He forbids us the cold pleasures of a vengeful spirit. In isolation, "an eye for an eye" might seem to tolerate the thought, "I'll give him back everything he gave, just as the law says." But Jesus forbids it. Indeed, he requires the opposite attitude, as we shall see.

## DO NOT RESIST AN EVIL PERSON (5:39A)

Follow the flow of Jesus' thought for a moment. Slightly paraphrased, he says:

- The law says, "Eye for eye, and tooth for tooth."
- But I say, "Do not resist an evil man."

Jesus then presents two pairs of illustrations of his principle. The first pair says, "Do not react to the galling blow. Do not strike back, even if someone strikes your face, even if they add insult to injury. Moreover, if someone steals your coat, offer them your shirt too."

The second pair says, "The ban on retaliation holds, but beyond that you must positively do good to your enemies. If someone forcibly extracts service from you for a little while, freely serve him after your release."

Clearly, "Do not resist" is a general principle, not an absolute requirement, for elsewhere the Bible teaches that we should resist some things. For example, James and Peter both command Christians to "resist the devil" (James 4:7; 1 Peter 5:9). Paul declares that he "opposed [Peter] to his face" when he compromised his Christian principles (Gal. 2:11).[3] Paul also resisted Simon Magus when he interfered with Paul's gospel proclamation (Acts 13:8–12). So there are times to resist evil on a spiritual level.

The Bible also shows that we must sometimes resist evil with physical effort. David showed that he was God's anointed king when he resisted armies that invaded Israel (e.g., 2 Sam. 5:6–25). The Lord also told Joshua that no one would be able to resist him in battles for the land of Canaan (Josh. 1:5). Later, it was a sign of Israel's shame and disobedience that they could not resist invasions from the nations around them (Judg. 2:11–15). Israel always tried to defend itself from attack and often succeeded, with God's help. In short, the Bible does not teach pacifism or that the sword is intrinsically evil. As Paul says:

> The authorities that exist have been established by God. . . . For rulers hold no terror for those who do right, but for those who do wrong. . . . He is God's servant to do you good. But if you do wrong, be afraid, for he does not bear the sword for nothing. He is God's servant, an agent of wrath to bring punishment on the wrongdoer. (Rom. 13:1–4)

God does not bless war, and neither should we. But the Bible often tells us to defend the defenseless, starting with widows and orphans (Ex. 22:22; James 1:27; cf. Jer. 49:11). Defensive wars do that very thing. War is terrible, but a defensive war can and should be an act of love—love for one's own people, even love for one's enemies. The defender uses the minimum of force necessary to drive out the invader. The defender even loves the foe as he defeats him, for a nation will not find spiritual blessing if it lives by theft and murder. It is good for the invaders themselves if they are humbled by defeat. The same is true of terrorists. They should be stopped for their own good, as well as everyone else's.

But we may not harbor hatred for our enemies. When a lesser power or a terrorist attacks a greater nation, the greater nation is filled with cries for vengeance: "Bomb them back into the Stone Age. There is only one thing a terrorist understands—brute force." A case can indeed be made that terrorists do not understand anything but force. But thwarting terrorism is one thing, bloodlust is another.

So then, disciples must resist spiritual evil and they may even resist some physical attacks. What then does Jesus mean when he says, "Do not resist. Turn the other cheek"? Let Jesus' deeds interpret his words, above all at his trial. When the high priest interrogated Jesus, he did not resist. When charged with threatening to destroy the temple, Matthew says, "Jesus remained silent" (26:63). When Pilate questioned him, he gave no answer. He did not defend himself (John 19:9–11). At the trial, the servants of the high priest "spit in his face and struck him with their fists. Others slapped him" (Matt. 26:67). Pilate's men did the same. "They spit on him . . . and struck him on the head again and again" (Matt. 27:30). Mark says, "Then some began to spit at him; they blindfolded him, struck him with their fists, and said, 'Prophesy!' And the guards took him and beat him" (Mark 14:65).

The prophet Isaiah foretold this.

> I offered my back to those who beat me,
>     my cheeks to those who pulled out my beard;
> I did not hide my face
>     from mocking and spitting.
> Because the Sovereign Lord helps me,
>     I will not be disgraced. . . .
> . . . I know I will not be put to shame.
> He who vindicates me is near. (Isa. 50:6–8)

Peter tells us that Jesus' action was an example for us: "When they hurled their insults at him, he did not retaliate; when he suffered, he made no threats. Instead, he entrusted himself to him who judges justly" (1 Peter 2:23). Jesus said, "No servant is greater than his master" (John 13:16). If Jesus waited for the Father to vindicate him, then we can be still and wait for the Lord to vindicate us.

"Do not resist" therefore means that we do not retaliate, physically or legally, when an evil person harms us personally. But we do resist evildoers who tempt us to sin. We resist oppressors who ravage the helpless. If possible, we show personal kindness to evildoers. We do not make self-defense our first goal. This is clear from the two illustrations of nonretaliation.

## TURN THE OTHER CHEEK (5:39B)

To understand Jesus correctly, we need to visualize the blow that Jesus describes. It is a blow to the right cheek. If a right-handed person strikes a blow (and most men are right-handed), his right hand strikes his foe's left cheek. A right-handed person strikes the right cheek with the back of the hand. The back-handed blow is an insult, an affront to honor.

Jesus wants us to endure a first insulting blow, and then a second, for his sake. This especially applies to the insults that a disciple bears for his faith in Christ (Matt. 5:11). In Jesus' day and throughout the ages, disciples have suffered insults for their faith. But we do not fight back to protect our honor.[4]

Notice that Jesus does not say why a disciple must turn the other cheek. He does not say that it brings glory to God, or convicts evildoers, or instills repentance and faith. He does not say that the violent man will repent or feel remorse. It is simply the Lord's way. His life is our model, just as his words are our guide.

## IF SOMEONE SUES YOU (5:40)

Once again, we need to understand the culture in order to follow Jesus. Rightly or wrongly, someone is suing a disciple for a debt. The adversary seeks compensation by taking the disciple's clothing. Clothing was valuable and expensive in antiquity. Ordinary people had only shoes and one or two changes of clothing. People normally wore an inner garment, called a tunic, and an outer garment, called a robe or a cloak. The law permitted the seizure of a tunic, but not a robe. It was his covering, his blanket at night, and no one could take it from him (Ex. 22:26–27; Deut. 24:12–13).

Jesus says that if someone attempts to take our tunic, which may be his prerogative, give him the robe, though it is never his prerogative. Again, we must recognize the hyperbole. Jesus is not commanding us to give away everything until we are left cold and naked. He is commanding us not to devote ourselves to defending our honor and avenging all affronts.

He chooses the lawsuit to illustrate the point because it is so offensive to be taken to court. False accusations are much the same. If you want to make someone angry, accuse him of something he did not do. Children get angry when parents blame them for something their sibling did. Supervisors get angry if someone beneath them accuses them falsely. The critic is wrong, and who is he to criticize anyway? Watch yourself, too, when a family member accuses you unjustly. Imagine this scene:

> WIFE: Why did you eat my banana? I told everyone not to eat the last banana. I needed it for lunch.
>
> HUSBAND: I ate the last banana, but you didn't tell me not to eat it.
>
> WIFE: I certainly did. Just ten minutes ago, I called out, "Nobody take the last banana. That banana is my lunch for tomorrow."
>
> HUSBAND: Ten minutes ago I was in the shower. How am I supposed to hear you talking about your precious banana when I'm in the shower? If you would think before you talk once in a while, you wouldn't accuse me of such nonsense. . . .

Even at home, we are so quick to defend our honor, so quick to retaliate, at least verbally. The last remark, "If you would think once in a while," is pure retaliation. Jesus says, in effect, "Stop fighting for honor. Turn the other cheek. Let others defraud you; let God defend you."

That is easier said than done, because it defies human nature. But it is consistent with a believing heart, a heart that trusts God for vindication. A man who has been humbled by his sin, a man who knows he is guilty and redeemed by grace alone, will not protest too much at a false charge. We are like criminals who are guilty of one hundred crimes, but who, oddly enough, are not guilty of the charges at hand. Still, even if we did not commit the act in question, we did something else just like it. In a rough way, we merit the charges.

Some say a man must defend his honor. They will endure many things, but will not remain silent when someone assaults their integrity. For a public figure, that may be true, for a leader must be trusted. As Proverbs says, "A good name is more desirable than riches" (22:1). But we may not fight over every wound to our pride.

## Go the Second Mile (5:41)

The final two examples add to the ban on retaliation. Jesus requires us to show kindness to those who insult us. The first illustration is particularly galling, and obedience is especially hard. Roman law let soldiers commandeer local citizens in an occupied land and make them carry their equipment for a thousand paces.

What an affront: to be forced to help a foreign oppressor carry the tools he uses to oppress you! At one level, this is Jesus' answer to the Zealots, a group of Jews who were committed to the violent overthrow of Roman power. Jesus implicitly opposed armed revolution, here and elsewhere (e.g., Luke 19:41–44). At a pragmatic level, it was sound advice, because in those days the Romans were invincible and implacable. The Stoic philosopher Epictetus (*ca.* A.D. 50–120) advised that if a soldier commandeers a man's donkey, "let it go, do not resist nor grumble. If you do, you will get a beating and lose your little donkey just the same."[5]

The reasoning of Epictetus is strictly pragmatic. Resistance, he says, is futile. But Jesus has something more in mind. After the Romans forcibly extract a kilometer of service, Jesus says, freely give them another.

Jesus provides no rationale—at the moment. But it is not hard to find. Jesus turned the other cheek to those who struck him and served those who mistreated him.[6] Above all, Jesus died for sinners, even for the Roman soldiers who executed him, if they would repent and believe. Recall Jesus' prayer for his executioners, "Father, forgive them, for they know not what they do" (Luke 23:34 ESV).

The logic becomes explicit a few verses later, when Jesus says, "Love your enemies and pray for those who persecute you, that you may be sons of your Father in heaven" (Matt. 5:44–45). Disciples are generous because our God is generous and we conform ourselves to him.

## GIVE TO THE ONE WHO ASKS (5:42)

The last illustration confirms that Jesus is, above all, stressing the need for a generous heart. Of course, endless requests for help can stir up anger, as lawsuits and forced service do. Still, the topic of nonretaliation is fading as Jesus commends generosity in lending.

When we read, "Give to the one who asks you, and do not turn away from the one who wants to borrow from you" (v. 42), we wonder, "Is there a limit?" There is. Jesus does not want us to walk home from court unclad, nor to give away money we need to feed our families. There is no love in giving so much that we foster dependency. We do not love a man by teaching him to abuse our generosity.

Still, we should give generously. The law of Moses commanded Israelites to lend generously (Deut. 15:7–11; cf. Ps. 37:26; Prov. 28:27), without interest, to their needy brothers (Ex. 22:25–27; Lev. 25:35–38; Deut. 23:19–20). When a brother is in need, God said, be generous, for he was generous when his people were in need in Egypt. God is compassionate (Ex. 22:27); therefore, we must be compassionate. God liberated Israel from slavery; therefore, we must liberate brothers from their poverty (Deut. 15:14–15).

Most churches are fair, at best, at giving to the one who asks. We gladly help Christian friends in need. If a friend has a baby or surgery, most of us are quick to help with a meal or a visit. But we are less adept at helping a fellow Christian whom we do not know, including the needy who cannot directly ask us for help. We give money to needy Christians abroad, but compassion to people in our own communities can be quite weak if we have no connection to them.

Some churches have compassionate individuals, but do not grasp the value of group action. Most evangelical churches have a very limited ministry of mercy to the poor and needy in their own area. Tim Keller suggests three reasons for this:

1. We let individual ministries—personal care and growth and discipleship—overshadow social dimensions of the gospel.
2. We have not developed bridges to the needy members of our community. If we started a clothing pantry, we would have a hard time finding the people who need clothes. We do not

have many connections to the poor, even though there are poor people within a few miles of almost every church.

3. We have done little to encourage the friends of mercy. We fail to present a vision of ministry to the poor. Many churches are ripe for change if the right people receive encouragement and direction.[7]

Jesus said, "The harvest is plentiful but the workers are few. Ask the Lord of the harvest, therefore, to send out workers into his harvest field" (Matt. 9:37–38). Many churches could begin to approach the poor by praying before they propose a program. If we develop an eye and a heart for the needy, the programs may spring up almost spontaneously.

The Greeks said that it is impossible to be happy if one must serve. But Jesus said, "I am among you as one who serves" (Luke 22:27). He gave both to his friends (his disciples) and to strangers, such as us. James says that kindness to the needy is proof that our faith is genuine (2:14–17). So let us pray that God would open eyes and hearts to the needy, even those who cannot ask for help.

## CONCLUSION

When Jesus says, "Turn the other cheek," he commends a way of life that runs contrary to human nature. The news accounts of strife between antagonistic nations are drearily similar. One side fires a gun or sets off some explosive device. It strikes a combatant, but also a child or a woman. So the other side, filled with outrage, shoots and bombs back, killing more combatants and civilians. Soon, the cycle of violence is spiraling upward again.

The desire to strike back in order to defend our honor or our loved ones is understandable. It is natural to desire to see justice done, to see evil punished, to see marauders and terrorists stopped. But we must rein in the impulse to get even, especially at a personal level. We must eschew self-defense in order to break the cycle of violence.

The values of a disciple are the values of his Lord. The values of the kingdom are the values of the King. We look to Christ. We turn the other cheek because he turned the other cheek. We give generously to all because he gives generously to all. We go the extra mile because he went the extra mile, even with us. For when we (and not just the Romans) were his enemies, he won us with his love. Jesus does not prohibit the administration of justice; he will overthrow Satan himself one day and punish him! But, as God's children, we share in his supreme righteousness when we stop standing on our rights, when we forgo revenge and do good to all. We are strong, for Jesus is strong, but we also give, for Jesus gives.

# 9

# LOVE YOUR ENEMIES

## *Matthew 5:43–48*

FEW TEACHINGS IN SCRIPTURE are more memorable and more challenging than this: "Love your enemies and pray for those who persecute you" (Matt. 5:44). It is alien to our thought, our practice, and our nature.

We are pleased with ourselves if we love our family and friends, though even that is a struggle at times. Even decent and happily married men occasionally wonder how they got tangled up with the woman they wed. Our children irritate us when they seem to acquire our faults rather than virtues (besides picking up novel evils from unknown sources). Is it easier to love friends and neighbors? Friends tend to be cooperative, and we find them through common interests. Friends also trade favors. If I invite a friend to dinner today, he will probably return the favor next week. As for neighbors, we can endure their flaws if we keep our distance from them. We can tolerate a pencil-tapper for ten minutes a day, so we can love them in a distant way.

But love our enemies? What could motivate that? At best, we try to be polite and stay out of their way. Why would we want to love those who strive to do us harm? But let us listen to Jesus, so that we might understand and, with God's help, obey. He says:

> You have heard that it was said, "Love your neighbor and hate your enemy." But I tell you: love your enemies and pray for those who persecute you, that you may be sons of your Father in heaven. He causes

97

his sun to rise on the evil and the good, and sends rain on the righteous and the unrighteous. (Matt. 5:43–45)

# LOVE YOUR NEIGHBOR AND HATE YOUR ENEMY? (5:43)

This is the final teaching in the major section, Matthew 5:20–48, which presents Jesus' teaching on the true meaning of the law. He began that part of his sermon by saying, "Unless your righteousness exceeds that of the scribes and Pharisees, you will never enter the kingdom of heaven" (5:20 ESV). Jesus defines this surpassing righteousness more in terms of motives than in terms of external deeds. So, for example, he says nothing new about the act of murder, but he insists that his disciples banish its motive, the anger and contempt that lead to it. Likewise, he says nothing new about the act of adultery, but addresses the lustful eyes and thoughts that lead to it. Jesus is consistent in this, but he is also a spiritual fitness trainer. He keeps adding weight to the workout. As we have seen, his teaching becomes ever more challenging. In 5:27–32, he tells husbands to love their wives by shunning lust and divorce. In 5:33–37, he commands us to respect our neighbors by telling them the truth. In 5:38–42, he urges mercy, not vengeance, toward those who harm us. Finally, in 5:43–47, he mandates that we love even our enemies. This is not a repetition of the previous point, for others can harm us by accident, ignorance, or neglect. An enemy harms us with malice, hoping to wound. Jesus says, "Love that enemy."

In this part of his sermon, Jesus introduces each section by reminding his audience of what they have heard before. Five times Jesus says, "You have heard that it was said . . . ," and once he says, "It has been said. . . ." Each time he summarizes the law before he explains its full sense (Matt. 5:21, 27, 31, 33, 38, 43). Each time Jesus quotes or summarizes the law before correcting a superficial reading of it (5:21, 27) or removing a distortion of it (5:31, 33, 38). But in the last instance Jesus combats a darker error. For what "you have heard"—"Love your neighbor and hate your enemy"—is half a quotation of the law and half a fabrication.

"Love your neighbor as yourself" *is* from the law of Moses (Lev. 19:18). Indeed, Jesus says it is the second great commandment (Matt.

22:39). It is the sum and fulfillment of the law—the royal law (Rom. 13:8–10; James 2:8).

But "hate your enemy"? How could anyone think that the Bible commands hatred of enemies? In two ways. First, "Love your neighbor" could be taken to mean, "Love *only* your neighbor and don't bother with the rest." It is possible to interpret "Love your neighbor" in a way that removes our obligation to those who live at a distance. But the same chapter of the law that commands us to love our neighbor also commands us to love the stranger "as yourself" (Lev. 19:33–34). The parable of the good Samaritan makes the same point.

But second, certain Bible passages do appear to approve of hating one's enemies. For example, God commanded Israel to destroy the Canaanites totally, without treaty and without mercy (Deut. 7:2; 20:16–18). The Lord also promised to defend Israel, to fight her enemies, to put "curses on your enemies who hate and persecute you" (Deut. 30:7). Further, several psalms rejoice in God's judgment on those who hate God and his people. Psalm 11 says, "The LORD examines the righteous, but the wicked and those who love violence his soul hates" (Ps. 11:5). Psalm 139 says:

> Do I not hate those who hate you, O LORD,
>     and abhor those who rise up against you?
> I have nothing but hatred for them;
>     I count them my enemies. (Ps. 139:21–22; cf. 26:5)

If a critic tries to dismiss this as second-rate Old Testament teaching, remember that Revelation says the same thing. When Babylon, the symbol of rebellion against God, falls by his judgment, the heavenly host shouts, "Hallelujah! The smoke from her goes up for ever and ever" (Rev. 19:3). She was ripe for judgment, for she slaughtered the prophets and the saints (18:24), corrupted the earth with her adultery (19:2), and boasted in her strength (18:7). Babylon would buy or sell anything to get rich, even the "bodies and souls of men" (18:13). Her sins were piled up to heaven (18:5). Satan's ally, she joined the war against the Lamb (17:14). She will never repent (17:12–16). Therefore, angels rejoice at Babylon's fall, for it means the end of her oppression of mankind, the end of her rebellion against God.

The settled enemies of God must fall and shall fall. When their rebellion is implacable and irreversible, they are ripe for God's judgment, which is just and true (Rev. 16:5–7; 19:2). On judgment day, God's patience ends.

This is how we must understand the psalms and prophecies that approve of God's judgment. Believers hate violence and wickedness. Some people give themselves over to such sins, so they are properly called "the violent" or "the wicked." The Bible never commands us to hate individual enemies, but there is a place for righteous wrath toward God's settled enemies. On judgment day, we will rejoice at their downfall, for their end is inseparable from the victory of God and his saints. Thus, when we view the wicked as a class, from an eternal perspective, our love for them ceases.

In daily life, however, we have no right to adopt the eternal perspective. We cannot classify people. The man standing before us may be wicked, but we do not know whether he will repent or not. Remember the conversion of Paul. Once the archenemy of the church, he became its great apostle. Paul's salvation demonstrates God's "unlimited patience" (1 Tim. 1:16). Therefore, we should be patient with sinners too. Still, no one should presume upon that patience:

> Or do you show contempt for the riches of [God's] kindness, tolerance and patience, not realizing that God's kindness leads you toward repentance? But because of your stubbornness and your unrepentant heart, you are storing up wrath against yourself for the day of God's wrath, when his righteous judgment will be revealed. God "will give to each person according to what he has done." (Rom. 2:4–6)

Therefore, sinners must hope in God's mercy. Yet they must take warning, for God's mercy will eventually run out. For now, however, disciples leave judgment to God and show his mercy to others, just as he showed mercy to us.

## LOVE YOUR ENEMIES (5:44)

When Jesus said "Love your enemies," most Jews would have thought first of the Romans, who occupied and defiled their land. What good could ever come from loving the Romans? Would the Romans love the Jews back? No, but "Jesus does not promise that love will turn enemies into friends."[1] Our love of enemies is independent of the person loved, independent of their rank or attractiveness. None of that matters. Results are immaterial.

The law always points toward love. It extends from friends to neighbors to enemies. Still, "Love your enemies" seems daunting. How can we love those who hate us, who plan evil for us? The quick reply is that the love mentioned here is "agape," which is not an emotion, but a will to perform sacrificial acts. Some say, "Let agape love be defined by what follows." What follows is deeds that we perform for our enemies. We pray for them, do good to them, and greet them (Matt. 5:44–47). Because agape love is dispassionate, they say, we can love our enemies.

But it is not quite that simple. First, the Greek noun *agapē* and the verb *agapaō* are sometimes used to describe human affections and desires (see Matt. 5:46; Col. 3:19; 2 Tim. 4:10; 2 Sam. 13:1 LXX). Second, when Paul says, "If I give all I possess to the poor and surrender my body to the flames, but have not love, I gain nothing" (1 Cor. 13:1), he is addressing attitudes, not deeds. So then, love of enemies includes inward attitudes, not just outward deeds.

One cannot genuinely pray for someone without hoping for their good. When we pray for an enemy, animosity dwindles and compassion increases. Love is an act of a whole person reaching out to whole persons.[2] God's love is the source and the model for love of enemies. Augustine said that God's love is incomprehensible and unchangeable in that he began to love us before we were reconciled to him through the blood of his Son. Our sin made us his enemies. Yet because our iniquity had not entirely consumed his handiwork, "He knew . . . how . . . to hate what we had done, and to love what he had done [in creating us]."[3] Therefore, to love our enemies is to live like a child of God.

## SONS OF THE FATHER IN HEAVEN (5:45)

"Love your enemies," Jesus says, "that you may be sons of your Father in heaven" (Matt. 5:44–45). Jesus does not mean that acts of love are the instrument we use to gain the status of sons. Rather, we *demonstrate* that we are God's children when we love as our Father loves. Even so, the goal is not chiefly to demonstrate something to God. Rather, Jesus wants us to aspire to divine love.

To love our enemies is to pursue a life patterned after God. Protestants are sometimes reluctant to talk about imitating God because it sounds moralistic or perhaps Roman Catholic to them. But the idea of imitating God is biblical. It is our destiny and our obligation to be conformed to the character of God (Rom. 8:29; 1 Cor. 15:49; 1 John 3:2–3). Paul says:

> Be kind and compassionate to one another, forgiving each other, just as in Christ God forgave you. Be imitators of God, therefore, as dearly loved children and live a life of love, just as Christ loved us and gave himself up for us. (Eph. 4:32–5:2)[4]

God is our pattern when we love our enemies and pray for our foes. God "causes his sun to rise on the evil and the good, and sends rain on the righteous and the unrighteous" (Matt. 5:45).[5] Because the natural order is under God's control, we discover his character by observing it (Ps. 145:8–9). God creates and sustains all things (Heb. 1:2–3). Whatever meteorologists may say, the Bible calls rain God's gift to mankind (Ps. 104; Matt. 5:45). When God gives the rain and sun that we need for life, it demonstrates his love for us (cf. Matt. 6:26–30).

If we believe this, we should shower enemies and friends with acts of loving-kindness. Like God, we should give without regard for a return. Alfred Plummer says, "To return evil for good is devilish; to return good for good is human; to return good for evil is divine. To love as God loves is moral perfection."[6] It runs against human nature to clean up the mess left behind by a spouse, a child, a neighbor, or a neighbor's dog. But the standard is God's nature, not ours. Furthermore, if we give for the sake of giving, as God does, we gain endurance. Lack of results will not deter us, and the love of God will sustain us.

## LOVING THOSE WHO LOVE YOU, GREETING THOSE WHO GREET YOU (5:46–47)

Now Jesus defines divine love negatively, by comparing it to the lesser standard of ordinary decency. Sadly, we are inclined to congratulate ourselves for small, commonplace acts of kindness. I once had knee surgery and endured considerable pain for about three weeks. One day, as I congratulated myself for staying 98 percent free of the grumpiness that typically accompanies persistent pain, I realized that my family had stayed 99 percent free of the grumpiness that typically accompanies caring for an in-house patient. I had nothing to boast about. I was only returning decency for decency.

Jesus says there is nothing especially commendable in returning a favor. It does not count as a sign of love or virtue. If we love those who love us, we deserve no reward. Tax collectors do the same. If we greet our friends, we deserve no notice. Even pagans do the same.

When Jesus says that even tax collectors and pagans do the same thing, he refers to some of the most despised people in his day. Tax collectors were Jews who collaborated with Rome. The taxes they collected funded the Roman occupation of Israel. Furthermore, pagans neither believed in God nor obeyed his law. If even pagans return kindness for kindness, disciples must certainly do more.[7]

This reveals the weakness of the ordinary decency that counterfeits godlike love. Humans are prone to think well of themselves for every token of decency, but to return a favor is nothing more than politeness and may be mere self-interest, since we know that one act of kindness begets another. There is no special merit in doing a favor for those who favor us. God need not reward that kind of love; the neighbor takes care of it (Matt. 5:46).

Many churches seem cold and unwelcoming to visitors, but almost every church thinks it is friendly. Why? Because the members are friendly with their friends. They greet everyone who greets them. This is not noteworthy. Genuine love keeps an eye open for the quiet, the awkward, and the friendless, and seeks them out.

At work, we know it pays off to return calls. If we share valuable information with someone, he or she may subsequently share information with us. Self-interest ought to dictate that workers serve customers with courtesy. Courtesy is not meritorious.

I saw this afresh a few days after the knee surgery I just mentioned. I had to travel through Atlanta's sprawling airport to speak at a conference that I could not postpone. I was struggling to carry a bag and walk with crutches, and could only watch in detached wonder as airline personnel repeatedly glanced at me and then turned their backs toward me. One woman from the airline yelled at me to move faster and get out of her way. But one gate agent was conspicuous for her helpfulness. I asked for her name, so I could commend her to her superiors, but she refused. She said, "I don't deserve recognition. I am only doing my job."

She was right, and it set me thinking. Who had shown me extraordinary, divine love? Earlier, when every seat was full at a crowded gate, a businessman got up and insisted that I take his seat. He then stood against a wall until the plane boarded. That was love, because he owed me nothing. Yet that was only love of a stranger. Jesus loved us when we were his enemies (Rom. 5:1–11), and he tells us to love our enemies. So let us not be satisfied with common decency. Even pagans can show decency. Let us aspire to love strangers, even enemies, for it is a godlike thing to do. Frederick Buechner put it this way:

> The love for equals is a human thing—of friend for friend, brother for brother. It is to love what is loving and lovely. The world smiles.
>
> The love for the less fortunate is a beautiful thing—the love for those who suffer, for those who are poor, the sick, the failures, the unlovely. This is compassion, and it touches the heart of the world.
>
> The love for the more fortunate is a rare thing—to love those who succeed where we fail, to rejoice without envy with those who rejoice, the love of the poor for the rich, of the black man for the white man. The world is always bewildered by its saints.
>
> And then there is love for the enemy—love for the one who does not love you, but mocks, threatens, and inflicts pain. The tortured's love for the torturer. This is God's love. It conquers the world.[8]

## PERFECT AS THE FATHER IS PERFECT (5:48)

By now, careful listeners suspect that Jesus' moral ideal is splendid but unattainable. Jesus confirms our hunch when he says, "Be perfect, therefore, as your heavenly Father is perfect" (Matt. 5:48). Some try to soften this command by appealing to the Greek, for the Greek word for "perfect" actually means "mature" or "complete," not "sinless." But it is hardly a relief to learn that we need not be perfect, but only as mature as God!

This reminds us that the Sermon on the Mount is for believers, for men and women who have already entered the kingdom of God. No one can earn entry into the kingdom by keeping Jesus' standards. But the disciple takes his failure to God and pleads for mercy. He contemplates God's standards and pleads for grace. There is nothing else to do.

Lutheran theology rightly stresses that Jesus' moral demands reveal our sin and inability to keep the law. Luther said that Jesus incites a pre-evangelistic despair that prepares one for the gospel. Indeed, when we appreciate the extent of God's requirements, we realize how pitiful our moral achievements are. That compels us to plead for mercy. We ask God—who is the standard—to forgive us for breaking the standard, and he grants that forgiveness.

But God offers hope for success, not just mercy for failure. Look at verse 48 again: it is a command, yet Jesus states it in a way that gives us hope. The command to "be perfect" describes what Jesus requires of his disciples. Yet, to be precise, the Greek is a future indicative: "You *shall be perfect*, as your Father in heaven is perfect." In Greek and English, the future is used both to predict ("It will rain") and to command ("You *will* attend this meeting").[9] Since Jesus is giving ethical instruction, it is best to think of the future indicative in verse 48 first as a command. (Matthew also uses future indicatives for commands in 5:21, 27, 33, 43.)

But Jesus' teaching also points to the future. He makes promises. The meek *will* inherit the earth, those who mourn *will* be comforted, and those who hunger and thirst for righteousness *will* be filled (5:4–9). Therefore, we can read "You shall be perfect" as a promise, as well as a command: we shall be perfect.

In the Greek, again, the term "you" is emphatic. Jesus does not speak to mankind in general, but to his disciples. He charges *us* to be perfect, just as our Father in heaven is perfect. The phrase "your heavenly Father" makes two points. He is in heaven, which puts him far above us. But he is our Father, which puts him near us. The standard is high, yet not completely out of reach. If we read Matthew 5 merely as a set of moral demands, it is unattainable. But it also paints a portrait of kingdom life, of life in the family of God, and that is the life that disciples experience in some measure.

So Jesus says we must aspire to be like our Father. In the physical family, it is natural for a child to be like his father. It is also logical in the spiritual family, for God, our Father, is remaking us in his image. He has loved us with an everlasting love. The love he shows is the love he commands.

It is our duty to love our enemies and pray for them. But it is also our goal to be like the Father. It would be blasphemy to claim such a goal on our own, but God commends it to us and empowers us for it. We *are* the children of God. We shall, by his grace and Spirit, find some desire and ability to love our enemies. Therefore, let us *examine* ourselves. Do our good deeds surpass those of the *quid pro quo* world? Do we love the undeserving, as God does? Or do we still do good only to get good in return?

To live as Jesus lived, we must identify our enemies, those who make us think of revenge. Those enemies offer us the opportunity to love as our Father loves. For God loved us when we were strangers and alienated from him. He loved us when we were his enemies. Our animosity could not thwart his love. He loved us, gave us new life, and drew us to himself as his adopted children. He has poured his transforming grace into our hearts, so we can love our friends, our neighbors, and even our enemies.

As Matthew 5 moves to this climax, Jesus leads us to peer ever deeper into our hearts, that we may know ourselves. In the next chapter, the focus will shift away from the disciples' internal life and toward the life of a disciple in this world, in the presence of God.[10]

Discipleship
Worship
WORD & Prayer
Witness
Serving
Tithing

# 10

# HOLY ONE OR HYPOCRITE?

## *Matthew 6:1–6, 16–18*

IT WOULD BE HELPFUL if we could find a way to judge if the people we meet are or are not holy. If we meet someone at a Bible study or even at a monastery, it may be a good sign. But who knows? He might be a sinner who is merely contemplating repentance. We cannot judge holiness by the way someone looks. Ostentatious clothing will raise questions, but both saints and sinners generally dress according to the norms of their culture. We might be able to tell more by looking in someone's car. Is the radio preset for at least one Christian station? What kinds of recorded music float about the cabin? But most people listen to all kinds of music. Perhaps we could learn more if we attached a position locater to the car's frame to see if it goes to church on Sunday or not. Would that be enough? No, because Jesus says a man can give every appearance of righteousness and not be righteous at all.

## RIGHTEOUSNESS EXCEEDING THAT OF THE PHARISEES, REVISITED

In Matthew 5, Jesus described the *moral* demands of discipleship. Disciples ought to keep the law and ought to do so for the right reasons. Now Matthew 6 describes the *religious* demands of discipleship. Jesus says that true disciples perform their religious duties from the heart.

In Jesus' day, there were three signs of piety, three tokens of religious devotion: gifts to the poor, prayer, and fasting. A popular book from around 200 B.C. said, "Prayer is good when it is accompanied by fasting, almsgiving and righteousness" (Tobit 12:8). Jesus mentions the same three practices, but his emphasis does not fall on the deeds themselves. Rather, he first warns his disciples not to miss the point of doing them: "Be careful not to do your 'acts of righteousness' before men, to be seen by them. . . . So when you give to the needy, do not announce it with trumpets, as the hypocrites do in the synagogues and on the streets, to be honored by men. I tell you the truth, they have received their reward in full" (6:1–2).

We must clarify Jesus' teaching. He does not mean we must always hide our good deeds. He does not say that it is wrong to be seen praying. Rather, it is wrong to pray in order to be seen. He does not say it is wrong to be seen giving a gift to the needy. But it is wrong to give in order to be seen giving. As Jesus went on to say, "When you give to the needy, do not let your left hand know what your right hand is doing, so that your giving may be in secret. Then your Father, who sees what is done in secret, will reward you" (6:3–4).

If we regularly invite the divorced and the widowed to holiday dinners, or if we invite the singles and college students to share a Sunday meal, then someone will eventually discover it. It is no sin for the word to leak out that we are hospitable. But it is hypocrisy to be hospitable so that people will discover and praise our hospitality. True hospitality looks to the joy of the lonely and the needy, not the glory of the host. The desire to be recognized for doing good must not displace the simple desire to do good.

In the Sermon on the Mount, Jesus compares his disciples to the Pharisees and pagans. We surpass the pagans, because their religion consists of mechanical forms. Jesus says, "They think they will be heard because of their many words" (6:7). Surpassing the Pharisees would seem to be harder, for they kept the law's external demands scrupulously. But Jesus requires his disciples to obey God with better motives. He says that some fulfill their duties in order to feel good about themselves or to gain a reputation for piety.[1] But God takes no pleasure in the man who does good in order to be seen doing it:

- That man gives to the poor, not so much to help them as to be seen helping them.

- He prays, not so much to commune with God as to be seen on his knees.
- He fasts, not so much to devote himself to God as to be seen fasting.

Perhaps no one sets out to be a hypocrite. The hypocrite may start well, doing good innocently. Later, he thinks, "It would be good if others knew what I do. My example might inspire them." Finally, he takes steps to insure that others see and praise his piety. We trade the goal of pleasing the Father for the goal of pleasing men.[2]

There is another kind of hypocrisy. A hypocrite may first fool himself and then deceive others. This hypocrite may be sincere at one level, but at another level he suspects that he is fooling himself. Henri Nouwen, a professor of pastoral theology at Notre Dame, Yale, and Harvard, describes the way today's holy man can deceive himself: "As I entered into my fifties . . . I came face to face with the simple question, 'Did becoming older bring me closer to Jesus?' . . . I found myself praying poorly, living somewhat isolated from other people, and very much preoccupied with burning issues."

Everyone told him he was doing well. Nonetheless, Nouwen says, something inside him told him that his soul was in danger, that the Spirit was being suppressed, that something had to change.[3] Nouwen did change things, leaving academia to live and to serve, many hours each week, in a community for people with great mental and physical challenges. He did so to avoid becoming a subtle kind of spiritual hypocrite. This hypocrite performs frantically for others. He impresses others with his ministry, even while his own soul withers away. Nouwen understood that we miss Jesus' point if we condemn others for hypocrisy and don't watch ourselves.

Every pastor, every missionary, runs the same risk. We can starve our own souls while nourishing others. We can drown our spirit in a sea of spiritual cares. We can toil away impressively, so that everyone says, "You are doing well." At our worst, we can drink in the compliments and think, "So, it must be true."

Yet let us not run too rapidly to the present application of Jesus' message. Scripture will exert its maximum influence only if we retain our enthusiasm for the original words.[4] Let us labor to discover precisely what the Lord said in his day, so we can hear him clearly today.

## HOLIER THAN THOU?

Jesus warns against hypocrisy, but he never says that we should avoid expressing our faith in traditional, visible ways. Indeed, he assumes that his disciples will manifest their faith in activities such as giving and praying. He does not say, "If you give to the needy . . ." Rather, he says, "When you give to the needy . . . When you pray . . . When you fast . . ." (6:2, 5, 16). When we do such things, we must beware of practicing them "in order to be seen" (6:1 ESV). Yet, since a righteous person is equally righteous in public and in private, good deeds will inevitably be seen in public. As Jesus teaches his disciples how to give to the poor, pray, and, fast, he points this out. He speaks in a string of verbal echoes and refrains that make his point as memorable as a poem:

- When you give (or pray or fast), do not do it as the hypocrites do (6:2, 5, 16):
- To be honored or seen by men (6:2, 5, 16).
- "They have received their reward" (6:2, 5, 16 ESV).
- Rather, when you give (or pray or fast), do it "in secret" (6:4, 6, 16).
- "And your Father who sees in secret will reward you" (6:4, 6, 18 ESV).

That is, if we perform for man's praise, we will receive it. In conversation, we can find ways to tell stories about our work in the soup kitchen, if we are intent on it. The audience may be impressed and may praise us, but that will be the end of the praise. The Father will not honor us in the next life, for we offered our good deeds to humans and not to him. But if we act righteously in secret, for the audience of One, he will see and reward us. So let us avoid displays of holiness.

Our culture also dislikes displays. It despises Christians who have a "holier than thou" attitude. Disciples should certainly strive to be holy.

110

Since so many people have no interest in holiness, disciples will be holier than others. But we must avoid public posturing.

We serve the living God. If he sees us, nothing else matters.

## GIVING TO THE POOR WITH THE RIGHT MOTIVES
### (6:1–4)

Jesus said, "When you give to the needy, do not announce it with trumpets . . . in the synagogues and on the streets" (6:2). So far as we know, no one literally had trumpeters precede them as they prepared to give gifts. But, Jesus says, picture a man with a bag of silver coins, walking down the street with trumpeters blowing their trumpets ahead of him and calling out, "Alms for the poor! Alms for the poor! Come and get it!"

People always have ways of calling attention to their gifts. In Jesus' day, the wealthy paved city streets and had their names inscribed on highly visible stones. Today, if someone gives a large gift to a university, a hospital, or another institution, a building may be named after him. A moderate gift can earn a plaque on the wall inside the building, and a humble gift can earn a name on a brick under the plaque. The hypocrite longs for such attention. The world is his stage; he hopes to impress people, to win their applause. But Proverbs 27:2 (ESV) says, "Let another praise you, and not your own mouth; a stranger, and not your own lips."

Pastors and mission workers are also prone to self-promotion. After all, since all ministries rely on donations, we feel obligated to publicize our ministries, so people will support them. The challenge is to promote God's work without promoting ourselves.

When Jesus says, "Do not let your left hand know what your right hand is doing" (Matt. 6:3), he adds a new point. Not only should we avoid telling *others* about our righteous deeds, we should not even tell *ourselves*. We should have a blissful lack of self-consciousness because self-consciousness can decay into self-righteousness.

When we do something good, Jesus says, we can seek one of three goals: the praise of society, the praise we give ourselves, or the praise of the Father. Hypocrites seek glory from men. They love "praise from men more than praise from God" (John 12:43). But we can also do good so that we will feel good about ourselves, and not really for the sake of others.

111

When I fly, I like to help older and shorter people who struggle to get their carry-on language in or out of their overhead compartments. I like to help, but I must confess that I also like to feel benevolent. My left hand sees what my right hand does. When we perform some good deeds, we can stand outside ourselves and admire it, as we do when we host a party and judge it a success. Whenever we watch ourselves this way, the journey to righteousness is incomplete.

Those who possess great skill often lack self-awareness of it. Michael Polanyi said, "The aim of a skillful performance is achieved by the observance of a set of rules which are not known as such to the person following them."[5] One can be an accomplished musician or artisan without mastering the theory behind the craft. The violin-making skills of Stradivarius died unarticulated. This can happen because we pay the most attention to skills when we begin to acquire them, such as when learning to drive—or when something is amiss, such as when our athletic performance slips. Once a skill is established, our awareness of it recedes. The musician attends to the piece of music, not the location of her left index finger.

So it should be with righteousness. When it has become second nature, there is little self-awareness. Of course, when we write a check for kingdom work, both the right hand and the left hand engage in the physical process. When we help someone, we have some awareness of our acts. But true righteousness has no vanity, no calculation, no self-congratulation, no egotism. This is what Jesus had in mind when he said that he would commend the righteous on judgment day. They will not remember when they took care of the hungry, the thirsty, or the stranger (Matt. 25:37–40).

Some object that Jesus is contradicting himself, for he also said, "Let your light shine before men, that they may see your good deeds and praise your Father in heaven" (Matt. 5:16). How then can he prohibit the display of righteousness in our passage? John Stott replies that Jesus is speaking about different things:

It is our human cowardice which made him say "Let your light shine before men," and our human vanity which made him tell us to beware of practicing our piety before men. A. B. Bruce sums it up well when he writes that we are to "show when tempted to *hide*" and "hide when tempted to *show*." Our good works must be public so that our light shines; our religious devotions must be secret lest we boast about them.

The goal both times is the same, that the glory go to God. Our good works are public, so that God may be praised for transforming his people. Our religious acts must be private, so that the glory goes to God and not to ourselves.[6]

Someone may also ask, "If Jesus wants us to be righteous for the sake of God, why does he say that the Father, 'who sees what is done in secret, will reward you' (6:4)? Doesn't the promise of a reward reintroduce selfish motives? If we do good for the sake of God, why should we be interested in a reward?"

If we say giving earns a reward from God, this turns the act of giving into a business investment: I give to God and he gives back, with interest. At worst, this is wholly selfish, a manipulation of God for selfish advantage. At best, it pollutes an act of kindness by giving it a selfish turn at the end. It makes the right hand think hard about what the left is doing. It makes giving a self-imposed spiritual discipline, presented to God for proper recompense. Like eating our vegetables, it is good for us.

C. S. Lewis answers that there are two kinds of reward, which I will call extrinsic and intrinsic rewards. An extrinsic reward has no natural connection to the thing done to gain the reward. Prize money for winning a piano competition is an extrinsic reward. In contrast, intrinsic rewards do have a connection with the deed performed. In pick-up basketball, the intrinsic reward for winning a game is staying on the court. Between a man and a woman, the reward for true love is a marriage where love grows and deepens for many years. The reward for youthful academic excellence is a scholarship that allows further study. These are intrinsic rewards. It seems then that the reward for service must be intrinsic—the satisfaction of serving others and relieving needs.[7]

## Praying with the Right Motives (6:5–8)

Jesus says we must not pray "to be seen by men," but he does not forbid public prayer. Moses, Daniel, Ezra, and others prayed publicly.

Jesus let his disciples see him pray. The apostles and first Christians often gathered to pray together. They heard each other pray for boldness in their testimony and for success in their mission (Acts 4:23–31; 13:3; 14:23; 20:36). When disciples pray, they simply do not care if anyone sees it or not.

Hypocritical prayers do want to be seen. "Do not be like the hypocrites," Jesus warns (Matt. 6:5). They love to stand and pray during public worship. Crafting elegant phrases to express lofty thoughts, they hope to impress the gathered assembly with their piety. Hypocrites also love to pray outside, "on the street corners" (6:5). By custom, pious Jews living in Jerusalem were supposed to stop, drop, and pray when a trumpet blew in the temple for the daily afternoon sacrifice. The hypocrite was pleased to find himself in a public place then, so all would see him fall to his knees and pray.

Perhaps the hypocrite even arranged to be in a public place at that hour. Perhaps the hypocrite prayed sincerely at first. Then someone praised his well-phrased prayer, so that he gained a reputation for devotion. In time, he hoped to be seen or heard praying. Jesus says that if we pray to gain the approval of men, we will gain that—and nothing more. If a prayer is blind to God, God is blind to that prayer.

It is better to "go into your room, close the door and pray to your Father, who is unseen," for prayer is essentially private (6:6). Public prayer has all the distractions of a public situation: limits on time, the effects of an audience, and more. In private prayer, we can ask questions, groan, or pause and admit our confusion. A secluded place is best for that. Hypocrites pray with at most one eye on God and at least one eye on their reputation. But if we attend to God in prayer, he gives us his ear: "Then your Father, who sees what is done in secret, will reward you" (6:6).

It is the genuineness of a prayer that lets it surpass the prayers of hypocrites and pagans. Jesus rightly says that the pagans babble and use "many words" (6:7). First Kings 18:25–29 describes the prophets of Baal who prayed all day long, with shouts and bloodletting, for fire from their god. They invoked his name over and over and cut themselves, hoping to rouse him and gain his attention. Some written records of pagan prayers have survived to our day. They might invoke the names of many gods, in the hope of finding one who was both paying attention and well-disposed to what might be a simple request for health or safety. Our prayers may not be more impressive, but they have a nobler object—to speak to the living God—and a better spirit. For we do not pray to display our skill to many, but to reach an audience of one. More importantly, we do not imagine that we can extract a blessing from a reluctant deity. We trust that the Father knows what we need before we ask (Matt. 6:8).

## Fasting with the Right Motives (6:16–18)

In a later chapter, we will survey the biblical teaching about fasting. For now, listen to Jesus' warning against fasting with an improper motive, the desire to be seen by men. He says, "When you fast, do not look somber as the hypocrites do, for they disfigure their faces to show men they are fasting. I tell you the truth, they have received their reward in full. But when you fast, put oil on your head and wash your face, so that it will not be obvious to men that you are fasting" (Matt. 6:16–18).

Jesus invites us to imagine a scene where a shallow woman is preparing to fast. She doesn't want to boast openly about her fasting, but she thinks, "If I look a little ragged, maybe someone will ask why. So I won't wash my hair, and I'll skip my makeup. No, better yet, I'll smear a little brown and gray under my eyes."

When she arrives at work, her friends notice at once. "Lucy," they exclaim, "what happened to you today? You look terrible. Are you all right?"

"Oh, yes," Lucy slowly moans. "I'm fine . . . but I am a little hungry, I guess."

"Well then, can we get you something to eat?"

"Oh, no, no. You see, I'm fasting."

"Lucy, you are so holy!"

"Well, maybe."

The desire to be noticed is understandable but deadly. Jesus said, "Whoever exalts himself will be humbled" (Matt. 23:12). If anyone fasts "to be seen by men," it is an act of self-exaltation. But true fasting is self-humbling. Like genuine generosity and genuine prayer, genuine fasting is, by nature, self-effacing and self-denying.

Jesus says that the Father rewards this kind of fasting: "Your Father, who sees what is done in secret, will reward you" (6:18). Jesus does not say that fasting earns a reward from God. Rather, God grants a reward. Besides, if we fasted to gain a reward, it would be an attempt to manipulate God, for it sacrifices something to God in order to get it back, with interest.[8]

In Matthew 6, Jesus shifts his focus slightly. In chapter 5, he teaches his disciples to look inward, to their character and their motives. In chapter 6, he teaches us to look upward, to live to please God, rather than to please ourselves or impress our neighbors.[9] If we seek God and please him, he will grant the finest reward—his presence and pleasure.

# THE DISCIPLE'S PRAYER

*Matthew 6:5–13*

IT IS SWEETLY AMUSING to watch a little child miss the point of an event. The first time I took my youngest daughter to a professional baseball game, she drank in the sights and sounds in wide-eyed wonder before she uttered a word. At last she spoke: "Look, Daddy! All the seats have numbers!" I read the story of Nebuchadnezzar to another child, then three years old. She listened intently, eyes glued to the picture of the king as he ordered his servants to throw Shadrach, Meshach, and Abednego into a fiery furnace. She jabbed an angry finger at the royal figure. "The king is very mean," she exclaimed. "He has nice shoes, though."

## THE POINT—PRAYING FOR GOD'S SAKE (6:5–8)

Adults can miss the point, too. Jesus steers us to the main point of prayer by way of contrasts. The Pharisees and the hypocrites love to be seen praying in public. Their prayer is ostentatious and selfish. The disciples' prayer is secret and godly (Matt. 6:5–6). People are not especially eager to be seen praying today. But in Jesus' day, prayer, fasting, and almsgiving were three great signs of piety. Devotion to prayer signified righteousness. But Jesus warned his disciples not to miss the point of the spiritual disciplines: "Be careful not to do your 'acts of righteousness' before men, to be seen by them" (Matt. 6:1).

Jesus does not forbid all public prayer. He occasionally prayed in the presence of his disciples; prophets and apostles sometimes prayed in public, too. It is not wrong to be seen praying. But it is wrong to pray in order to be seen.

As we saw in the last chapter, it is better to pray in an inner room, with the door closed (6:6). Public prayer is not sinful, but the essence of prayer is private conversation with God, and a quiet, secluded place is best for that. Because hypocrites pray with an eye on their reputation, they miss the essence of prayer. Jesus says that if we attend to God, he will reward us.

By avoiding hypocrisy, we surpass the righteousness of the Pharisees. Our prayers may not be technically superior, but we pray for a nobler reason. We do not pray for show or to fulfill a religious duty, but to commune with God.

Pagan prayer fails in a different way. Atheists do not pray at all, and agnostics may do nothing more than toss up a petition "in case someone up there is listening," but many pagans do pray. In Jesus' day, they prayed mechanically, heaping up empty words. Their problem was not repetition *per se*; after all, Jesus blesses those who pray persistently (Luke 18:1–7). Their problem was their *mindless* repetition—a tongue that wagged while the mind slept.

To this day, some religions practice "meditation" that repeats a simple sound over and over to attain a trancelike state. And some Christians repeat the Apostles' Creed or a liturgy or even the Lord's Prayer so mechanically that they hardly even hear themselves speak. Genuine prayer is sincere, not hypocritical. It is thoughtful, not mechanical.[1]

## THE TRAITS OF TRUE PRAYER

### True Prayer Is Private (6:6)

As we said, public prayer is permissible, but genuine prayer finds its voice in private. Public prayer has the distractions of a public situation and the influence of an audience. In private prayer, we can stumble, correct ourselves, and admit that we do not know how to pray. We can pause to think or leave a thought unfinished. But these things are not suitable for public prayer.

### True Prayer Is Simple (6:7)

Pagan prayers of Jesus' day sought to manipulate the gods with what Jesus calls "many words" (Matt. 6:7). The petitions of pagan prayer were apt to be very short and simple, such as "Grant me safety on my journey." This simple prayer might grow to "many words" in two ways. First, they might invoke the names of many deities, hoping that at least one might be propitious enough to grant their request. Second, they might make the same request over and over. We again recall the prophets of Baal in their contest with Elijah on Mount Carmel (1 Kings 18). They cried to Baal "from morning till noon" (v. 26). They shouted and danced and slashed themselves, growing ever more frantic in a futile attempt to gain Baal's attention (v. 28).

Some people still think that God is too busy or indifferent to hear every prayer. They hope to shake him from his lethargy, to shout above his deafness, or to locate the formula that captures his attention. The problem in prayer is not that God is too busy for us, but that we feel too busy for him. God does not remove himself from us; we remove ourselves from him.

We do not need to master techniques that guarantee effective prayer. We should reject the idea that our prayers must be "good enough" to merit God's attention. Our words will never be good enough to merit God's attention! But God is kind and compassionate enough to listen.

The pagans had their ideas about how to garner God's attention, and we have ours. Some Christians think that their fervor, their sincerity, or their technique may gain them God's ear. Some think, "If I rise early in the morning and pray on my knees, in the cold, without coffee, then God will hear me."

But such prayer performances may not be seeking God at all. They may be seeking God's benefits or may even be trying to manipulate him. Instead of pleading for mercy, they attempt to force God to be merciful. Persistent prayer is certainly good, but God does not answer prayer because our persistence impresses him. He answers prayer because he loves us. True prayer seeks to commune with God, not to extract benefits from him.

True prayer rests in God's generosity, not in our efforts to earn rewards. True prayer waits on God's wisdom, rather than assuming that

Would God answer our prayer if it would do harm vs or someone else

we can accurately assess our needs. True prayer trusts God and finds its confidence in him.

### True Prayer Is Confident (6:8)

We can pray with confidence if we know that our "success" depends on God's wisdom and attention, not on our performance in prayer. There is a saying, "Be careful what you ask for; you might get it." That is, if we ask for the wrong thing, God just might give it to us. So, this reasoning goes, a man should not pray to become the governor of California. He might be elected, run the state to ruin, and then be turned out of office while millions watch. Of course, we should be careful with our requests. But we insult the Lord if we suggest that he will give us what we ask for, even though it will harm us. Why would he do such a thing?

Does God lack discernment? Is he like an overindulgent parent, giving out candy because his children request it over and over, despite the fact that it rots the teeth and bloats the flesh? No, God knows our needs. He gives good gifts to his children (Matt. 7:11).

Is God cruel? Will he say, "You asked me for something foolish. OK, I will grant it. But you will realize your folly when you see the results. That will teach you to make rash requests."

The Lord is neither ignorant nor cruel. He knows and loves. Jesus says, "Your Father knows what you need before you ask him" (6:8). If we ask amiss, the Spirit perfects our prayers. "The Spirit himself intercedes for us with groans that words cannot express" (Rom. 8:26). Sometimes our prayers are misguided or poorly expressed. But God knows what we intend to say and what we ought to say. If we become inarticulate, we can pray, "Lord, you know my heart. You know what I ought to say." He *does* know. He is pleased to respond to what we intend to pray or should pray. God forgives and mends our prayers as surely as he forgives and mends our other failings. This lets us pray confidently.

## THE PATTERN OF TRUE PRAYER

We come now to the opening of the prayer itself. The first half of this pattern for prayer is thoroughly God-centered, as Jesus tells us to pray,

"Our Father in heaven, hallowed be your name, your kingdom come, your will be done on earth as it is in heaven" (Matt. 6:9–10).

### True Prayer Is Familial

The words "Our Father in heaven" reveal the first element of Christian prayer. It is *family* speech, for we address God as "our Father." In Jesus' day, this was radical. Jewish prayers stressed God's sovereignty, lordship, glory, grace, and covenant. On rare occasions, the Old Testament refers to God as "Father" (Deut. 32:6; Ps. 103:13; Isa. 63:16; Mal. 2:10), but no prophet taught the people to pray to God as "our Father."

When Jesus called God "his own Father," some Jews were offended (John 5:18). Pious Jews held God in such awe that they used circumlocutions to avoid saying his name, for fear of misusing it. Therefore, we must pause to consider something remarkable—Jesus teaches us to address the holy, almighty Lord as "our Father."

When we meet a great person or someone holding high office, we find it difficult to call him by his first name. Whether we like our president or not, we do not call him "Bill" or "George," but "Mr. President." But if titles are proper for such people, then the Creator and King of heaven certainly deserves titles of respect. But God is personal. Therefore, he requests a personal title: Father. Nothing shapes our prayers more than this word. It explains why prayer is simple and why sinners can approach God with confidence.

God's fatherly nature connects prayer to the gospel. Many Christians are reluctant to pray because they feel unworthy. God's presence frightens them, due to their sin. For some, the difficulty is their repeated requests. They understand that the Lord forgives the sinner who comes to repent of sin. But they cringe at the thought of asking God for mercy, again and again, for the *same* sin. Projecting their impatience onto God, they recoil at the thought of asking forgiveness for a sin they commit repeatedly.

They think, "I ask for forgiveness and for strength. Then I commit the same sin and return, the next day, with the same request. I am making no progress whatsoever." Almost every Christian struggles with one particular sin. Our tongues may curse, boast, lie, and gossip. Our hearts may be filled with pride, envy, or lust. We may crave alcohol, drugs, or sensual indulgence. We may be short-tempered and critical. Doubt and dark thoughts may hold our minds captive. And we wonder how we can enter God's presence with this load of sin.

But remember the gospel. Jesus is more than a teacher. He came into the world to "save his people from their sins" (Matt. 1:21). Jesus did not come simply to tell people to stop sinning. The prophets could handle that. The Son of God entered history to *save* sinners. "He was delivered over to death for our sins and was raised to life for our justification" (Rom. 4:25).

Jesus hints at this with the simple command to call God "Father." Understand this, and doubt dissipates. How do parents treat their children when they come confessing their weaknesses? Are we shocked? Do we banish them? Do we say, "Come here so I can punish you, then disown you"? Even sinful human parents know how to comfort and forgive. How much more will God the Father treat us with mercy and grace?

Some cannot bear to bring the same sin and failure to God over and over. But do you think he is surprised to see you confessing this sin again? Did he not know our weaknesses, our sins, long ago?

We ask, "Can God love me when I fail him as a Christian?" He can. He sent Christ, knowing the sins we would commit—both before coming to faith and after coming to faith. That is his unconditional love, a love that exceeds all human love. Do not misunderstand: the Father grieves over our sins. But the gospel says that God loved us while we were yet sinners. Surely, he loves us now that we are his sons and daughters.

Consider the institution we call a report card. Suppose a child comes home with two A's, a B, a C, and an F. The good father says, "I certainly am pleased with your A's. Well done. And I grieve over that F. But you know I love you just the same, whatever your grades may be." A wise father asks his child to do his best and says, "If you do your best, I will be satisfied. And if you do not do your best, I will be disappointed, but I will still love you."

Wise parents participate in the divine nature (2 Peter 1:4). They share in the wisdom of our Father in heaven. Our sins grieve him, but they do not nullify his love. God knows that we are sinners and knows it down to the details. He knows that obedience is easy for us in one area, but hard in another. He knows that one of us gossips and that another struggles with pride. He know that one person loves God, but breaks his commandments, while another keeps the law, but has many doubts.

God knows that some of us have wounded ourselves with past sins. He knows that if our drinking alcohol leads to alcoholism, we will be alcoholics until the day we die. He knows that longings for alcohol may torment the alcoholic until his last day on earth. He knows that those who are promiscuous for a few years may be plagued by sexual temptation for many years. Some accidents make our bodies limp for years, and some sins make our spirits limp even longer.

God says, "Come to me. Don't bear that burden of guilt. Bring it to Jesus. He has borne it for you. Come to me, child, and rest in my love." That is the gospel, applied to prayer. God is personal, loving, and powerful. Therefore, we rightly take every need to him.

Many church members struggle with pride; indeed, whole churches are so prone to pride that people are reluctant to confess their sins or admit their needs. Such pride deprives us of the church's support in time of need. During a discussion of divorce among Christians, an elder said, "I remember looking at a couple and thinking, 'They must have the perfect marriage.' A month later, they were getting a divorce." Pride makes us pretend we have a great marriage. Because of pride, some couples would rather look healthy than be healthy. Why should we hide our struggles, spurning help, until we finally snap? Everyone struggles somewhere. The church is a society of sinners and weaklings. If God calls himself Father, that means we are his children. Indeed, he calls us his children dozens of times in Scripture (e.g., Deut. 14:1; Pss. 34:11; 103:13; Isa. 8:18; 54:1; John 1:11–12; Rom. 8:16–21; Gal. 4:28–31; Eph. 5:1, 8; Heb. 2:13–14; 1 John 3:1–10).

When God says, "You are the children of the LORD your God" (Deut. 14:1), he is saying two things: "I love you" and "However strong you are compared to others, you are weak enough to need my help. Like children, you should have enough sense to say, 'Help me.'" Why deny our need of God's strength? We are children, humble and weak enough to need God's help. We are also believers, wise and confident enough to ask God, our Father, to help us.

### True Prayer Is Corporate

Jesus teaches us to call God "Father." To be precise, we should pray to him as "*our* Father." We do not pray abstractly to "the Father" or individualistically to "my Father," but corporately and communally to "our Father." This phrase reminds us that we belong to the family of God. In the New Testament, only Jesus calls God "Father." He speaks of "my Father" about forty times (see Matt. 10:32–33; 11:27; 26:39, 42, 53; John 10:17–18, 29, 37; 14:20–23; 15:23–24). He also speaks of "the Father" dozens of times (see Matt. 11:25–27; 23:9; 24:36; 28:19; Mark 13:32; 14:36; Luke 9:26; 10:22; 22:42; 23:34, 46; John 5:17–26; 6:27–46). But here, he teaches us to pray to "our Father."

### True Prayer Is Transcendent

We pray, furthermore, to "our Father *in heaven*," reminding us that true prayer is also transcendent. Our prayers reach escape velocity. We pray to the sovereign King, the Father who dwells on high. The address "our Father in heaven" means that God is both near to us, for he is our Father, and beyond us, for he is in heaven. So then, true prayer is private, confident, simple, familial, corporate, and transcendent; we pray to *the* Father, to *our* Father, and to our Father *in heaven*. Through it all, biblical prayer is God-centered.

We have all kinds of questions about prayer: If God is sovereign, why pray? Can we change his will? Should we try? Why is it hard to pray about things like sex, debt, and fear? Why is it easy to pray for missionaries? Why is it easier to pray for our children than for our parents? Why is it easier to pray for a friend's health than for our own? What does God think of long prayer lists with request after request? These are good, honest questions, and the Lord's Prayer answers some of them indirectly. But regardless of any unanswered questions, Jesus does teach us the essentials of prayer.

## THE CONTENT OF TRUE PRAYER

The Lord's Prayer is a guide or pattern, not a formula or mantra. It tells us *how* to pray, not precisely *what* to pray. So we may repeat these words in a liturgy or use different words. True prayer begins with God, our Father in heaven. Because his concerns rank first and our desires rank second, Jesus instructs us to pray first for his honor, his will, and his kingdom.

## Hallowed Be Your Name

The first petition, "Hallowed be your name," must be understood broadly. We should strive to use God's name correctly, but his name also represents his person. To honor God's name is to honor God himself. Thus, true prayer is God-centered. Prayer can help *us* center; it helps us meditate on spiritual matters. But prayer is not the same as centering or meditating. Prayer brings us to God, the Creator, the Redeemer, and the sovereign Lord.

The prayer "Hallowed by your name" is similar to the third commandment, "You shall not take the name of the LORD your God in vain" (Ex. 20:7 ESV). We honor God's name when we pray sincerely, not as a ritual or incantation. We honor God by praising him warmly, by discussing his ways reverently. We never say "Oh my God" merely to express surprise. We say "My God" when we are crying out to the Lord, not when we cry out because we just thumped a finger.

We also honor God's name with godly conduct. If we call ourselves Christians, we honor or dishonor his name with every public deed. Our conduct says, "This is the way we live when we come under Jesus' influence." That is why I am reticent to put a Christian bumper sticker on my car. I am not a bad driver, but I doubt that my driving is good enough to represent the name and glory of God. To put it differently, if we put a pro-life message on our car, we need to drive in a consistently pro-life way.

We honor God's name by honoring his person. When we pray "Hallowed be your name," the Greek word for "hallowed" would usually be translated "sanctified." We are not praying that God's name should become holy; it already is holy. Rather, we are praying that his name and person be revered. We pray that God's name, which embodies his essence and character, will be *treated* as holy. This means we honor God's name in public, and pray that the world will honor him too. We also strive to honor God in private.

I once had a bedtime conversation with one of our children when she was eleven. "Daddy," she began, "I don't seem to be praying well in family devotions."

"That's OK," I replied. "Sometimes it's hard to pray with a group. It can be hard to pay attention."

"No, I mean even when I'm alone, I just pray the same things over and over: 'Thank you for this day, thank you for the good things you give us.' I hardly pay attention to myself."

It is this thought or feeling, I told her, that the Lord's Prayer immediately addresses. It teaches us to start our prayers by praising God for who he is, from our heart.

My daughter's eyes lit up. She got the point and wanted to pray at once. She began, "Dear Lord, you are so cool." A few days later, she switched again: "Dear Lord, you are so awesome."

"Hallowed be your name" is a large petition. We pray that we will speak well of God and that our lives will cause others to bless his name as well (Matt. 5:16). We pray that we can focus on God's nature, not just on our needs, when we pray. In prayer, we say, "I admire you. I adore you."

The first petition also illumines some of the obstacles to prayer. The chief obstacle is unbelief. If someone doubts that God exists, or thinks that he is impersonal or weak, it is hard to pray. Such people can only lob up a prayer and hope for the best.

Mature Christians get confused, too. We can master information about God and cease to focus on him. We can be so busy studying God's word that we lose sight of the God who speaks. Others make prayer into a discipline—a personal "quiet time." Daily prayer is good, but I wince when people say, "I missed my quiet time this morning, so it's been a dreadful day." If we need a quiet time to guarantee a good day, we miss the point again. We pray to meet God.

### Your Kingdom Come

This petition overlaps with the first, for God's name is honored whenever his rule is more evident. "Your kingdom come" means that Christ is King and that we want his rule to become more evident every day.

"Your kingdom come" is also an evangelistic prayer. We pray that the blessings of salvation will flow, that the church will grow in size and influence, that Christians will grow in maturity, and that we would obey Jesus in every sphere of life.

We also pray that Christ will return. If we seek God in prayer, we long to see him face-to-face. To pray "Your kingdom come" is to pray for the restoration of all things, that his kingdom will come in its perfect form. Finally, to pray "Your kingdom come" is to ask the Lord to reign now, in our lives.

### Your Will Be Done

This petition bridges the theocentric and personal aspects of the Lord's Prayer. It contains two elements. First, we ask to know God's will. Second, we ask that we and others would have the desire and the strength to do it.

We ask first that God would make his will clear. "The will of God" can mean two things: his moral will (his precepts) and his will for history (his decrees). God's precepts are his revealed will, his principles and rules for holy living, such as the Ten Commandments and the law of love. God's decrees are his eternal counsel or plan for human history.

Clearly, it is right to pray that God's will be done in both senses. We ought to pray for obedience to God's moral will. We may also pray that the Lord would perform his will and show us his will for the elements of life—where to live, what career to pursue, whom to marry, how to educate our children, how to use our gifts, and how to spend our time. This prayer is akin to a prayer for wisdom and discernment, a prayer for wise friends and counselors.

"Your will be done" also looks to a more distant day, when Christ returns, and his will shall be done perfectly. Until then, we pray that God's will should be more visible on earth, with more love, freedom, and joy, with less sin and frustration. We pray that earth will look more like heaven and less like hell. We pray for loving homes and for justice and truth in society. Finally, to pray for these blessings is to commit ourselves to work for these goals.

The first half of the Lord's Prayer is so God-centered that it prompts us to scrutinize our prayers. What do we pray for? Do we praise or thank God for a moment, and then move to a string of petitions? Do we ask, again and again, for health, peace, and prosperity for one person after another? Let us not miss the point of prayer. Let us pray above all that the person of our Lord be blessed.

# 12

# THE LORD'S PRAYER: OUR PETITIONS

*Matthew 6:9–15*

ANDY BENES, a pitcher for the St. Louis Cardinals, ended the 2001 baseball season with a sore knee and a string of bad performances. The 2002 season began even worse. His knee was still sore, and opposing batters were pounding him. After a series of disastrous games, he was removed from the pitching rotation. The team hinted that he should consider retirement, but Benes wanted to finish his career in the right way. So he rested his knee, and then returned to the minor leagues to recover his form. He also prayed that the Lord would let him finish well and retire in St. Louis, the city that his wife and children called home, with dignity.

Throwing in the outfield one day in the minor leagues, he began to experiment with a pitch called a split-fingered fastball. It ordinarily takes months, even years, to master a new pitch for use in major-league competition. Further, a split-fingered fastball is a difficult pitch that few professionals can ever master. But it seemed to work at once for Benes. He tried it that very night. He got a double play the first time he threw it, and easily retired several more batters with it. Success followed success; within weeks he was back with the Cardinals, refining his new pitch. He ended up being their most effective starting pitcher in the last two months of a season that ended with a division title.

God answered Andy Benes's prayer; he retired with dignity after that season. Six months after his retirement, he said, "That pitch was like a gift God dropped from heaven. If I had to throw a split-fingered fastball today, I'm not sure I would know how to do it."

## OUR HESITATION TO PETITION GOD

In the last chapter, we saw that the first part of the Lord's Prayer is God-centered. We pray to the Father, personal yet great, dwelling in heaven. We ask that he honor his name, that he bring his kingdom, and that he accomplish all his plans and purposes.

In the second half of the Lord's Prayer, Jesus declares that we also have a right, indeed an obligation, to take our needs to him and ask for his blessing. Many people find it difficult to ask for help. Young adults hesitate to ask their parents for help, and older parents hesitate to ask for aid from their children as they age. We feel awkward asking friends for favors, especially if we have often needed help. Yet we know that we should lay aside our pride and seek the assistance we need.

This principle is also true spiritually. If relatives and friends gladly assist us when they can, surely our Father in heaven gladly helps his children. It is no surprise, then, that Jesus says we should present our needs to God. Oddly, some Christians find it easier to pray for a sick relative or distant missionary than for themselves. But the Lord both invites and commands that we petition him for aid, both for ourselves and for others.

This seems simple enough, but things can go wrong in several ways. First, we hesitate to bring our requests because we have unworthy desires. Think of the male interest in automobiles, for example. A while ago, I needed a new car. I began to read reviews and watch advertisements in the paper. During my quest, I came upon a review for a certain car, which the expert called "the perfect car." It was fairly expensive, but who would not want to own "the perfect car"? Yet it seemed impossible to pray, "Father, you know I need a car, and I humbly ask that you grant me 'the perfect car' and, furthermore, that someone sell it to me at half price, since I can afford no more."

Second, we hesitate to bring our requests because we doubt that God will act, even for a worthy desire. Suppose a family member, recently the epitome of health, falls ill with a life-threatening disease. Strangely, we may choke on our prayers. What if God denies our requests? Could we bear the thought that God would fail to heal our loved one? Sometimes we want to avoid such questions, so we do not pray at all.

Third, we hesitate over the scope of our petitions. Is it right for adults to pray about the common cold, or for children to pray for sick puppies? Do we insult God's dignity with such concerns? Or does he want us to take everything to him? (I believe children may certainly pray for sick puppies, although God may answer more for the sake of the child than for the dog.)

These are good questions, and Jesus answers them, in principle, in the Lord's Prayer.

*Principle 1*: Prayer is God-centered. In prayer, we speak to God, our Father in Heaven.

*Principle 2*: There is a place for self-interest in prayer. Indeed, Jesus commands his disciples to pray for their needs. But there is a God-given priority and pattern for those needs.

## THE NATURE OF OUR PETITIONS

Prayer must never seek to manipulate God. We do not extract what we want by piling up words or repeating his names, as if they were magical incantations (Matt. 6:7). Prayer does not and cannot induce the Lord to abdicate his throne. God is not like a weak parent who backs down if his children badger him long enough. He will not break down, if we whine enough, and say, "All right, you can have what you want, but you may not like it when you get it."

The Father knows what we need before we ask him (6:8). "He is neither ignorant, so that we need to instruct him, nor indifferent, so that we need to persuade him."[1] He loves us, knows us, and gives what we need. As Calvin said, believers do not pray to inform God about things unknown to him, or to urge him to do his duty as though he were reluctant. "On the contrary, they pray in order that they may arouse themselves to seek him," to meditate on his promises, and to relieve themselves of their anxieties "by pouring them into his bosom." By prayer they declare that from him alone they expect all good things.[2]

Calvin's statement suggests how prayer changes things. It does not cause change in the sense that utterly unplanned events suddenly occur, so that even God is surprised. But prayer does change things, for it changes *us*. God does not change, nor do his plans change, but prayer does change our relationship to God.

Suppose a family moves and their teenage daughter changes schools. The academic programs of the old school and the new school do not match perfectly. The father consults the school's leaders and concludes that his child must take a summer school course so that she can enter the proper "track" in the fall. The class is best for her, but summer school feels like punishment to her, so she objects: "Daddy, I don't want to go to summer school. Please don't make me."

Because the father loves his daughter, he will not change a decision that is in her best interest. Yet he still wants to discuss the matter with her. The conversation may be frustrating before it is satisfying, but the father wants his child to understand and do her best, even in an unpleasant experience. Likewise with us, prayer may not change God's will, but it does change our attitude toward his will. It alters our attitude toward events.

Suppose again that an older boy has an automobile accident. No one is hurt, but the boy lost control of his car while driving recklessly, and he is not taking responsibility. He blames the road conditions; he blames another driver. The father is grateful that the boy is healthy, but he will pursue his child—sternly, if necessary—until he admits his mistakes and learns from them. When the young man does repent, the tenor of the father-son relationship will change. The shift will not occur because the father's values or principles have shifted, but because the son's repentance lets the father show another side of his character. The father remains the same, but their relationship changes when the son repents.

Similarly, we may approach God in a state of rebellion, feeling nothing but his frown. But through prayer, we may see our errors and repent, so that we soon feel God's pleasure. What changed? Did the Lord suddenly become nicer? No, God did not change; we did. And because we changed, he could stop leading us to repentance, with his temporary frown, and show us his pleasure. When we pray, we change, and that alters our relationship with the Father.[3]

There is, however, one more way to think about the effects of prayer. While the Lord does not necessarily grant a request because the petitioner is especially noble or sincere or fervent, our prayers do matter deeply in the sense that they are a vital means that God uses to accomplish his purposes. So, for example, if he ordains that a student will receive an A in a class, he also ordains the means of diligent study. If he ordains someone's salvation, he also ordains the means—the testimony of a friend or the sermon of an evangelist. Similarly, the Lord does act in history in response to our petitions (see Hezekiah in 2 Kings 20) or to cries of repentance (see the Ninevites in Jonah 3), even while those prayers are part of his will. This is what the Westminster Confession of Faith means when it say that God's sovereign will does no violence to "the liberty or contingency of second causes" (3.1) and that his will includes both the ends of human history and "all the means thereunto" (3.6).

## THE SPIRIT OF OUR PETITIONS

Prayer begins with a desire for God's honor. We also have a family relationship with him. Family members attend to their relationships. Therefore, we pray that mankind will honor God when we say, "Hallowed be thy name." We pray that God will be revered and loved. We pray that that reverence will lead to discipleship throughout the world. We pray, "Your kingdom come, your will be done."

After seeking God, our prayer continues with expressions of our needs. Since God is fatherly to us, we rightly describe our needs to him. As Calvin said, prayer does not inform God about things unknown to him. Rather, prayer rouses us to seek him. We relieve our anxieties by pouring them out to him. We name our fears, needs, and hopes. We do not simply ask for things. Jesus instructs his disciples to pray for three types of need: for the food we need for daily life, for grace to cover our sin, and for deliverance from temptation. This trio balances our material concerns with our spiritual concerns. We can upset this balance in two opposite ways.

First, we may read the first petition as an invitation to selfish prayers, so that we approach God as the cosmic Giver, glad to hear and indulge our fancies. We must not ask for anything sinful. We must not pray for God's wisdom as we plan to rob a bank. We must not pray for the demise of a rival. But as long as we make honest requests, we should present our needs to God.

Second, we may notice that five of the six petitions concern the person and work of God, and conclude that we should not mention personal needs. We may also try to avoid selfishness by praying only for others. Some believers excel at prayer for others, but never state their own needs and desires. They faithfully pray for pastors and missionaries, but hardly pray for their own service to God.

Then there are topics, such as money and sex, that we hesitate to mention in prayer. We may balk at prayer about money, since the topic seems unspiritual. Yet if a man chronically spends more than he earns, and cannot stop, or if a woman is trapped by debts and cannot escape, why not present it to the Father? Moreover, if God has blessed us with abundance, we should pray about its best use. Whatever our situation, God is not shocked to hear about our problems. If earning, spending, saving, and retiring occupy our thoughts, if financial calculation guides too many decisions, we should pray through it.

We can also pray about our sexuality, although we may not be accustomed to doing so. We can thank God for making us male and female. We might pray for blessed intimacy with our spouse. We might ask that we discipline our thoughts. Again, do we think that God will be shocked to hear about our struggles? Do we think we can hide our sins from him by not mentioning them in prayer?

We can pray about our emotions. Anger, fears, regrets, grudges, secret hopes and dreams all affect our walk with God. To pray about them is to pray "Your kingdom come." Our Father has redeemed us. He wants to enlighten every corner of our lives.

## THE CONTENT OF OUR PETITIONS

### *Give Us Today Our Daily Bread*

In this petition, we confess that we depend on God. There is a scene in the old movie *Shenandoah* where Jimmy Stewart eats a meal with his children shortly after his wife has died. She had handled all the prayers, but now the children tell him he must pray before dinner. He is no Christian, and his words reflect it. He prays roughly like this: "Dear

Lord, thank you for this meal. We plowed the ground, we planted the seed, we pulled the weeds, we harvested the wheat, we ground the flour, we baked the bread, but thank you, Lord, for this meal."

A believer sees it differently. We pray for our daily bread, knowing that God created plants for our food. We know he put us in families, where we learned to work. He gave us the strength to plow, plant, and harvest. We do not view these as accidents, but as gifts from God. Therefore, we pray, "Give us today our daily bread," and we thank him whenever we eat.

Notice that Jesus tells us to ask for the bread we need for this day, every day. Today, in the affluent West, bread is optional food; we eat it if we need calories, and shun it if we do not. It is a snack to keep us busy before the entrée arrives at a restaurant. But in Jesus' day, bread was the stuff of life, the one food people ate every day. The message is, "Pray each day for the food you need to live in the coming day." Bread represents all food (Num. 21:5; Deut. 8:3, 9; Ps. 136:25; Isa. 33:16). It represents our basic daily needs. If we have food and covering, we should be content with that (1 Tim. 6:8). Just as God gave the Israelites manna every day, so he will feed us each day as we rely upon him.

We miss the urgency of this prayer today. Americans live in a land of plenty. Indeed, we have so much food we worry more about obesity than hunger. We buy large quantities of food in well-stocked stores and stuff it into capacious refrigerators and freezers. We plan ahead, so that our food seems to come from our work and our kitchen. In Jesus' day, it was more obvious to a laborer that he should pray daily for his daily bread. A common laborer lived on a payment for that day's work. If he could find no work or if his employer withheld his wages, he might go hungry. Western culture has changed enough (monthly paychecks are an example) that we do not feel the urgency to pray for food daily. But our food still comes from God, and we honor him when we acknowledge it.

Observe, too, that Jesus does not say, "Ask for everything you will ever need." We should pray for what we need, one day at a time. At night, we pray for the morrow. In the morning, we pray for the dawning day. Jesus exhorts us to petition God for our daily needs, not our daily greeds. We pray for every need, not for every desire. In fact, Scripture tells us not to pray for wealth. Proverbs 30:7–9 says:

Two things I ask of you, O LORD;
    do not refuse me before I die:
Keep falsehood and lies far from me;
    give me neither poverty nor riches,
    but give me only my daily bread.
Otherwise, I may have too much and disown you
    and say, "Who is the LORD?"
Or I may become poor and steal,
    and so dishonor the name of my God.

Paul adds, "People who want to get rich fall into temptation and a trap and into many foolish and harmful desires that plunge men into ruin and destruction. For the love of money is a root of all kinds of evil. Some people, eager for money, have wandered from the faith and pierced themselves with many griefs" (1 Tim. 6:9–10).

These passages show that to pray for wealth is to pray for temptation. But we pray, "Lead us not into temptation." Proverbs says wealth tempts us to forget God. Paul says that the quest for wealth can entrap us. So let us not pray for riches.

This does not mean that it is evil to be prosperous. If someone invents a useful product, patenting laws may make him a rich man. If someone provides a uniquely excellent resource or service, she may prosper. But becoming wealthy through hard work is different from working hard to become wealthy. The goal of the first is service for others. The goal of the second is self-service. The first man will have to strive to resist temptation. The second man is asking for temptation.

It is a mistake to ask for too much. It is also a mistake to ask naively, with a hand perpetually stretched out, waiting passively for God's next donation. The teaching about daily bread reminds us that sometimes we must *ask and act*. In this regard, prayer for food and prayer for wisdom are identical.

James says, "If any of you lacks wisdom, he should ask God" (James 1:5). Solomon prayed for wisdom: "Give your servant a discerning heart to govern your people and to distinguish between right and wrong" (1 Kings 3:9). But Solomon also worked for his wisdom. He examined and described plant life and taught about all kinds of animals (1 Kings 4:33). That is, Solomon became wise because God gave him a gift *and* because he worked by watching how the world works (Prov. 7:7; 24:32). One proverb says, "He who walks with the wise grows wise" (13:20). Spend time with a wise parent and you will become a better parent. Spend time with a wise businessman and you will become a better businessman. Thus, we should pray for wisdom and work for wisdom.

Similarly, Scripture tells us to ask for food and to work for food. Paul says, "If a man will not work, he shall not eat" (2 Thess. 3:10). Moses teaches us to pray: "Establish the work of our hands for us—yes, establish the work of our hands" (Ps. 90:17). We pray and we labor.

### Forgive Us Our Debts, As We Also Have Forgiven Our Debtors

The first petition asks God to provide our chief physical need, food. The second petition asks for our chief spiritual need, forgiveness of sin. As before, we can misread this request. Some think that "Forgive us our debts, as we also have forgiven our debtors" means that God will forgive us if and only if we forgive others. Those who hold this view also appeal to Matthew 6:14–15, where Jesus says, "For if you forgive men when they sin against you, your heavenly Father will also forgive you. But if you do not forgive men their sins, your Father will not forgive your sins." The best way to understand these verses is to take all three together.

First, the gospel itself forbids that we say God grants us mercy if and only if we grant mercy to others. That would make God's mercy—and salvation itself—a reward for our prior act (our "work") of showing mercy to others. That cannot be right, since God's mercy is never a reward for our good deeds. If we call forgiveness a reward, we contradict the gospel, which says that God's mercy is a gift. Forgiveness is essential to our salvation, and the entire Bible teaches that we do nothing to merit our salvation. Indeed, if forgiveness from God turned on our forgiveness of others, we should despair, for even the most tender and understanding Christians occasionally find it hard to forgive.

Jesus' point is that God forgives the penitent. That is, if we understand how precious it is to be forgiven, if we know how much it cost God to forgive, then we will forgive others. The forgiven have motives to forgive. We thank God for his gift, we admire the beauty of his way, and we hope to do the same for others.

John Stott says, "Once our eyes have been opened to see the enormity of our offense against God, the injuries which others have done to us appear by comparison extremely trifling. If on the other hand, we have an exaggerated view of the offenses of others, it proves we have minimized our own."[4]

Sadly, we even let trivial offenses bother us. If someone neglects to thank us for a favor done, or makes a mess we have to clean up, or takes credit for work we performed, we can become agitated. Yet we commit the very sins we resent in others (Rom. 2:1–3). We sin and excuse ourselves, then hold a grudge against someone else who does the same thing. But when we forgive someone else, it shows that we understand what it cost God to forgive us. It shows that we savor God's mercy.

Jesus commands us to pray for forgiveness every day. This is proper, for we know that we sin every day. But repentance is not as easy as it sounds. When we sin, we can respond in several ways, and not all of them involve repentance:

- We can excuse our sin, especially by blaming others. If we get angry, someone provoked us. If we fail, someone tempted us. We even blame God for our sins: "When tempted, no one should say, 'God is tempting me.' For God cannot be tempted by evil, nor does he tempt anyone; but each one is tempted when, by his own evil desire, he is dragged away and enticed" (James 1:13–14).
- We can deny our sin. We redefine our actions, so they sound better. The impenitent never argue, they have animated discussions. They never shout, they make their points emphatically. They don't steal, they borrow indefinitely without telling the owner. If anyone points out the error, that person is judgmental.
- We can succumb to shame and run away. We can collapse in guilt and self-recrimination. We can give up because we decide that we are unable to change.
- We can resolve to try harder. We can stir ourselves to redouble our efforts until we collapse in failure and shame again.

- Or we can ask the Lord for mercy. Some wonder if God will forgive us when we commit the same sins over and over. He will. Remember, "Forgive us" is part of Jesus' model prayer. We pray this way daily. If we can ask for bread daily, we can ask for forgiveness daily.

The question "Will God forgive again?" is sensible, but it underestimates the gospel. God's grace is greater than our sin. The gospel goes to sinners, to the poor in spirit. We rest in God's love, not our performance. The Lord is pleased when we obey, yet he loves and forgives, whether we obey or not.

### Lead Us Not into Temptation

The third petition proceeds logically from the second. The man or woman who is free from the guilt of sin also wants relief from its tyranny. The previous petition asks for release from the guilt and penalty of sin. This one seeks release from its power and corruption.

When we pray, we confess that we cannot remain loyal by our own will. Remember, Proverbs 30:8 says, "Give me neither poverty nor riches," because both lead to temptation. In essence, we are asking that God would remove us from paths of temptation.

Again we see a place both to pray and to work. We pray for deliverance from temptation, yet Scripture also commands us to flee from it (1 Cor. 6:18; 10:14). We ask God to lead us away from temptation, yet we must *avoid* temptation. We must make no provision for the lusts of the flesh. We should structure our lives so that it is harder to sin.

Children become irritable when they are deprived of sleep, but so do adults. So if we are prone to foul moods, we should do more than pray for a sweeter disposition; we should get more sleep.

Still, some testing is inevitable. Indeed, God himself tests us on occasion. God tested Abraham when he asked him to offer up his son Isaac (Gen. 22:1; Heb. 11:17). Jesus does not mean we should pray that we will never face any hardship. Rather, we should pray that we will be ready to endure tests and hardships faithfully.

The same situation can be a test on one day and a temptation on another. Suppose a man who is accustomed to cursing vows to reform his speech. If a rude driver cuts him off in traffic a day after his vow, it will tempt him to curse. But if the same thing happens years after he has purged profanities from his lexicon, the incident will be less a temptation than a test—an occasion for him to prove his resolve.

So we do not shun every test. Yet we sense that there are some tests that we cannot pass. If we do not escape them, they will entrap us. These we should not face squarely, in direct combat. We should retreat, even flee, from them. We ask the Lord to lead us away from the temptations that will defeat us. We pray that our Father will so arrange our life that we can remain loyal to him. We do not look for a trouble-free life. Disciples face the tests that are common to mankind. But we do ask God to spare us from tests we cannot endure (1 Cor. 10:13). When we ask God to "deliver us from evil" (Matt. 6:13 ESV), we ask for deliverance from the traps of "the evil one" (6:13 NIV) as well.

This prayer also hints that our interests and God's interests coincide. When we pray, "Deliver us from evil," we know that our holiness hallows his name. When we resist evil, we do his will and his kingdom comes. God is for us and we are for God. In prayer, proper self-interest and proper devotion meet.

Incidentally, this petition partially explains why some prayers go unanswered. If a request leads to temptation, God will not grant it. Of course, God will not hear a prayer for aid as we sin, such as, "Father, grant my fingers skill as I attempt to break into this safe." But even if we ask for something that is good, he will not grant it if it would lead us into sin.[5]

## CONCLUSION

The Lord's Prayer is comprehensive. It chides hypocrites whose grand prayers parade their spirituality. It rebukes pagans who repeat the names of the gods, trying to force them to grant favors. As a believer's prayer, it begins with God's glory and ends with his generosity.

This prayer addresses the full range of human need. Jesus bids us to take every need to the triune God. We pray for daily bread, and the

Creator meets our physical needs. We pray for forgiveness, and the redeeming Son meets that need when we turn to him by faith. We seek deliverance from evil, and the Spirit meets our moral need by leading us away from temptation.

In the Lord's Prayer, God meets us and brings us to himself. Proper self-interest and love of God meet. We pour out our needs to God because we trust him, and he answers us because he loves us.

# 13

# FOOD, FASTS, AND FEASTS

## *Matthew 6:16–18*

SOMETHING HAS GONE AWRY in Western society's relationship to food. If we listen to the media, we hear two contrary messages. On one hand, marketers and advertisers invite us to gormandize. Chomp the chewiest cheeseburgers, wolf the fattest French fries. Guzzle the partiest soda and the hardiest beer. Consume!

Others call for refinement. Satisfy your palate with select spices and sauces. Dine on dainty delicacies. Still others want to ban all the animal fats ladled into tacos, pizzas, ice cream, and steaks. Meanwhile, advertisers promote low-carb, low-fat foods so we can reverse the damage caused by the aforementioned cheeseburgers. Medical analysts weigh the pros and cons in the diet wars. All the while, the honest blessings of broccoli, peaches, rice, asparagus, and beans are oft neglected.

We are the victims of our own success. During the last century or so, we have learned to produce a bountiful food supply. In democratic nations, at least, starvation does not loom. We produce all the food we want, and more. In fact, we hardly know how to manage the abundance. Still, at root, food is a simple thing. Let us begin with a short theology of food.

## FOOD AT CREATION

God initially gave Adam every seed-bearing plant and fruit tree on the earth. "They will be yours for food" (Gen. 1:29). Later, when God reestablished the human race after the flood, he said, "Everything that lives and moves will be food for you. Just as I gave you the green plants, I now give you everything" (Gen. 9:3).

In God's original design, appetites and needs matched. God placed the food and drink that we need within our reach and invited us to take it. He measured our needs and appetites to fit the foods he placed in this world. He provided plants and soil, sun and rain, so we could work and live.

Today, despite the disorder caused by sin, some of that harmony remains. The Bible says, "The laborer's appetite works for him; his hunger drives him on" (Prov. 16:26). God gave us hunger as a gift. It drives us to work, so we can eat.

Angels do not need to think about the next meal. Neither God nor angels have physical needs; they do not eat, drink, or sleep. We do. The Lord expects us to feed and care for our bodies (Eph. 5:29). We should work, so we can eat (2 Thess. 3:8–10). Like animals, we must eat, drink, sleep, and procreate. Yet, unlike animals, we think about more than food. We belong to the material realm, so we need food, but we also belong to the spiritual realm, so we need more than food.

## FOOD AFTER THE FALL

In the beginning, there was no struggle to find food, no problem of scarcity. After the fall, Adam's race has had to eat by the sweat of the brow. We battle with weeds and wild animals, blights and droughts. Still, God restrains the chaos, so we can eat. Ordinarily, God feeds the world indirectly. He establishes and maintains structures for this world so that people and animals can find nourishment (Ps. 104; Matt. 6:26). As he governs the world, he has the capacity to prosper a nation's herds, harvests, and bakeries, or to withhold his blessing, as he wishes (Deut. 28:4–5; cf. Hos. 11:4).

Occasionally people cannot feed themselves. Then their friends and neighbors must come to their aid (James 2:15–18). Indeed, the Bible even says, "If your enemy is hungry, feed him; if he is thirsty, give him something to drink" (Rom. 12:20). When necessary, God feeds his people more directly. God sent bread—manna—from heaven to feed

Israel in the desert (Deut. 8:3). He also fed the prophet Elijah when he had no food (1 Kings 17:4).

The Bible recommends a certain mind-set when we consider food. First, if we have plenty, we should thank God, enjoy it, and share it. In the Old Testament, God even ordained feasts, so people could celebrate God's bounty in his presence. Second, we should strive for contentment, whether in plenty or in want. From his prison cell, the apostle Paul said, "I know what it is to be in need, and I know what it is to have plenty. I have learned the secret of being content in any and every situation, whether well fed or hungry, whether living in plenty or in want" (Phil. 4:12). We should be content if we can meet our basic needs. "Godliness with contentment is great gain. For we brought nothing into the world, and we can take nothing out of it. But if we have food and clothing, we will be content with that" (1 Tim. 6:6–8).

If we suffer want, we are tempted to anger or despair. When Job had lost his wealth, his health, and his children, when only his wife remained, she asked why he clung to his integrity. "Curse God and die." That is, savor your bitterness; despair and die (Job 2:9).

But abundance brings temptation, too. Jeremiah says that when God gave Israel an abundant harvest, they forgot him: "They have become rich and powerful and have grown fat and sleek" (Jer. 5:27–28). The issue is not plumpness *per se*. In other places, God says he makes people rich (1 Kings 3:13; 2 Chron. 32:29) and fat (Isa. 10:27)! Physically, great girth brings great risks. But the prophet is watching the heart, not the waist. He knows the danger of false confidence in stockpiles of food or wealth.

## FOOD AS AN IDOL

In a way, food is simple. We should eat to live; we should not live to eat. But there are problems. Our mastery of our bodies is imperfect. They do not do what we ask. They crash into people and drop dishes. We also eat when we are not hungry. If we look closely, we can see that the root problem may be idolatry. Calvin said that the human heart is a factory of idols. When we lose contact with the Lord, we put other things in his place. We can take anything that is good and make it into an idol. Food is no exception. We turn to it for the benefits that God provides.

- We eat to find peace. We eat to medicate ourselves, to overcome feelings of anger, depression, and loneliness. We eat when we need comfort. When we do not or cannot find proper comfort, we eat what some call "comfort food."
- Abundant food can be a token of strength, wealth, prosperity, and self-sufficiency. Today one farmer, equipped with good seed, land, and machines, can feed one hundred people. That farmer and that farmer's nation can become proud. We can think, "Behold the work of our hands and all that we have provided for ourselves. Do we still need the help of God?"
- Food can become *the* source of joy and meaning. It is fine if food is one source of pleasure and meaning. But what if we eat all that we need, then continue to eat for the physical pleasure of it? It is good to find joy in a shared meal. Some love to prepare food for others; others prefer that chefs prepare it for them. But there is a problem if we live to eat, rather than eating to live.

A woman once told me that she had a problem with cookies: "A plate of cookies, put out in a public place after lunch, positively torments me. I am not hungry. I do not *need* a cookie . . . (she paused to poke her plump belly), but I cannot bear the thought of someone else eating that cookie. So I walk past it, then I think about it, and come back and eat, because I'm afraid someone else will take it and I won't get to taste that cookie." That is a brilliant analysis of our battles with desire. She said it of food, but the basic ideas apply in so many areas. We are tormented by something we desire, but we know we do not need it and should not take it. We pass the pleasure by, then return to it, afraid we will lose it.

The story is the same with food, sex, and material possessions. When we cruise the Internet, when we cruise the mall, we act like my friend and her cookie. Whether we are obsessed by food, sex, sports, or possessions, we fight the same battle with the idols. How can we win the spiritual battle? We gain insight from Jesus and his ways with food.

# JESUS AND FOOD

Jesus ate and drank freely. He was popular throughout much of his ministry, so he was in demand as a guest at banquets. In his desire to reach everyone, he often attended them. He mingled, ate, and drank enough that critics called him a glutton and a drunkard. It is safe to assume that Jesus enjoyed a good meal, as we all do.

Jesus ate with the prosperous, but he also fed the hungry. Once he fed bread and fish to five thousand people when they followed him to a desolate place and had no food (Matt. 14:13–21). On another occasion, he fed four thousand in a time of need (Matt. 15:29–39).

Jesus enjoyed food and knew our need of food, but food was no idol for him. He fasted for forty days and forty nights to prepare for his mission. Matthew says, "After fasting forty days and forty nights, he was hungry" (4:2). Indeed he was. When I fast, I can persuade myself that I am hungry after forty minutes, not forty days. Tomatoes are the size of pumpkins, apples and peaches the size of beach balls when my hungry eyes spy them in the kitchen. Why did Jesus inaugurate his ministry by fasting? Why not gather his strength by eating and resting? Scripture answers: he gathered his strength by fasting and praying.

The apostles understood, as should we, that Jesus set a pattern. A time of prayer and fasting preceded the commissioning of Paul and Barnabas for their mission of preaching the risen Christ to the Gentiles. Acts says, "After they had fasted and prayed, they placed their hands on them and sent them off" (Acts 13:3). Paul and Barnabas did the same thing in turn for the next generation of leaders: "Paul and Barnabas appointed elders for them in each church and, with prayer and fasting, committed them to the Lord" (14:23).

## WHY FAST? CURBING OUR APPETITES

Fasting was a well-established practice in Israel. Moses fasted on Sinai when God established his covenant with Israel. Jehoshaphat the king, Esther the queen, Ezra the scribe, and Paul the apostle all fasted in time of need, as they called on the Lord.

We fast to follow Jesus when he says, "Man does not live on bread alone, but on every word that comes from the mouth of God" (Matt.

4:4). There was a saying in the city of Corinth, "Food for the stomach and the stomach for food" (1 Cor. 6:13). That is, if the body has an appetite for food or for sex, it must be satisfied, and the sooner the better. The materialist says, "If we have a drive, a desire, and a way to fulfill it, we should. Self-denial is pointless, even absurd." We fast, in part, to show that we are not animals. We are not slaves to our appetites. More than that, we fast to show that we have a hunger that exceeds our hunger for food.

Jesus *assumes* that his disciples will fast. He says, "When you fast," do not do it to impress men with your piety. Fast so that only God sees you, "and your Father, who sees what is done is secret, will reward you" (Matt. 6:16–18).

But why should we fast? According to John Piper, we fast to nourish our hunger for God and to reduce our hunger for the world.[1] We ought to fast because our physical appetites are so intense that they threaten to overwhelm our hunger for God. Piper writes: "The greatest enemy of hunger for God is not poison but apple pie. It is not the banquet of the wicked that dulls our appetite for heaven, but mindless nibbling at the table of the world. It is not the X-rated video, but the prime time dribble of triviality we drink in every night."[2]

When Jesus tells us what keeps us from entering the kingdom, from joining him at his banquet table, he does not mention Satan. He does mention a plot of land, several yoke of oxen, and a newly married wife (Luke 14:18–20). To quote Piper again, "The greatest adversary of love to God is not his enemies but his gifts. And the most deadly appetites are . . . for the simple pleasures of the earth. For when these replace an appetite for God himself, the idolatry is scarcely recognizable, and almost incurable."[3]

When Jesus explains why some hear the word of God, but do not respond to it, he says, "They are choked by the cares and riches and pleasures of life" (Luke 8:14 RSV). Again, he says, "The desires for other things come in and choke the word" (Mark 4:19). The pleasures of this life are not evil things; they are part of God's bountiful creation. They are grapes, blueberries, guacamole dip, and humus. They are football and soccer, silk and wool, comedy and drama, classical music, classic rock, hip-hop or jazz, according to your taste.

Our basic desires or drives are good in themselves, but they get perverted by sin. The problem begins when we form the habit of satisfying desires soon after we feel them. Hungry? Why wait until supper? Why not grab a candy bar, an apple, or a handful of nuts right now? The problem deepens when we declare ourselves content when we have met every craving.

We fast because fasting says, "I do not live for my appetites. I set aside physical desires, so that I may seek God in prayer, that I may desire God and his blessing." When we fast, we battle the relentless stream of appetites. We demonstrate that we do not live by bread alone. When we fast, the body grows weak, and that reminds us that we do not live by our strength, our provision, and our planning.

I do not excel at fasting. My metabolism is high, and I get very hungry very fast. Nonetheless, fasting is good for me. I am a self-disciplined type, and fasting reminds me that I do not prosper by diet, exercise, and disciplined labor alone, but by the blessing of God. When we fast, we declare, "Lord, you are my strength."

### *How to Fast: Practical Matters*

1. Fast *regularly.* Jesus assumes his disciples will fast. He says "when you fast," not "if you fast" (Matt. 6:16). Jesus fasted and he predicted that his disciples would fast after he left them (Matt. 4:2; 9:15). Fasting has its ups and downs as a discipline. The Puritans loved corporate fasts, but in recent decades, fasting fell into neglect. Richard Foster found that not one book was published on fasting from 1861 to 1954. John Wesley wisely observed, "Some have exalted religious fasting beyond all Scripture and reason; and others have utterly disregarded it."[4]

2. Fast *prayerfully.* Almost every culture has some concept of fasting. Many fast to show sorrow. Others fast to deprive themselves, thinking self-deprivation pleases their gods. Today some fast for their health, to purge and recalibrate their bodies. Such fasting may be beneficial. But Christians fast to dedicate themselves to God and to prayer. We need not pray all day; we need not forsake all regular activities. But we do pray more as we fast.

3. Fast *secretly.* Praise from men can be addictive. It is gratifying to be noticed for our accomplishments. Jesus says, "When you fast, do not

look somber. . . . Wash your face, so that it will not be obvious to men that you are fasting" (6:16–18). If you aim to be noticed and praised by men, you will probably succeed. People of faith will notice and admire your discipline. But the Bible calls it pride and hypocrisy.

Someone may ask, "How is it hypocrisy for people to know what you are doing? What is wrong with letting your deeds show? That is simple honesty." But the public display of our works poisons the well. When we fast or give away money and seek credit for it, we do it to impress others and not to seek God. We pretend to act for God, when really we act for ourselves and our audience. We are posers, feigning love for God.[5]

4. However, we may fast *corporately*, so that believers can join together to pray for a great matter. The people of Israel did this, the apostles did this (Acts 13–14), and in times past the church often did this. As long as the essential motive is to seek God, there is no harm if others discover that we are fasting, especially if they are seeking God the same way, beside us.

5. Fast *humbly*. There is a proud religion—legalism—that makes its rules and imposes them on others for the glory of exercising authority. It says, "Do not handle, do not taste, do not touch!" There is also a self-made religion that features "self-abasement and severe treatment of the body." These, Paul says, "are of no value against fleshly indulgence" (Col. 2:21, 23 NASB). The fleshly indulgence that Paul has in mind here is actually the sin of pride, not gluttony. C. S. Lewis said:

> Fasting asserts the will against the appetite—the reward being self-mastery and the danger pride. . . . Ascetic practices which, in themselves, strengthen the will, are only useful insofar as they enable the will to put its own house in order, as a preparation for offering the whole man to God.[6]

Fasting is a means to an end—saying good-bye to the power of our possessions, so that we may give ourselves to the reign of God (Luke 14:33). Apart from that end, fasting can be rebellion, a desire to master the animal self and to secure the triumph of the will.

6. Fast *creatively*. If a diabetic cannot fast for physical reasons, she can lay aside television to devote herself to God. Some people eat a slice

of plain bread when they fast. It cuts their hunger, so they think about food less and remember their goal. The issue is broader than food. Fasting includes "abstinence from anything which is legitimate in and of itself for the sake of some spiritual purpose."[7] We could "fast" from any physical blessing that threatens to become our first love. One person could fast from televised news for a week and devote that time to God. Another could fast from shopping for anything but food.[8]

### The Goals, Motives, and Rewards of Fasting

God tested Abraham when he took Isaac to the mountain. The test demonstrated, both to God and to Abraham himself, that Abraham loved God more than anything. When we fast, it leads us to ask: "Do I love God? Do I hunger for him? Do I long for him? Or have I been content with his gifts?" Fasting makes us consider what we do with our unhappiness. As Foster says, we use "food and other good things" to cover up the sins inside us. If pride or sensuality, if "anger, bitterness, jealousy, strife, fear—if they are within us, they will surface during fasting. At first, we will rationalize that our anger is due to our fasting." But eventually we will realize that the anger is ours, and that knowledge can lead us to seek healing in Christ.[9]

This revelation of anger and bitterness questions us. Will we cover our distress with food? Will we eat fine fare so that the good feelings balance out the bad? Or will we take our hunger to the Lord? He is the bread of life. Every meal points to him. He is the one who truly satisfies our longings. When we drink from his well, we never grow thirsty.[10]

Fasting may seem a little strange, even to Christians, if the desire for the Lord has dimmed. Why might a believer not desire God? "Because you have nibbled so long at the table of the world. Your soul is stuffed with small things, and there is no room for the great."[11] But our appetite for God can awaken if we deny ourselves some pleasures of the world, even honest ones.

There are several motives for fasting. First, since fasting shows sorrow, especially over sin, we fast to repent, to mourn, and to humble ourselves before God. Second, we fast to seek God's blessing. When we fast we deny ourselves our ordinary means of strength and ask God for strength. Finally, we can fast to identify with the needy. Isaiah says the fasting that God sees is this:

> to loose the chains of injustice
>     and untie the cords of the yoke,
>         to set the oppressed free . . .
>     . . . to share your food with the hungry
>         and to provide the poor wanderer with shelter. (Isa. 58:6–7)

What counts, Isaiah says, is humility, repentance, and kindness to the oppressed. But praise from men can be a powerful thing, and sacrificing a meal seems remarkable. As we saw in chapter 10, it would be painful to skip a meal if no one noticed the sacrifice.

The desire for notice is understandable, but deadly. Jesus said, "Whoever exalts himself will be humbled" (Matt. 23:12). To fast in order to be seen is to exalt oneself. Genuine fasting is self-abasement. If genuine generosity seeks the good of the poor, genuine prayer and fasting seek the Lord. True giving, fasting, and prayer are all, by their very nature, self-forgetting and self-denying.

Jesus says that the Father rewards fasting: "Your Father, who sees what is done in secret, will reward you" (Matt. 6:18). This is important, but easily misunderstood. Jesus does not say that fasting earns a reward from God. Rather, God grants a reward. If we fasted for a reward, fasting would become a business investment: we sacrifice for God, and he gives back, with interest. At worst, that would be manipulation. At best, it would pollute an act of devotion by giving it a selfish twist. Fasting is not a spiritual discipline presented to God for proper recompense. The reward the faster receives is God himself. When we fast properly, we love him more and love the world less. By fasting, we learn to seek first the kingdom of God.

## HEAVENLY FEASTING

This talk of self-denial, seeking God, and rewards in heaven (Matt. 6:1) may not make a great deal of sense to a skeptic or a doubter. Let me address skeptics for a moment. It is agreed that all men die. If there is a God—and even doubters suspect that there is—then when we die, we may meet him. The Bible asserts that we do indeed encounter him when we die. To all who love him, to all who trust in Christ Jesus for their salvation and long to see him, he says "Come" to dwell with him forever. To the rest, who do not trust him or seek him, he says, "Depart from me." If you do not love the Lord in this life, you will not love him in the next.

Before he died, Jesus promised his disciples that he would eat with them again (Luke 22:16). That meal, which comes at the end of time, is called the wedding feast of the Lamb. In heaven there will be no more hunger and no more of the cravings that we battle. But there will be feasting in the presence of Christ. For then our strongest hunger will be satisfied by the Lord himself.

So then, let us fast from time to time, as the Lord leads. Take time to pray about an important matter. Remind yourself that he is your strength. Teach yourself to long for larger and more lasting pleasures—for the feast where the Lord Jesus is host.

# 14

# GOD OR MAMMON

*Matthew 6:19–24*

FOR SOME YEARS, the arbiters of taste have informed the culture that conspicuous consumption is out of favor, that the wealthy ought to be fairly discrete in their displays of wealth and in their talk about it. During the 1980s, American culture went through a different period. The stock market rocketed upward in value. The media celebrated wealth. In a major movie, the star delivered a pivotal speech with the theme "Greed is good." People spoke about their desire for money with remarkable candor. One poll asked people what they would do for a million dollars. Forty-two percent said they would be willing to spend time in jail, never see their best friend again, move permanently to a foreign country, or throw their pet off a cliff. When people wanted to inquire about another person's wealth, they asked, "How much is he worth?"—as if his worth and his net assets were the same.

This awe of wealth was widespread. When Philippine kleptocrat-dictator Ferdinand Marcos fell in 1987, the Filipinos discovered that his palace was filled with the plunder of a nation, valued at billions of dollars. Throngs of Filipinos descended on the palace, but they did not burn or pillage. No, they filed past his fabulous possessions, not with indignant shouts, but with hushed silence. Although Marcos had amassed his fortune at their expense, the people remained in awe of the wealth.

Jesus taught more about wealth than about any other social issue—more than marriage, politics, work, sex, or power. His teaching about money stands in a discussion of discipleship and loyalty to God. Few people set out to live for wealth. No one wants to *serve* wealth; we want wealth to serve us! Yet the love of money can gradually take control of our hearts. This is the danger, the false god, that Jesus addresses.

## TWO TREASURES (6:19–21)

### Treasures on Earth

Jesus begins with two simple commands: Do not store up for yourself treasures on earth. Do store up treasures in heaven. Next, he offers two reasons not to store up treasures on earth: There moth and rust destroy (two evil agents do one evil thing). There thieves break in and steal (one evil agent does two evil things).

Jesus forbids the hoarding of treasure, whether the hoarding is for selfish indulgence today or for the future. He forbids the forms that hoarding took in antiquity: valuable clothes, which moths might eat, and precious metals, which might corrode. If he spoke today, he would address our houses, cars, furnishings, and retirement plans.

Jesus mentions two kinds of loss. First, we suffer the *passive* harm of rust, moths, and decay. Things fall apart. Entropy is relentless. Wood rots, threads fray, metal rusts, and inflation erodes savings. There is a worm, one millimeter in length, with a fourteen-day life span. Researchers have determined that necrosis sets in after eleven or twelve days, and the worm begins to get flabby. Worms, like everything else, fall apart.

Second, we suffer *active* harm. Jesus says thieves break in and steal. Thievery represents all violent acts that destroy property: wars, fires, floods, and all the rest. Burglar alarms, rust-proof paint, and hedge funds can slow the decay of wealth, but they cannot stop it. Money flies from our hands. Even if it grows in this life, it leaves us when we die. Solomon said, "Naked a man comes from his mother's womb, and . . . so he departs" (Eccl. 5:15). Therefore, we should store up treasures in heaven, where they are safe, guarded by the God who also guards us.

Jesus does not ban savings or financial planning or ownership of property. Indeed, the Bible praises those who work and prepare for winter, for the lean season (Gen. 41; Prov. 6:6–10). Parents should save for their children (2 Cor. 12:14). The Bible expects us to use God's good creation joyfully. God "richly provides us with everything for our enjoyment" (1 Tim. 6:17).

But Jesus does ban the godless, selfish accumulation of goods—heaping up possessions and savings beyond the ability to enjoy or spend them. James warns those who live in luxury and self-indulgence, "You have fattened yourselves in the day of slaughter"—that is, judgment day (James 5:5). The same godlessness that leads to hoarding also leads to a hard heart—to neglect of the needy and exploitation of the poor (James 5:4–6).

Jesus also forbids the dream that life consists in the abundance of our possessions (Luke 12:15). He warns us not to tether our hearts to this world. When Jesus says, "Don't lay up treasures," he does not forbid joyful living or financial planning. He does forbid greed and love of money and selfish luxury.

Some people are confused by this. They ask, "How do I enjoy this world without loving it? How do I enjoy wealth without living for it?" Jesus says, "Store up treasures in heaven." The New Testament stresses that we store up treasures in heaven by giving generously of them on earth. If we live in covenant faithfulness, in loyalty to the Lord, we will be Christlike and give sacrificially. The Bible says:

- "Good will come to him who is generous and lends freely, who conducts his affairs with justice" (Ps. 112:5).
- "A generous man will prosper; he who refreshes others will himself be refreshed" (Prov. 11:25).
- "A generous man will himself be blessed, for he shares his food with the poor" (Prov. 22:9).
- The rich should "be rich in good deeds, . . . generous and willing to share" (1 Tim. 6:18).
- "Whoever sows sparingly will also reap sparingly, and whoever sows generously will also reap generously." Give "not reluctantly or under compulsion, for God loves a cheerful giver" (2 Cor. 9:6–7).

Because God is generous and full of grace, we must be generous (2 Cor. 9:8). The motivation is not duty or compulsion, but joy in God's gifts. God saves liberally and provides for us daily. Our generosity keeps the cycle going. That does not mean that if we give money away, we will automatically receive yet more in return (no matter what certain advocates of the prosperity gospel say). But liberality is part of the blessed life. God makes us "rich in every way," so that we "can be generous on every occasion" (2 Cor. 9:11). By our generosity, we lay up treasures in heaven. When we give our money to God's causes, we show where our heart is.

### Treasures in Heaven

Jesus says that we ought to store up treasures in heaven, rather than on earth. The reasons, he says, are the positive counterparts of the reasons not to store up treasures on earth. Moth and rust do not destroy there, and thieves do not break in and steal. Heaven is the safest place to store our treasures. Our treasures are safe there, and we are safer when we put them there, "for where your treasure is, there your heart will be also" (Matt. 6:21). If we place our treasure in heaven, our heart will follow and be as safe as the treasure.

We lay up treasures in heaven by investing in God's causes and God's people. The effects of such investments last forever. We store treasures in heaven by worshiping God, growing in knowledge and grace, and growing in love for God and neighbor. Financially, we store treasures in heaven by using money for kingdom causes, by giving money to the church, to missions, to Christian schools, to the poor. When we store treasures in heaven by investing our money in God's people, our investment will bear dividends for eternity. The Greek roots of the word "philanthropy"—meaning "love" and "mankind"—are apt. By giving, we demonstrate our love for mankind.

The value of stocks and real estate rolls up and down. The only truly safe investment is in the kingdom and the people of God. People live forever. If we put our effort into accumulating this world's treasures, the heart probably will not be satisfied. Some years ago I gave a talk on money at a men's retreat. A friendly, well-dressed fellow in his early forties approached me afterward. His career had gone very well, he told me without pride. "In fact," he added, with a wry grin, "I find that I am making twice as much money as I ever dreamed possible. But somehow it still isn't enough."

It is unusual to earn twice as much money as one could dream possible, but it is not unusual to confess, "It still isn't enough." Solomon said, "I denied myself nothing my eyes desired; I refused my heart no pleasure. . . . Yet when I surveyed all that . . . I had toiled to achieve, everything was meaningless" (Eccl. 2:10–11). Cooks like to say that hunger is the best seasoning. If so, then a simple hamburger tastes better to a hungry man than a gourmet meal tastes to a well-fed man. As Solomon says, "Whoever loves money never has money enough" (Eccl. 5:10). But if wealth never satisfies us, how can it become a god? Jesus explores that in the next verses. There he shifts from the question "Where shall we put our treasure?" to "Where shall we fix our eyes?"

## TWO VISIONS (6:22–23)

In Matthew 6:21, Jesus addresses the inner attitude, the heart. In verses 22–23, he speaks of the eye when he says, "The eye is the lamp of the body." It might seem that Jesus is changing subject, as he shifts from the heart that desires to the eyes that see. But the terms *heart* and *eyes* can both refer to the inner person that sets life's direction. Notice how the words *heart* and *eyes* are almost interchangeable in Psalm 119:

> I seek you with all my *heart*;
> > do not let me stray from your commands. (v. 10)

> Open my *eyes* that I may see
> > wonderful things in your law. (v. 18)

> Turn my *heart* toward your statutes
> > and not toward selfish gain. (v. 36)

> Turn my *eyes* away from worthless things;
> > preserve my life according to your word. (v. 37)

The Bible says the issues of life proceed from the heart. Here Jesus says the body finds its direction, for good or ill, through the eyes. A person with good sight walks in the light. A healthy eye gives direction to all of life. The eye affects the whole body, just as the heart directs all of life. Ambition to serve God throws light on everything. Ambition to serve oneself plunges all into darkness. It creates pride, makes us self-indulgent, and crushes charity.

## Where We Set Our Heart

Jesus urges us to examine our eyes: "If your eyes are bad, your whole body will be full of darkness" (Matt. 6:23). Greed flows from a greedy heart. If we see someone hoarding wealth, living for wealth, Jesus wants us to focus our attention on their heart. If the eye sees little but material wealth, why so? Because their eyes are dark, because their heart is set on this earth.

We expect unbelievers to live for money. Atheists *cannot* store treasures in heaven. If there is no God and no heaven, why store wealth there? It would be absurd. Secular people inevitably store their treasures on earth. How could it be otherwise? They cannot trust God to protect or reward them when they deny his existence. Unbelief destroys the capacity to heed this command. Secular people believe that they must provide for themselves, for no one else will. If there is no personal God, no Father in heaven, hoarding is perfectly sensible. Who wants to run out of money in their one and only life?

This passage is diagnostic. If a man cannot tear his eyes away from money, if he lives for wealth, it is because his eye and heart are corrupt. If the eye is dark, there is no hope, unless God grants renewal. No one can *do* what is right unless he can *see* what is right. Therefore, Jesus' message is not, "Try harder," but "Examine yourself." So if you fail to follow Jesus, if you hoard and do not give, examine yourself! You cannot do what is right without the ability to see it. On the other hand, if you know that you belong to Jesus, and yet you act as if you live for money, that is neither your true heritage nor your true self. You know better. God has set your heart on better things. You will find peace and rest when your heart goes where it belongs. Yet there is another side of the issue . . .

In the original Greek of Matthew 6:22–23, there is a deliberate ambiguity. A literal translation of Jesus' words brings out the issue: "The light of the body is the eye. If, therefore, your eye is good [or "sound"], your whole body will be light. But if your eye is evil, your whole body will be darkness."

The words for "good" and "evil" can both have different meanings that make sense here. The word translated "good" is *haplos*. Its most basic meaning is "whole" or "healthy," and it can also mean "clear" or "simple" or "generous" (see 2 Cor. 8:2; 9:13; James 1:5).[1] The meanings "simple" and "generous" overlap: the generous person gives simply, not expecting any favor in return. The word translated "evil" is *ponēros*. It can mean "sick, in bad condition," or "evil, wicked," or "jealous, envious." Jesus has chosen words that might merely describe an eye that is healthy or unhealthy. But he has also chosen words that apply to attitudes toward wealth—generosity or jealousy.

So we could translate 6:22–23 two ways. First, if your eye is *healthy*, or if your eye is *generous*, then the whole body will be full of light. Second, if your eye is bad, or if your eye is *evil* or *jealous*, then your whole body will be full of darkness. In first-century Palestine, as in many cultures, the "evil eye" was the jealous or covetous eye, the grudging spirit, that looks with envy on the possessions of others.[2] Thus, Jesus warns against the jealous eye while inviting us to hear him in two ways:

### Where We Fix Our Eyes

First, Jesus poses a diagnostic question: if your eye is perpetually set on riches, ask yourself, "Why am I fixated on material things?" The answer is, "Because you have given your heart to material things." It is right, therefore, to repent and ask God to redirect your heart toward him.

Second, Jesus warns us about the danger of jealousy or envy. He commands, "Do not set your eye upon material treasures or upon the riches of others." It is a sin and can corrupt your heart.

The first point is surely the central one. If we find that our eyes are fixed on wealth, we must examine ourselves. Some people focus their lives on wealth because money is their god. But others love God and have fallen into bad habits. We spend too much time looking at the wrong things. We spend too much time in the mall or poring over mail-order catalogues. We behold costly homes, cars, furniture, and clothes.

To be practical, when an advertisement directs a man to "picture yourself behind the wheel" of the latest, greatest car or truck, or hybrid vehicle, he should not so picture himself. When a magazine directs a woman to consider a kitchen renovation, she should not begin to plot out every purchase. Remember, the Bible says that we should flee temptation. Therefore, we should not stir up envy by eyeing our friends' cars or fabrics or vacations. Let us be careful where we set our eyes. Let us be careful with advertisements and with visits to our more prosperous friends. It is one thing to admire a beautiful home, another to envy it.

In Christ, we have a good, clear, generous eye. The child of God, renewed by the Spirit, has no divided loyalties and no ulterior motives. We seek our neighbor's good, not his goods. When Jesus commends the clear eye, he urges disciples to live out their true identity. One way to do that is to set our eyes on the right things. The discipline of the eye reflects a heart that is set on the kingdom.

There are two lessons here. First, if you cannot take your eyes and heart off material things, if you live only for this world and its satisfactions, you must ask, "How is my heart?" Second, by setting your eyes in the wrong place, on the possessions of others, on graphic displays of affluence, you can harm your soul. Rather, let us be content with what we have.

## TWO MASTERS (6:24)

Gordon Dahl once said, "We worship our work. We work at our play. And we play at our worship." Of course, if we worship our work, we will serve it, heart and soul.[3] Using a Hebrew poetic form (chiasm), Jesus states this as a choice in Matthew 6:24:

No one can serve two masters.
    Either he will hate the one and love the other,
    or he will be devoted to the one and despise the other.
You cannot serve both God and Money.

Many people doubt this statement. The antithesis—God versus money (traditionally translated "mammon")—seems inappropriate. They wonder why God and prosperity cannot coexist. Why must they choose between God and money?

To be sure, some people *try* to serve two masters. They honor God on Sunday (if convenient), serve mammon from Monday to Friday, and reserve Saturday for themselves. But this mind-set regards faith as a hobby, like gardening. One can certainly have a job and a hobby or two. Or they view God as an employer, not a master. Surely a man can work for two employers, schedule permitting. But no one can *belong* to two masters. No slave can be the property of two owners, "for single ownership and full-time service are of the essence of slavery."[4] By definition, a master can demand service at *any* time. Therefore, we cannot serve two masters.[5]

This is suggested by the name Jesus chooses for money. The term *mammon*, which means "trusted thing" or "that which one trusts."[6] The name is apt, for we are prone to trust money. Remember the prayer, "Give me neither poverty nor riches. . . . Otherwise, I may have too much and disown you and say, 'Who is the Lord?'" (Prov. 30:8–9, cf. Hos. 13:6). Jeremiah commands, "Let not . . . the rich man boast of his riches" (Jer. 9:23). Ezekiel says, "Because of your wealth your heart has grown proud" (Ezek. 28:5). Job says a man can speak to gold and say, "You are my security" (Job 31:24). It is all too easy to set the heart on riches (Ps. 62:10).

### Living for Money

Money is not the kind of god that demands exclusive loyalty or direct worship; no prostration is necessary. Money is a god in a polytheistic land. It just wants a spot in the pantheon; a few other demigods can reside there too: status, power, pleasure. It is satisfied with casual worship and a few holy days.

Few people openly live for money, but I did encounter one while in grad school. Hoping to locate a summer job that paid enough to cover the next year's tuition, I searched for unpalatable seasonal work and decided to try pest extermination. I got an interview with a young, energetic owner. He shook my hand, sat me down, and asked, "What is your purpose in life?" Momentarily speechless at this opportunity to share my faith, I quickly launched into an explanation of a Christian's purpose in life. A minute later, the exterminator interrupted, "Listen," he lectured, "my purpose in life is to make money, and I want to know if you want to make money." At one level, I understood perfectly. After all, no one starts a pest-control business in inner-city Philadelphia to meet interesting people and visit interesting places. But his bluntness was exceptional. Not many declare, "I live for mammon." Most people prefer to mask their allegiance. They live for mammon, but they say, "I look at my house as an investment" and "I only want to provide the best for my family." It is no sin to produce or gain wealth by honest means, for God created the world with the capacity for wealth creation. The problem is making wealth a god, and serving it with heart, soul, mind, and strength.

Jesus presents a choice between two ways of life. Will we store treasure on earth or in heaven? Will our eyes be light or dark? Will we serve God or mammon? This question speaks equally to the rich and the poor, for both can look to wealth for security. Everyone is susceptible to greed. Anyone can think that they would be happy if they had just a little more.

This is why Jesus calls money a rival god. People trust in their trust funds. They find security in their securities. They expect wealth to grant them the blessed life. Some even give money a divine name—"the Almighty Dollar." But like every false deity, money disappoints its worshipers. One day its devotees awaken and say, "I have it all, but it isn't enough. I still don't know the meaning of life."

### Living for the Lord

To be a Christian is to turn "to God from idols to serve the living and true God" (1 Thess. 1:9). In Matthew 6, Jesus names two great idols that threaten to separate us from God. When he taught about praying, giving, and fasting to impress people, he named reputation and status as rival gods. We cannot serve God and status. It is hypocrisy (6:1–6, 16–18).

Here Jesus labels another choice. God and mammon offer alternative ways of life, and they battle for our loyalty. Jesus forces a choice: Will we store up treasures on earth or in heaven? Will our eyes be generous or envious? Will we serve God or mammon? We know whom the Lord wants us to serve. He has told us where the lasting treasure lies. But, for the moment, he presents a choice, not a command: You can store up treasures on earth or in heaven, but not both. You can serve God or mammon, but not both.

Certain traits identify those who live for mammon. Some save and save, for they feel secure only when they have a hoard of wealth. Others spend and spend, because they believe money, well spent, can gain them the good life, a life of peace and pleasure. They give away very little—perhaps one to four percent of their income—just enough to avoid feeling guilty about their greed.

Another set of traits marks those who live for God. They like to give money away, and like it better if no one notices. They are generous with their skills, giving them away (as volunteers) when appropriate, instead of charging for everything. They give the basic tithe and more, if possible.

Not many, even among the noblest disciples, can entirely avoid the love of money. What shall we say when we detect service to mammon in ourselves? The same self-examination that reveals a disciple's sin also reveals deeper truths. Every believer knows and is known, loves and is loved, by God.

Money also seeks our love. It attempts to bind us to itself with promises of wealth. But wealth is an elusive lover; the object of affection slips just out of reach. As Hosea says, "She will chase after her lovers but not catch them; she will look for them but not find them." Devotees of mammon forget that God provides our grain, wine, and oil (Hos. 2:7–8).

The prosperity gospel does us no favors in our battle with mammon. But even the apparently innocuous interest in stewardship can be problematic. The concept of stewardship is sound, but it can lead us to think of ourselves as "the one to whom God (wisely) entrusted his wealth" and the ones entrusted to administer it.[7]

To love God rather than wealth, we must trust him, rather than worrying. We must not hoard, and must instead give freely to the church and to the poor. By giving, we show that our heart is fixed on the Lord, not on a corruptible cache here on earth (Luke 12:33). Consider the heart issue this way: If an agent dragged you into court and accused you of loving Jesus, could your checkbook and credit cards be summoned as evidence against you? If auditors examined your finances, would they find proof of your love of God? If our vacation and restaurant bills exceed our giving, what might that signify?

To give our heart to God means to trust him to provide for our needs. We can scan a dark future and worry, or we can consider the birds of the air and the lilies of the field, and become calm, because God cares for us much more (Matt. 6:25–32). If we love God rather than mammon, it will show in each sphere of life—in our heart, mind, and strength.

### Our Mind and Money

To love God with our minds, we first strive to think God's thoughts about wealth. The Bible says, "Everything God created is good, and . . . to be . . . received with thanksgiving" (1 Tim. 4:4–5). Yet Christians should never be engrossed in money (1 Cor. 7:31–35). We should believe that riches are a good servant, but a bad master, and that there is profit in learning contentment whether with a little or with much (Phil. 4:11–12; 1 Tim. 6:6).

To love God with the mind, is, second, to accept his laws about money. Mammon tries to establish its own laws, of course. When it supplants God, it reduces everything to buying and selling, value and profit. Money says people can be bought and sold as slaves (Rev. 18:13). We still say, "Everyone has his price." Even Jesus had a price tag: thirty pieces of silver. We give our mind to God when we know and live by his laws for wealth. We use it to meet basic needs: "If we have food and covering, we will be content with that" (1 Tim. 6:8). We give generously because God said that "those who are rich in this world . . . [should] be generous and willing to share" (1 Tim. 6:17–18).

To love God with the mind means, third, to speak about money in ways that reiterate his truth. For example, we should not start to make our financial decisions with "Can we afford it?" Instead, we should ask, "Does this glorify God? Does it make me a better servant?" Parents must especially take care not to answer their children's petitions for toys and games simply by declaring, "We can't afford it." Those four words end the conversation very effectively at some ages and keep parents from seeming insensitive. But the subliminal message is, "The adults don't make the decisions in this family, money does." When we make decisions, we should let God and his law have the final word, not money. Wealth makes a useful servant, but a poor master.

## Our Strength and Money

We serve God with our strength by refusing to select a career designed strictly to make us rich (James 4:1–4; 1 Tim. 6:6–10). We love God with our strength, first, by laboring to supply our needs (2 Thess. 3:6–10). Second, we accept only those jobs that are constructive and lawful. No Christian should be a professional gambler, for example. Third, we should do good to all in our work, by offering them something of value.

## Our Heart and Money

Christians, by nature, love God more than money. We have committed our hearts to the Lord by entering into his covenant. The challenge comes in the realm of diligence and consistency. We can lose sight of the antithesis between God and money. We can drift, a little bit at a time, toward loving and serving money. We can lose our discernment and our clarity and make one decision, and then another, on the basis of money and possessions. Let us pray, therefore, that the Lord keeps our eyes clear, that he fills us with his light and truth and love. May he finish the good work that he has begun in us.

# 15

## Not Worry, but Trust

*Matthew 6:25–34*

JESUS INAUGURATED HIS MINISTRY by proclaiming, "Repent, for the kingdom of heaven is at hand" (Matt. 4:17 ESV). He went throughout Galilee, proclaiming that kingdom (v. 23). The Sermon on the Mount starts the process of unfolding what Jesus meant when he proclaimed the coming of the kingdom.

The first section (5:3–16), containing the Beatitudes, is essentially an overture to the sermon. The first and last beatitudes proclaim that the kingdom is a present possession for Jesus' disciples. The first one says, "Blessed are the poor in spirit, for theirs *is* the kingdom of heaven." And the last one says, "Blessed are those who are persecuted because of righteousness, for theirs is the kingdom of heaven" (5:3, 10).

In the next section (5:17–48), Jesus declares that he came to fulfill the law. Further, whoever breaks a commandment is least in the kingdom, and whoever practices and teaches Jesus' commands "will be called great in the kingdom" (5:19). Jesus' teachings on murder, anger, adultery, truthfulness, and love explain the character of kingdom righteousness.

Early in chapter 6, Jesus instructs his disciples to pray that the kingdom will come (6:9). The entire sermon may reach its climax when Jesus commands, "But seek first his kingdom and his righteousness, and all these things will be given to you as well" (6:33). Before this climax, chapter 6 describes three of the forces, the false gods, that keep people from seeking the kingdom. The first is reputation or human honor (6:1–18).

The second is wealth (6:19–24). The third is security (6:25–34), which Jesus tackles in terms of worry.

At one level, worry is simply a human folly, roughly on the order of eating or drinking in excess, or staying up too late at night. Like overindulgence, worry is a self-destructive state we think we should be able to control. After all, we know that worry is pointless—no one can add even an hour to his life by worrying (v. 27). It "accomplishes nothing except to put God out of the picture."[1] But, at another level, worry, like sensual indulgence, can be a symptom of allegiance to false gods. Self-indulgence may reveal a commitment to sensual pleasures. And worry can reveal a commitment to our personal security. That is, we may wish to ensure our personal security for ourselves, instead of trusting God.

## The Context: God, Money, and Worry

Jesus' teaching in 6:25 begins with the word "therefore." That is, there is something in the previous passage that forbids worry. It emerges when we look closely at the context. Matthew 6:24 gave us a choice—"You cannot serve both God and Money." Ordinarily a choice is not a reason. But if we follow Jesus' logic in 6:19–24, we see that it is. In that passage, Jesus told us to weigh and choose between two alternatives, two gods:

- We can store up treasures on earth or in heaven. We can store up and enjoy treasures on earth for a season, knowing we must battle the moths that eat and the rust that corrodes them. Or we can store up our treasures in heaven, where they are safe with God forever. Which treasure will be more lasting?
- As we chart our life's course, we must decide where to set our eyes and affections. We can set our hearts on wealth or on God. We can set our eyes on material goods or on the kingdom. We can live with generosity and openness or with stinginess and greed. Which object of our affection and attention promises a better life?
- So choose, Jesus says. Will you serve God or mammon? Weigh it carefully, and after you choose, persevere in it. Serve that God. Be devoted to him and give no thought to the other.

Since Jesus addressed his sermon primarily to believers (5:1–2), we know that his audience has already decided to serve God, not mammon. That is, Jesus' disciples wanted to serve God and store up their treasures in heaven. But, like us, they needed to understand the implications of that commitment. Here, Jesus explains some of the *consequences* of our decision to follow God. He says that God cares, physically, for those who care for him, spiritually.

If God is our Lord, we need not worry about our material needs. He frees us from the mental consequences of loyalty to mammon. That is, if we live for riches, we live for a weak god, who cannot protect what is most precious to us. Therefore, it is natural for those who serve mammon to worry about their wealth, whether it be much or little. Conversely, our love for God makes us secure and ends worry, in principle.

## THE STRUCTURE OF MATTHEW 6:25–34

Our passage presents a positive message through a prohibition. Negatively, Jesus forbids that we worry about food, drink, clothing, or any other material need. Positively, we must trust God. He knows our needs; he loves us and cares for us. Because he knows we are prone to worry, Jesus supplies us with logical arguments and lifelike illustrations to calm our hearts and teach us to trust him.

Jesus' teaching has substantial repetition. But, as he repeats key ideas, he develops them further, so they strengthen the main point: we have good reasons to trust God and stop worrying.

| 25a | Command 1 | Do not worry about your life, your food, drink, and clothing. |
|---|---|---|
| 25b | Reason 1 | Life is more than food and clothes. |
| 26 | Reason 2 | God cares for the lower creation—the birds. You are more valuable than they. |
| 27 | Reason 3 | Worry changes nothing. |
| 28–30 | Reason 4 | God cares for lower creation—even lilies and grass, short-lived as they are. We are more valuable, as even men of little faith should know. |

| 31 | Command 2 | Do not worry about what you will eat, drink, and wear. |
| 32 | Reason 5 | The pagans (sensibly) chase these thing, since they are godless. But your Father knows your needs, so that you need not chase them. |
| 33a | Command 3 | Seek first God's kingdom and his righteousness. |
| 33b–34 | Reason 6 | All the things the Gentiles chase will be given to you. |
| 34 | Command 4 | Therefore do not worry. |

## THE FIRST COMMAND NOT TO WORRY

> Therefore I tell you, do not worry about your life, what you will eat or drink; or about your body, what you will wear. Is not life more important than food, and the body more important than clothes? (6:25)

The word "therefore" tells us to connect this statement to Jesus' previous teaching in 6:24. So, if we serve God rather than mammon, we also know him as the Creator and Redeemer. He demands our service, but provides far more than he demands. His provision spells the end of worry. Earlier, Jesus invited his disciples to ask God to meet their needs, confident that he is fatherly and knows our needs even before we ask (6:6–9). So we can stop worrying.

Still we worry, and in predictable ways. We worry when things are out of our control. When we can do nothing else, we worry (and pray). If a flood is coming, worry dissipates if we can stack sandbags. If we fall ill, worry fades if we can research our disease. But when there is nothing more to do, we lapse back into worry.

We also worry when we love the wrong things. Jesus warns against seeking fulfillment or happiness in a sphere that cannot provide fulfillment, the sphere of transitory things. Since these things are subject to loss, they leave us vulnerable to loss. Our love for them is unavoidably tinged with fear. Socially, this sets one person against another, as we feel like rivals grasping for the same prizes. Personally, misguided loves wound us. We set out on a desperate, hopeless quest when we search for fulfillment where it cannot be found.

It is logical that we worry first about food and clothing, since they are essential to bodily life. Still, as Paul says, the love of money is a root of all evils (1 Tim. 6:10). It is a love for the wrong thing. It is a love that is "entangled in the web of unhappiness that it has spun for itself."[2]

### Reasons for a Worry-Free Life

#### Reason 1: Life is more than food and clothes (Matt. 6:25b).

Jesus quickly moves from his command to his reason. We should not worry about food and clothing, he says, because God cares for life itself, which encompasses food, clothing, and all the rest. If God cares for the greater thing, for life as a whole, then he certainly cares for the lesser things, the constituent parts of life that sustain us each day.

To put it differently, if we worry about food, drink, and clothing, we have hardly gotten started. What about war, pestilence, collapsing buildings, wild animals, floods, pollution, meteors, and more? If we believe that God cares for the great thing, life itself, then we should trust him to care for its parts. And when we are confident that God oversees our material needs, we are free to seek his kingdom.

#### Reason 2: God cares for creation—the birds.

> Look at the birds of the air; they do not sow or reap or store away in barns, and yet your heavenly Father feeds them. Are you not much more valuable than they? (6:26)

The second reason to stop worrying is the mirror image of the first. Here Jesus moves from the lesser to the greater. Since God cares for a lesser thing—the birds of the air—he will certainly care for us, for we are greater—more valuable—than they are.

The whole earth bears witness to God's love, if we let faith guide our sight. Birds work hard at times, but they put forth no properly organized effort. They are not farmers. They neither sow nor harvest nor store food, yet they avoid starvation. Like birds, we enjoy God's providence.

Yet we are more valuable than birds. Confident of his providence, we should seek him and his kingdom.

### Reason 3: Worry accomplishes nothing.

Who of you by worrying can add a single hour to his life? (6:27)

The original, translated literally, reads, "Who of you by worrying is able to add a span to his length?" There is a slight riddle here, since "span" can mean a span of time—an hour—or a span of length, which at that time was eighteen inches.

The point is that worry cannot accomplish even a little thing. Since it would be a rather large thing to add eighteen inches of height, Jesus must mean that we cannot add an hour to our life. Indeed, some say, the stress of worry may cost us a few hours of life. But certainly worry, by itself, cannot lengthen our life span. Therefore, we should commit our energies to places where it can make a difference, by seeking first the kingdom of God.

### Reason 4: God cares for creation—flowers and grass.

Why do you worry about clothes? See how the lilies of the field grow. They do not labor or spin. Yet I tell you that not even Solomon in all his splendor was dressed like one of these. If that is how God clothes the grass of the field, which is here today and tomorrow is thrown into the fire, will he not much more clothe you, O you of little faith? (6:28–30)

Once again Jesus looks to the lower creation, offering two examples this time, from creatures less weighty than birds. Jesus puts the traditional images of flowers and grass to a new use here. In the Old Testament, flowers and grass illustrate the "brevity and fragility of life."[3] Isaiah says that God's breath blows down plant life and human life alike. Only his word stands forever:

All men are like grass. . . .
The grass withers and the flowers fall,
     because the breath of the LORD blows on them.
     Surely the people are grass.

The grass withers and the flowers fall,
> but the word of our God stands forever. (Isa. 40:6–8; cf. Ps. 37:2)

There are two possible lessons that we can draw from creation. First, we can learn that life is feeble and fleeting, that we are defenseless. We are as short-lived as plants and as easily slain as animals:

As for man, his days are like grass,
> he flourishes like a flower of the field;
the wind blows over it and it is gone. (Ps. 103:15–16)

But, like Jesus, the psalmist directs us to the opposite lesson:

As a father has compassion on his children,
> so the LORD has compassion on those who fear him;
for he knows how we are formed,
> he remembers that we are dust.
As for man, his days are like grass,
> he flourishes like a flower of the field;
the wind blows over it and it is gone,
> and its place remembers it no more.
But from everlasting to everlasting
> the LORD's love is with those who fear him,
and his righteousness with their children's children. (Ps. 103:13–17)

Contemplation of the lower creation could make us miserable. We have eternity in our hearts, but we know that our life is short and easily extinguished. But both David (in Ps. 103) and David's Son (in Matt. 6) point us to the contrary lesson. If God lavishes such care on lilies, which bloom only for a few days, and on animals, which live a few years, then how much more will he care for us? Human beings live longer than most creatures. Still, we are as restricted by time as they are. But God's love goes from everlasting to everlasting. He wins our love in return, and bids us seek his kingdom and his righteousness.

The last phrase in Matthew 6:30 deserves our attention. If God bestows rich clothing on grass, how much more will he "clothe you, O you of little faith?" The phrase "you of little faith," which is just one word in Greek, is notable. Jesus' audience, like most church audiences today, consisted primarily of disciples, with a few of the curious tossed in. His listeners had faith, or at least an interest in faith. But they were worrying, which signals a lack of faith and trust in God. They have "a little" faith. But they need strong faith.

Strong faith does not come by introspection, by working up feelings of trust in God. Rather, Jesus says, stronger faith comes by contemplating God's ways with his creation. Watch the birds. Observe or contemplate the lilies and the grass.[4] The animals and plants point beyond themselves to God, their caretaker. Strong faith knows that he dresses the lower creation and will also dress us.

Indeed, God dresses them better than we could ever dress ourselves. At the height of his wealth and self-indulgence, Solomon could not dress himself any better than a lily or a zinnia (Eccl. 2:1–11). So why worry?

This message is vital, yet open to abuse. Some might think that Jesus' ban on worry requires believers to make no plans, to anticipate and prevent no troubles. But to plan, even to plan for potential trouble, is not necessarily to worry. We must pause, therefore, to consider how lack of worry and proper planning can coexist, in areas such as bodily care, financial planning, and life's troubles.

### Planning without Worry

*Bodily care.* Jesus does not forbid us to worry about our bodies because they do not need care, but because he cares for them. Our bodies are good. God designed them for us. They are "us" in one sense, and they are our instruments in another. Either way, because they are essential, God provides the food and clothing that preserve them.

So our bodies matter. Yet we should aspire to more than feeding, clothing, and comforting them. The Gentiles seek comfort and pleasure. We seek something more; we seek the kingdom.

As I watch friends and relatives from my parents' generation age, I see that some, sadly, neglect and abuse their bodies. Others exercise regularly and eat properly. But some become consumed with physical health. They embark on vain quests to nullify the results of aging. They are always visiting a doctor, always taking a new medication. When you ask, "How are you?" they offer a pharmacological report. The aged must care for their bodies without making them an obsession.

Youth can also make their bodies an obsession, honing them for competition, primping them to attract the opposite sex. Glancing through one of my teenage daughter's magazines a few days ago, I noticed a letter to the editor. "What happened to you?" the writer asked. "I thought you believed beauty was on the inside, but now I have the impression I have to be physically beautiful first. Is mascara more important than character?" Character *is* more important than mascara, and so is the kingdom.

Middle-aged adults can obsess over the decay of youth and its powers. Again, fitness is good. We are more than minds lodged inside alien bodies. Fitness helps our bodies remain dependable. But when people cut and inject and drug their bodies to lose weight or remove wrinkles, then we are not tending our bodies, we are enslaved to them.

*Financial planning.* Just as care for the body is good, so planning is good. Proverbs 6 tells the sluggard to go learn from the ant, who stores up food for winter. Proverbs 31 blesses the woman who sees winter coming and prepares clothing for her family. Paul tells men and women that they need to provide for their families (1 Tim. 5:8). He even tells parents that they should save up for their children (2 Cor. 12:14).

We know that more possessions bring more cares. But if possessions are few enough, it can also be true that fewer possessions bring more cares. So planning is good. The problem, again, is the obsession that frets over every financial decision, that dies a little with every financial setback, that always finds something to worry about.

When Jesus says that God feeds the birds, he is not encouraging sloth. Birds do work. They use their God-given wings and beaks and instincts. God feeds them by those means. Likewise, God grants us strength of body and mind, showers us with mental and physical gifts, and sends us parents and teachers to instruct us. He even makes laziness painful. "The laborer's appetite works for him; his hunger drives him on" (Prov. 16:26). God feeds us, but we are also responsible to work. It is right for us to plan to use our God-given abilities and training wisely.

*Human troubles.* If we hone our talents and work willingly, we may expect to be free from privation. We may even enjoy abundance. But God does not promise believers that they will never go hungry. (In Ps. 37:25, David says, "I was young and now I am old, yet I have never seen the righteous forsaken or their children begging bread," but this is a description, not a promise.) Jesus' analogy promises God's care, not a carefree life. After all, God clothes flowers and feeds birds, but flowers do fade and birds do fall to earth and die. Jesus does promise that God will guard us even in times of trouble, and is working all things for our good, so we need not worry.

That promise can fortify Christians who have suffered for their faith in pagan empires, in Communist countries, and in Muslim lands over the centuries. That promise braces believers who are caught up in pestilence and war. Shortly after World War II, a German evangelical pastor, Helmut Thielicke, reflected on this very thing.[5]

What could Jesus' promise of freedom from anxiety mean to those Germans living through the Allied invasion of Germany? "We know the sight and the sound of homes collapsing in flames. . . . Our own eyes have heard the sound of crashing, falling, and shrieking." In such times, the invitation to consider the birds and lilies seems inapt. Yet, Thielicke continued, we must "stop and listen when *this* man, whose life on earth was anything but birdlike and lilylike, points us to the carefreeness of the birds and lilies." The shadow of the cross already loomed over the Sermon on the Mount. So it is reasonable for us to trust the Father in a dark hour, because Jesus, our exemplar, did so as well. Moreover, Jesus blazed a trail through life's troubles, tasting death itself, and defeating it on our behalf.

We do suffer war, famine, and disease. But let us never blame them on God's inadequate provision. He supplies sun, rain, and fertile soil. He created nourishing plants and domesticatable animals. Wars create famine. Dictators and warlords use starvation as a weapon against their foes, even to suppress dissent among their own people. Starvation is rarely caused by lack of production. God gives enough for us to eat. Hunger is caused by sins of oppression, hatred, greed, and, sometimes, laziness.

# THE SECOND COMMAND NOT TO WORRY

So do not worry, saying, "What shall we eat?" or "What shall we drink?" or "What shall we wear?" (Matt. 6:31)

Jesus repeats that we must not worry about food, drink, and clothing. This is a daunting command, since they are life's essentials, not its luxuries. But notice that Jesus does not forbid that we care about the essentials. Indeed, he addresses our legitimate interest when he promises in verse 33 to supply them. He only forbids us to worry and chase after them. We must pursue our needs in ways that allow us to seek the kingdom first. So we must never meet our needs through jobs that require us to deceive customers, promote destructive products, or otherwise act immorally.

*Reason 5: Your Father knows your needs.*

For the pagans run after all these things, and your heavenly Father knows that you need them. (6:32)

Pagans logically toil and chase after material things, since they have little else to do with their lives. But when we know the King as our Father, who knows our needs and works to meet them, we can lead an anxiety-free life. Trust in God casts out worry. One can always imagine the future and find a reason to fret. Or we can ponder God's protection of his birds and flowers and find peace. The carefree believer is not reckless. But we are calm as we look at the near horizon, our daily food, and look ahead to the distant horizon, the eternal kingdom.

# THE THIRD COMMAND NOT TO WORRY

*Reason 6: The things the Gentiles chase will be given to you.*

But seek first his kingdom and his righteousness, and all these things will be given to you as well.[6] (6:33)

"Seek first the kingdom" is the great ideal, the commission and charter for disciples. And Jesus backs it with a promise. We can afford to seek the kingdom first because God will give us all the things that the Gentiles chase. Lest this be reduced to a mere slogan, let us explore how Jesus would have us seek the kingdom, drawing on his own instruction.

1. To seek the kingdom is to seek the King, to love him as Savior and Friend, to bow to him as Lord, to trust the God who has chosen us, redeemed us, and taught us to trust him.

2. To seek the kingdom is to pray for it: "Your kingdom come." We pray for kingdom causes, not just for local and personal concerns.

3. To seek the kingdom is to evangelize, that is, to bring others into the kingdom, to introduce them to our King's beneficent reign over all of life. To seek the kingdom is to desire that God be known and glorified as King throughout the earth.

4. To seek the kingdom is to submit personally to God's reign by obeying him. We seek the kingdom when we obey God at some personal cost. A Christian retailer seeks the kingdom when he closes his stores on Sunday, even though it is a good day for retail sales, so that he can worship and rest, and model the same for his employees.

5. To seek the kingdom at work means pursuing wages and profits in ways that please God, knowing that that may lead to less money, at least in the short run.

6. To seek the kingdom means to have an eye on social reform, so that society may at least approximate the justice that God desires. For example, it means that public officials should do all they can to stop the spread of state-sponsored gambling, and, if possible, reverse it.

7. To seek the kingdom is to pursue righteousness in public places and distant lands, if we can. It also means restraining something as small and personal as our tongue—checking a sarcastic remark or refusing to repeat a morsel of gossip.

The context suggests that seeking the kingdom especially means dethroning wealth and possessions as our first pursuits. We must not hoard treasures or live for pleasure, but put our treasures in heaven by giving to kingdom causes (Matt. 6:19–21). We should watch the way we think about wealth. Wealth is a *lesser* good—a useful servant, but a miserable master. We should even watch the way we talk about wealth. When we make a decision, we should speak in terms of God's way. We should not speak as if money makes our decisions, as if "We can afford it" or "We can't afford it" is a sufficient guide to most purchases. Let God's will be our guide, and let us speak that way.

To seek first the kingdom does not mean Christians lack ambition; rather, it means we have different ambitions. Everyone needs a purpose, a direction, an ambition in life. It is sad when twenty-year-olds drift in and out of college, shift from one job to another, or go from one relationship to another. It is sadder still when a mature adult drifts aimlessly.

Ambition has two sides. There is selfish ambition, the desire for success and control as an end in itself. Dictators embody ambition at its worst. For them, power is its own reward. Greedy businessmen can also acquire wealth far beyond all needs, simply to win the game of commerce. Such ambitions are evil. "Selfish ambition" is one of the works of the flesh (Gal. 5:20). It is vain, harmful to others, and disorderly (Phil. 2:3; James 3:14–16).

But there are other ambitions, including the aspiration to unfold what is strongest and best in oneself, to accomplish goals that may improve this world a little. The Bible commends such ambitions, including the ambition to preach Christ (Rom. 15:20), the ambition to lead a quiet, productive life (1 Thess. 4:11), and the ambition to please God (2 Cor. 5:9). Ambition is good, if it seeks God's kingdom and his righteousness.

## THE FOURTH COMMAND NOT TO WORRY

Therefore do not worry about tomorrow, for tomorrow will worry about itself. Each day has enough trouble of its own. (Matt. 6:34)

Our final verse restates the main command, "Do not worry," applying it to the immediate situation. We should not worry about tomorrow because we can stay busy enough attending to the tasks and troubles of today. When we live in "tomorrowland," we can fret over our woes or dream about our triumphs. Both can distract us from the goal of living for the kingdom in the present. The prospect of living for the King should be enough to keep our minds and hands well occupied.

# 16

## "Judge Not" and the Right Use of the Law

*Matthew 7:1–8*

P. J. O'Rourke, a writer who is half analyst and half humorist, toured Kuwait and Iraq before and after the 2003 war in Iraq. He loved Kuwait, but he judged Iraq to be a nation not worth saving. The Iraqis were so greedy and inept that they could not even line up properly to receive free food. Iraq was ugly, too. It "looked more like the target of a trash collectors' strike" than the target of a war. "There were burned-out military vehicles here and there, but garbage was everywhere." Trash and ordinary debris littered every public space. Hundreds of black plastic bags lined the streets. "The people of Iraq may have nothing, but they have the bag it came in." The air campaign was so precise that most of the damage was invisible. But "damage caused by the armor attack on the city was noticeable because it was newer, crisper, and more clean-edged than the general deterioration of Baghdad." Then there were Saddam's palaces. Built at enormous cost and perpetually empty—Saddam never stayed in them because it was too risky—they were, above all, hideous. "If a reason to invade Iraq was wanted, felony interior decorating would have done. Imagine Liberace as an inner-city high school basketball star who'd just signed an NBA contract and converted to Islam." O'Rourke knew Iraq's warlike past, but he could hardly imagine this feckless but combative nation ever amounting to much.[1]

This analysis may amuse or it may inform, but people will also object to it for several reasons. First, some will say the article judges wrongly. It is too harsh on the Iraqis, who have many fine people. Second, some will say the article uses the wrong method of judgment, for it makes light of a great issue. But most importantly, some will say that O'Rourke has no right to judge Iraq at all. He may say he dislikes Iraq and that Iraq does not adopt Western attitudes toward lines and trash. But how can he declare another nation greedy and warlike? How can he enter Iraq with his American prejudices, live there for a few months and pronounce his judgment on it? Even ignoring the fact that he criticizes a nation that his armed forces just invaded, the question is this: how does he dare to judge another culture?

## THE PROBLEM OF JUDGMENT IN CONTEXT: WHO HAS THE RIGHT TO JUDGE?

According to the prevailing mind-set of our age, no one has the right to judge—or, more specifically, to condemn—anybody else. Sometimes the reasons are personal. Feeling the need to defend themselves, people ask, "Who gave you the right to judge me?" There are also philosophical objections to judgment. If, as certain philosophers say, there is no objective, transcendent truth, then by what standard can one person judge another? Richard Rorty says that "truth" is what our peers let us get away with. If, as some social philosophers say, knowledge is power, then truth claims are actually power claims.[2]

Years ago, the best known text in Scripture was John 3:16 (KJV): "For God so loved the world, that he gave his only begotten Son, that whosoever believeth in him should not perish, but have everlasting life." But today, the best known passage might be Matthew 7:1, "Do not judge, or you too will be judged."

Paradoxically, our airwaves and our personal conversations are laden with criticism and invective, yet we also claim to be opposed to judging others. We declare that no one should tell anyone else how to live, and that no one should impose his or her standards on others. "Judge not" is the sort of statement that our culture would eagerly embrace, without bothering to discover precisely what Jesus meant by it. But was Jesus really opposed to all judging? Would Jesus condemn anyone who condemned others? Would Jesus let each man's conscience be his guide? The first step in discovering Jesus' intent is to put his teaching in its biblical context.

The last verse of Matthew 6 and the first verse of Matthew 7 both begin with prohibitions: "Do not worry" (6:34) and "Do not judge" (7:1). When Jesus says "Do not worry," he forbids a negative attitude toward our own affairs—worry. When he says "Do not judge," he prohibits a negative attitude toward others—a critical spirit.[3] Just before that, Jesus said, "Seek first his kingdom and his righteousness" (6:33). Here Jesus reinforces that command, saying in effect, "Do not criticize the unrighteousness of others. Address your own unrighteousness first, then perhaps you can address others."

## Judge Not

Jesus gives several reasons why we should "not judge." First, God is the judge of mankind. We have no right to usurp his role (7:1). Second, when we judge others, we invite judgment in return, both from God and from the people around us (7:2–3). Third, since we cannot evaluate ourselves very accurately, why should we try to critique the flaws of others (7:4–5)? So then, instead of judging the sins of our neighbors, we should ask God for grace to remove our own sins (7:7–11).

When Jesus says "Do not judge" (KJV: "Judge not"), he does not mean that we must never criticize anything. There is nothing wrong with saying that a certain movie is a waste of time, or that certain apples taste bad. Jesus does not forbid the *evaluation* of others. He forbids the *condemnation* of others. The grammatical form of Jesus' command (a present imperative) implies that disciples should refrain from continual judgment, from a censorious spirit. Occasional outbursts of judgmentalism are of course not acceptable, but it is especially dangerous to fall into the habit of criticizing anything and everything.

Still, people cite the saying "Judge not" as if Jesus never wanted anyone to disapprove of anything. But if we want to understand Jesus, rather than using his words for our purposes, we must remember that Jesus actually endorses judgment at times. He says, "Do not judge by appearances, but judge with right judgment" (John 7:24 esv).

Let me summarize the biblical teaching this way: Jesus prohibits a critical spirit, but does not forbid all use of the critical faculty. To follow Jesus, we must therefore discover why he says "Judge not" in Matthew 7, but says "Judge with right judgment" in John 7.

Notice first that Jesus tells his disciples to make judgments in the very chapter that says "Judge not." Later in Matthew 7, Jesus says, "Watch out for false prophets. They come to you in sheep's clothing, but inwardly they are ferocious wolves. By their fruit you will recognize them" (vv. 15–16). That is, disciples must discern—must judge—who is a false prophet and who is a true one.

Later in Matthew, Jesus says, "If your brother sins against you, go and show him his fault, just between the two of you. If he listens to you, you have won your brother over" (Matt. 18:15). To obey this commandment, we need to determine—to judge—that our brother has indeed sinned. If the sin is serious (another judgment!), then we must speak to the problem and ascertain if the sinning party listened and heeded or not.

Second, Jesus himself made judgments, including negative judgments. He said, "Woe to you, teachers of the law and Pharisees, you hypocrites! You clean the outside of the cup and dish, but inside they are full of greed and self-indulgence. . . . On the outside you appear to people as righteous but on the inside you are full of hypocrisy and wickedness" (Matt. 23:25, 28). Jesus did more than disapprove or warn. He declared that certain people were bound for eternal judgment unless they repented: "Woe to you, teachers of the law and Pharisees, you hypocrites! You travel over land and sea to win a single convert, and when he becomes one, you make him twice as much a son of hell as you are" (v. 15).

The apostles also say that judgment is necessary. For example, John says, "Dear friends, do not believe every spirit, but test the spirits to see whether they are from God, because many false prophets have gone out into the world" (1 John 4:1). Paul knew that teachers who propound major errors must be confronted (Gal. 2:11). Moses and Paul agreed that leaders must judge if a teacher is so dangerous that he must be removed from the assembly (Deut. 13:1–11; 1 Tim. 1:3–4; 6:3–5). Such judgments are necessary to preserve the church (Acts 20:28–29).

In the Old Testament, God appointed judges over Israel to protect his people. He gave the people judges to settle disputes and enforce the law (Ex. 18:13–26; 1 Sam. 7:16). He also established rules, so that they could judge properly. For example, he says, "You shall not be partial to the poor or defer to the great, but in righteousness shall you judge your neighbor" (Lev. 19:15). Over and over, the Bible commands fair, impartial judgment. Why? Because the Lord, "the great God, mighty and awesome . . . shows no partiality and accepts no bribes." Therefore, "Do not pervert justice or show partiality. Do not accept a bribe" (Deut. 10:17; 16:19).

God sets standards for judges because he is "the judge of all men" (Heb. 12:23). He knows the secrets of the heart (1 Cor. 14:25). Therefore, sinners should flee the judgment by repenting and believing in the Lord (Luke 3:3–14). Judgment day is coming.

Daily life also forces us to make assessments. There is always an issue in the news that divides the public, so that people ask their pastors and teachers for their judgment: cloning, gay "marriage," the justice of a certain war, the latest celebrity trial, the latest exposé of a televangelist. Christian leaders must evaluate—pass judgment—on these things. Do we favor or oppose gay marriage? Is the prosperity gospel a minor error or a heresy?

Responsible adults must make judgments or assessments daily. Whenever a father corrects a child, or whenever a teacher grades a test, judging takes place. These forms of assessment, or judgment, are inescapable. Therefore, "Judge not" apparently prohibits certain kinds of judgment, but not all. Sometimes it is legitimate, even mandatory, to exercise moral discernment. Yet there are times to refrain from passing judgment. The context of Jesus' teaching helps us decide when to refrain. The instruction to "judge not" comes after a long block of moral instruction. This setting suggests that Jesus wants to warn his disciples not to use his teaching to condemn others, although it is tempting to do so.

We are all prone to listen to stirring messages, and then apply them to someone else. Jesus' instruction certainly invites that abuse. His ethic is so profound and rigorous that it can be painful to apply it to ourselves. And if we do strive to follow his word, we inevitably notice that others fall far short, too. Either way, we are prone to apply the word to others, rather than to ourselves. Pastors often see this. After we preach, our beloved people greet us at the door and intone, "Powerful sermon, pastor. I just wish my brother had been present to hear it."

Gifted but lazy students invite rebukes. Talented but undisciplined athletes invite reproach. But to the judgmental person, everyone is a target for censure. Misdirected zeal for the teaching of Jesus makes everyone look like an underachiever, ripe for correction. Jesus forbids us to use his law to censure others.

To put it differently, consider how dangerous it is to attend a marriage seminar alone. Going without our spouse changes the way we listen. The talks can lead us to rejoice over our blessings in marriage or to godly self-examination. But, sadly, they can also lead us to list all the counsel the speaker had for our spouse, the one who really needed to hear the message. When we report on the conference, we say, "You should have been there, honey. The speaker suggested three ways for me to be a better husband and nineteen ways for you to be a better wife. Let me share the top five with you right away. . . . " But Jesus does more than prohibit judgment. He carefully explains why.

## WHY NOT JUDGE?

### Reason 1: You Will Be Judged (7:1)

When Jesus says "Do not judge, or you too will be judged" (NIV), or "Judge not, that you be not judged" (ESV), we must ask, "What is the judgment that we should avoid? Who will judge us, if we judge others?" Jesus means, "You will judged by God." His contemporaries so wanted to avoid taking God's name in vain, that they tried not to use it at all. One way to avoid using God's name is to say that something will be done (using a passive verb) without specifying the agent who will do it. This is called the divine passive. So when Jesus says, "Judge not, or you will be judged," he means, "Judge not, or else God will judge you."[4]

### Reason 2: The Measure You Use on Others Will Be Used on You (7:2)

A literal translation of Matthew 7:2 might read: "With the judgment you use to judge, you will be judged." That is, the standard we use to measure others is the standard that will be used to measure us. Paul says, "In passing judgment on another you condemn yourself, because you, the judge, practice the very same things" (Rom. 2:1 ESV). If we know God's standards well enough to judge others by them, then we know them well enough to be judged by them. When we measure others by a standard, it shows that we accept the standard, so that God can judge us by it. God can ask: If you condemn others for telling half-truths, do you tell half-truths? If you condemn those who break commitments, do you ever break a commitment? If you condemn theft, are you honest financially? If you hate careless remarks that hurt others, do you watch your words?

Since we all violate the standards that we use to measure others, we are all liable to God's judgment. But if we hope to receive mercy from God, we ought to show mercy.

Friends and family will also apply our standards to us. If a man tells his wife, "You always make me late," he may hear about it the next time he makes her late. James develops this theme when he says, "Anyone who speaks against his brother or judges him speaks against the law and judges it. When you judge the law, you are not keeping it, but sitting in judgment on it" (James 4:11). That is, someone who judges his brother actually judges the law. James reasons that anyone who judges or slanders a brother appoints himself to a superior position. To judge a brother is to deny that he is your peer. The judge drops his neighbor a notch and exalts himself two notches. The judge soon utters a misplaced but stinging criticism. The censure may be half right, but who gave him the right to judge? The judge exalts himself over others, and that violates the law of love.

As a result, the judge thinks that he enforces the law, while he actually violates the primary law, "Love your neighbor as yourself." The critic judges the law because he picks and chooses among its commands. He enforces one, by judging his neighbor, but ignores another, by failing to love his neighbor.

Only God has the right to judge mankind. If we judge others, we usurp God's role and forget to love. Thus, we invite judgment on ourselves. James specifically warns against judging a brother. He said this because we often level the harshest accusations against those who are nearest to us. Husbands and wives fall into cycles of reciprocal criticism. Siblings slander each other. "He hit me," says one, conveniently forgetting that he started it. We criticize our partners, whether at work, in church, or in sports, because a partner's flaws are so visible.

But, as Jesus says, if we judge others, that same standard will be used to judge us. We will have shown that we know right and wrong. Then, if we condemn others and do the same thing, we have no excuse. We are ripe for judgment.

### Reason 3: We Should Attend to Ourselves First (7:3–5)

Jesus asks, "How can you say to your brother, 'Let me take the speck out of your eye,' when all the time there is a plank in your own eye?" (Matt. 7:4). Let me comment on this in three ways.

First, Jesus is not saying we should never correct a brother who is caught in sin. He means that we can help others with their sins after we deal with our own sins. Jesus says, "First take the plank out of your own eye, and *then*" you can remove your brother's speck (v. 5).

Second, Jesus teaches us to consider our problems to be large and our neighbors' problems to be small. When Jesus says that we have a plank in our eye, he chooses a term that can refer to the main beam in the floor or roof of a building—a plank as much as forty feet long and five feet around. We tend to trivialize our sins and magnify the sins of others, but Jesus says that our sins should seem painfully large to us, while our neighbors' should seem small. If we offer help in that spirit, it will carry more weight.

Third, Jesus hints that we can be keen at discerning the flaws of others, but blind to our own sins. Our sin blinds us to our true appearance. We are ignorant of ourselves. We can recognize a friend by his posture or stride at a distance of one hundred paces, but we might not recognize our own posture or stride, if shown it. We do not even know what our voice sounds like. No wonder we can scarcely detect our flaws.

Suppose a weekend athlete loses an important game and starts to tell a friend about it: "We lost today, and it was ugly. The other team was red hot, but I can't remember when Jack played so poorly. . . . On second thought, I guess I didn't play my best either." Why do we tend to criticize a teammate first, before we move on to ourselves?

Or imagine a domestic scene. We think that someone in our family is a bit grumpy one day. But it is hard to be sure because the whole family got in late the previous night, so everyone is sleep deprived and prone to grouchiness. Even if our spouse is irritable, it is easier to overlook it when we are in a good temper. Since we cannot see ourselves clearly, we should judge ourselves, not others. That should be our daily practice. As Samuel Johnson said, "What we hope ever to do with ease, we must learn first to do with diligence."

## THROW PEARLS TO PIGS? (7:6)

Jesus' next statement—"Do not give dogs what is sacred; do not throw your pearls to pigs. If you do, they may trample them under their feet, and then turn and tear you to pieces"—is startling. After forbidding judgment in the previous paragraph, Jesus now seems to require that we judge certain people to be "pigs" or "dogs" and not give them our pearls.

In Jesus' day, pigs were unclean animals and dogs were wild, unclean scavengers, not pets, so the assessment is quite harsh. Indeed, the terms are so cutting that some scholars believe Jesus is using instructive irony, so that his intent is the opposite of his literal words. The sense, to paraphrase, would go this way: "If you view your criticisms as 'pearls' of wisdom and toss them at those whom you consider to be 'swine' and 'dogs,' those 'swine' will trample your 'wisdom' and those 'dogs' will perceive your attitude and turn and attack you."[5]

In favor of this view, it is true, first, that Jesus does use instructive irony occasionally (see Luke 15:7). Second, it seems odd to ask a disciple, who has just heard that he must not judge, to reverse himself and determine that certain people are pigs and dogs, who do not deserve our wisdom. Third, Jesus never called anyone a pig or a dog, so it seems odd that he would tell us to do so. Fourth, while Jesus did occasionally withhold his teaching from certain hostile people, he often engaged sinful people and social outcasts. Finally, since we do not know the heart, we cannot judge who is truly a pig and who is not. Since the person who seems least likely to listen is often the one who actually does so, we should share our truth with everyone.

This interpretation has much to commend it, but if the concept of instructive irony sounds too artistic, look at it this way. The teaching about pigs and dogs sounds like the overstatement Jesus often used: "If your hand causes you to sin, cut it off and throw it away" (Matt. 5:30). If we also have overstatement here, then Jesus does not actually want us to call anyone a pig, but he is teaching us that it may be necessary to assess our audience. There are times when the words of truth—such as the teaching Jesus has just given—will not get a fair hearing. Then we must be silent. Proverbs says, "Do not speak to a fool, for he will scorn the wisdom of your words" (Prov. 23:9). Similarly, Jesus tells his disciples that some towns will neither receive them nor listen to their words (Matt. 10:14).

Perhaps the passage is a paradox: we who must not judge must yet judge who will not hear our judgments. Jesus proposes another reason to shun judgment: it is futile to try to correct people who will not, in any event, receive it. We should not try to force our message "on those who show no inclination to accept it."[6] Should we offer God's truth to those who have demonstrated their contempt for God's truth?[7]

## ASK, SEEK, KNOCK: THE NEED FOR GRACE (7:7–8)

Jesus sets high standards for his disciples in the Sermon on the Mount, and true disciples know they fall short of them. Recall Jesus' standards: "Anyone who is angry with his brother will be subject to judgment" (Matt. 5:22). "Be perfect, therefore, as your heavenly Father is perfect" (5:48). "Be careful not to do your 'acts of righteousness' before men, to be seen by them" (6:1). The list of our failings is nearly as long as the list of Jesus' teachings. We lust (contrary to 5:28), fail to keep our word (5:33–37), store up treasures on earth (6:19), and worry (6:25). We boggle to think that our deeds must shine so brightly before men that they will praise God (5:16).

When we compare God's law to our failings, we should neither imagine that we can reach Jesus' standards nor deny the problem. Certainly we must not wield the law on others, to judge and condemn them—and perhaps to divert attention from our failings. Instead, we should turn to the Lord; we should, as Jesus says, "Ask and it will be given to you" (7:7).

We should ask for two things. First, we should ask God to forgive our sins. Jesus' standards are beyond us, but there is good news: Jesus did not come simply to deliver laws; he also came to deliver those who cannot keep his laws. He came to bear the punishment of those who fail to keep his law. He came to teach, but he also came to redeem those who cannot follow his teachings. He, on the other hand, perfectly followed his own laws. He offers his obedience and righteousness as an inheritance for all who are united to him by faith. When we become his children by faith, we inherit his spiritual riches.

192

We will examine Matthew 7:7–8 more thoroughly in the next chapter, but we need its essential message now. When Jesus says, "Ask and it will be given to you," he means the Father will give us aid. When he says, "Seek and you will find," he implies that we may not know exactly what we are looking for, but that God does and will provide. When Jesus says, "Knock and the door will be opened to you," he indicates that some door is closed to us. Perhaps we have tried and failed to open it. Perhaps we have concluded that we cannot open it, but God can and will open it for us. All three instructions invite us to plead with God for aid when we face Jesus' commands. We ask for his saving grace, to forgive our sins. We ask for the Holy Spirit to enable us to obey Jesus' commands, at least a little more, day by day.

In context, therefore, "Ask and it will be given to you" leads to the gospel. Advocates of prosperity theology think it leads to material blessing. If we ask with enough faith, they say, God will give us whatever we desire. But Jesus teaches us to seek our daily bread, not our daily caviar. Further, Jesus' topic is discipleship, not wealth.[8] When Jesus instructs his disciples to ask, seek, and knock, he means we should seek grace to cover our sin and strength to grow in holiness. God will grant that prayer. It is said, "One may be a truly industrious man, and yet poor in temporal things; but one cannot be a truly praying man, and yet poor in spiritual things."[9]

May we therefore be rich in Jesus' way: hearing his words, striving for holiness, sharing his word with others (to bless them, not judge them). And when we fail to find the riches of Jesus, let us not despair. Instead, let us ask, as Jesus says, for God favor. Let us knock at his door, seeking mercy and grace in the hour of need.

# 17

## ASK AND IT WILL BE GIVEN

WE ALL NEED a little encouragement from time to time. Someone once told me that a particularly demanding supervisor had written just two words on a report he had written: "Good work." There was nothing more, simply "Good work," but that comment made his week. When someone is looking for a job, the anxiety level can be very high. If he or she has gone to a couple of interviews and come home empty, a positive word can lift the spirits: "You are so talented; I know someone will recognize it soon." When we face a daunting task, it helps to know that someone thinks we are capable. And if we are ready for a task, it is a blessing that a capable friend is willing to help.

This kind of encouragement is just what we have in Matthew 7. In the Sermon on the Mount, Jesus bombards his disciples with uncompromising demands. The self-aware reader knows he cannot fulfill all of them. Jesus forbids anger and forbids lust. He commands that we keep our every word, that we give freely to those who would borrow. He prohibits worrying and forbids boasting. He says, "Let your light shine before men, that they may see your good deeds and praise your Father in heaven" (Matt. 5:16). He says, "Be perfect, therefore, as your heavenly Father is perfect" (5:48).

The breadth and depth of this standard would lead us to despair, if Jesus did not pause to bring encouragement. Fortunately, Jesus does strengthen his disciples' resolve at crucial moments in his message. He invites us to lay aside our fears. As he tells his disciples how to live, he also explains how they may reach toward his standards.

For example, in 6:19–24, Jesus tells his disciples how to think about wealth and how to use it. Then he adds crucial encouragement. If we seek first the kingdom, the King will provide the food and shelter we need to live. Therefore, we need not be anxious about tomorrow, because God will take care of it (6:25–34).

Then Jesus tells his disciples how to regard their neighbors (7:1–6). There is a kind of neighbor whose lawless, feckless life invites criticism and judgment. His moral failings are obvious, but even his clothes and manners are an affront. But Jesus tells us to refrain from hasty judgment. Perhaps if we remove our own sins first, then we can help our neighbor with his.

But it is no easy thing to withhold judgment or to still a critical tongue. Beyond the negative effects on others, censorious people often fail to see how Jesus' word speaks to their flaws. Jesus says we should apply the law to ourselves first, confessing to God our sin, our weakness, and our inability to reform ourselves. If we ask, he will listen and act. Hear the poetic balance and repetition in Jesus' promise (Matt. 7:7–8):

> Ask and it will be given to you;
>> seek and you will find;
>> knock and the door will be opened to you.
> For everyone who asks receives;
>> he who seeks finds;
>> and to him who knocks, the door will be opened.[1]

Furthermore, Jesus continues, the Father knows how to give good gifts, especially gifts of grace, to those who ask (7:9–11). We need that grace, for discipleship is not easy. The road that Jesus traveled was hard, and when he asks us to follow him, he bids us to take the hard road, too (7:13–14). Jesus' road is hard and his standards are high—indeed, they are beyond us. But, as we saw, the same Jesus who delivered these laws also came to deliver those who do not and cannot keep his laws. He came to give commands and to redeem those who violate them.

## Ask, Seek, and Knock

Jesus says simply, "Ask and it will be given to you; seek and you will find." When Jesus says that "it will be given" and "the door will be opened," he means that the Father will give us aid. He will open the door (7:7).[2]

Jesus draws our attention to the gifts that God gives in answer to prayer by mentioning them first and last in this passage. The first word is, "Ask and it will be given to you" (7:7). The last word is, "Your Father in heaven [will] give good gifts to those who ask him" (7:11).

Further, Jesus wants us to ask, seek, and knock *continually*. This is not clear in English translations, but the original text uses present imperatives for "ask . . . seek . . . knock," and that grammatical form in Greek signifies that an act should be performed continually. Scripture often encourages constant prayers for God's blessing. The Lord says, "You will seek me and find me when you seek me with all your heart" (Jer. 29:13). Jesus says, "I will do whatever you ask in my name. . . . You may ask me for anything in my name, and I will do it" (John 14:13–14). Finally, James says, "If any of you lacks wisdom, he should ask God, who gives generously to all without finding fault, and it will be given to him (James 1:5).

This teaching can be understood in two ways. We could put the accent on the one who asks and say, "Persist long enough and you will get what you desire." This "beggar's wisdom" suggests that our petitions can wear God out, so that he finally grants us whatever we want, even if he were initially disinclined to do so.

But Jesus places the emphasis on the God who hears, not on the man or woman who asks. He says that God loves his children and knows how to give them good gifts. If we ask, the Father will give what he knows we need. He says this three ways, and each seems to build on the other:

- "Ask" is a general term. In context, it means "Ask God in prayer."
- "Seek" implies that we may not know exactly what we are looking for or precisely how to pray (Rom. 8:26). A child asks a mother who is close at hand, but when the mother is not vis-

ible, the child seeks her. When we seek God, we will find him and discover what we should desire.

- "Knock" implies that we seek something that is inaccessible to us. We have tried and failed to attain something, to open a door. We cannot, but God can and will open it, if it is right for us.

Jesus follows the threefold command with a threefold promise. We should ask, seek, and knock because "everyone who asks receives; he who seeks finds; and to him who knocks, the door will be opened" (Matt. 7:8), for God will open it. Martin Luther explains that God "knows we are timid and shy, that we feel unworthy . . . to present our needs to God. . . . We think that God is so great and we are so tiny that we do not dare to pray. . . . That is why Christ wants to . . . remove our doubts, and to have us go ahead confidently and boldly."[3]

If we follow the pattern of Scripture, we will pray for God's material provision and for his spiritual gifts, with an emphasis on the latter. It is tempting for pastors to pray about buildings and budgets, but it would be better for us to pray for the spiritual life of our churches. Christian leaders might pray for their local church like this: that those who seek Christ will find him here, that the weary and lonely will find a welcome and a home, and that if we grow we will still welcome and disciple people one by one. We should pray that all will grow in knowledge and in obedience to God, that all will engage the culture, and that every teacher, lawyer, and businessman or woman will strive to serve God and neighbor at work. When things go wrong in the church, we should pray that we will trust one another and think the best of each other, preferring to think that an offense is inadvertent, not malicious (cf. 1 Cor. 13:7). We can pray that we will not probe old wounds and pick at the scabs that cover cuts from long ago, so that God can heal us and dark days may recede. God hears such prayers. He knows how to give good gifts to his church.

## FATHERS ON EARTH AND THE FATHER IN HEAVEN

Jesus wants to assure us that God hears us and will give us what is good. He begins by asking a couple of rhetorical questions about the way human fathers behave. "Which one of you," he asks, "if his son asks him for bread, will give him a stone? Or if he asks for a fish, will give him a serpent?" (Matt. 7:9–10 ESV). Sadly, there are a few such parents, but Jesus is thinking of ordinary parents. In the Greek, it is clear that Jesus expects a negative reply.[4] If a child asks for a loaf of bread, no father would say, "Here is something else that is earth-toned and round—a stone." And if a child asks for a fish, no father would say, "Here, have something else with scales—a snake."

Jesus then draws his conclusion, using a form of argument that he likes to use, called the lesser to the greater. It goes like this: if even sinful human fathers (the lesser) give good gifts to their children when asked, then the wise and good Lord (the greater) will certainly give good gifts to his children when asked (7:11).

This simple argument contains vital lessons about people and about Jesus. First, when Jesus says, "If you then, who are evil . . ." (ESV), he assumes, as the whole Bible does, that all humans are sinful. We are members of a race of sinners. We are radically selfish, inclined to rebel against God and to do evil toward our fellow man. But Jesus says that even sinful people can do what is right. Their hearts may be dark, but parents still care tenderly for their children. Fathers do not typically mock their sons, nor do mothers betray their daughters. Some parents do abuse their children. Still, as sinful as fathers are, few play devilish tricks on their children. And as sinful as mothers are, few offer their children inedible food. If human parents, crippled by evil, still treat their children well, then God, who is good, will certainly give good gifts to his children.

This passage tells us something important about Jesus. We know that Jesus identifies with us in our *weakness*, but here we see that he does not identify with us in our *sinfulness*. Jesus does not say "*we* who are evil," but "*you* who are evil."

Further, Jesus does not say that God gives us all we ask for or all we want. Rather, he gives us "good gifts." "Ask and it will be given" is not an absolute promise, as if God must give us whatever we ask. When we pray, we do not rub a magic lamp. What a burden it would be to know that we would receive everything we sought in prayer! The thought would paralyze the prayers of a sensitive Christian. Who would be wise enough to pray if God gave us whatever we asked for, whenever we asked?

Jesus knows the difference between wise and foolish requests. Most everyone is now thankful that the Lord declined some request they once made. Sometimes, therefore, we receive less than we ask. One summer on a road trip, our family played the game "If you were a superhero, what super power would you choose?" Naturally enough, choices included the ability to fly or the capacity to move forward or backward in time. I chose the power to move at the speed of light. That fall, after a physics class, one of my children told me, "Dad, did you know that to accelerate to the speed of light, an object must also have infinite mass and infinite impulse force?" Infinite mass and impulse force sound impressive, but I doubt that I would actually want either one. My interest in moving at the speed of light was, therefore, misguided. I would not want everything my request entailed. So it is with our requests, which explains why the Lord sometimes denies our appeals.

On the other hand, he sometimes gives us more than we seek. Solomon, we recall, sought wisdom to rule well. This pleased the Lord, who said he would give Solomon "a wise and discerning heart." Then, because Solomon craved wisdom rather than riches or long life, the Lord determined to give him the other blessings as well (1 Kings 3:5–15). He gave Solomon more than he asked.

In the context of the Sermon on the Mount, the Lord wants to give us his kingdom and his righteousness. The Bible, incidentally, never shows anyone praying for happiness, never tells us to pray for happiness, and never promises that we will be happy. It does promise that God will make us holy. In Luke 11:13, Jesus says that the Father will "give the Holy Spirit" to those who ask. He grants what we need to grow in holiness, not necessarily to have a carefree life. Paul says, "Christ loved the church and gave himself up for her to make her holy, cleansing her by the washing with water through the word, and to present her to himself as a radiant church, without stain or wrinkle or any other blemish, but holy and blameless" (Eph. 5:25–27).

We need this holiness. In Matthew 7:11, Jesus calmly assumes that we are "evil," even though we can do good things. Evil parents "forget themselves" and give liberally to their children, for God drops into human hearts "a portion of his goodness."[5] But these good deeds do not remove our sinfulness. Therefore, when we pray, we should first seek forgiveness of sin and deliverance from evil. Of all God's gifts, this is supreme: Jesus bore the punishment we deserve for our evil deeds. Then he offered to wrap us in his holiness, his good deeds, if we believe in him. Then, when God looks upon us, he sees Christ's righteousness, not our sin.

## ON THE DUTIES OF PARENTS

Since our passage describes the goodness of God the Father, we may consider what makes human parents good. After all, human parents should care for their children as God cares for his. The Bible assumes that parents give good gifts to their children, but we must define those gifts correctly. First, parents provide food (good healthy food, not just anything), clothing, and shelter for their children (1 Tim. 5:8; 6:8). Second, parents owe children an education, both academic and practical, that prepares them for a God-given vocation. Wise parents notice their child's skills and interests and nurture them. We teach them to do the small chores and the larger jobs that let them discover where they excel. Third, parents should instruct their children in the Christian faith and Christian living. On the first two points, our culture largely agrees with Scripture, but in the latter sphere, it will substitute any soul-enriching experience—piano lessons, travel to Europe, inner-city service projects, a spot on the soccer team or the debate team—for specifically Christian instruction.

Even as the Father in heaven brings us to spiritual maturity, so godly parents will offer their children every opportunity to attain spiritual maturity. They should read the Bible and pray with their children. At home, the principles of Christian faith and life should often be on our lips, as we tell our children about Jesus and his love. Moses told parents to talk about God's laws throughout the day: "Talk about them when you sit at home and when you walk along the road, when you lie down and when you get up" (Deut. 6:7).

Christian nurture also occurs within the Christian community. On Lord's Days, parents bring their children to Christian education designed for students and to worship designed for all ages. Wise parents collaborate with pastors and teachers. They help their children pay attention by quizzing them afterward: "What did you learn in Sunday School? What did you learn in church?" They know that most teachers offer excellent instruction, but that some present moralistic versions (or perversions) of the faith. Parents review sermons because reasonably bright children can surely grasp leading points of a sermon (linked, perhaps to an illustration) by the age of ten.[6]

Like the Father in heaven, Christian parents also try to discern when they should and when they should not give their children what they ask and indulge. Prosperous parents are prone to pamper their children, indulging their desires simply because they can. Parents of ordinary means may be tempted simply to pick a similar family and match what they do. Lest loving parents become doting parents, we need to teach our children the benefits of work, stewardship, and patience. In our culture, parents confuse love with indulgence, and instant gratification with provision. Christian parents make God their model. As he bestows gifts on his children, he keeps material and spiritual gifts in perfect equilibrium.

## THE GOLDEN RULE

The Golden Rule is widely cited and widely abused. An adult twist on the Golden Rule says, "Whoever has the gold makes the rules." A child's version says, "Do one to others before they do one to you." But a proper understanding of the Golden Rule begins with its context. Matthew 7:1–11 lists various obligations of a disciple. With our brothers, we should offer help, not judgment. With God, we pray with confidence, knowing he will care for us. But the same verses also sum up Jesus' teaching. After hearing all his exposition of the life of discipleship, Jesus says, apply it to yourself, not others. Take the log out of your own eye, instead of poking around in other people's eyes (7:1–6). Further, when we hear all the commands and feel overwhelmed, we must ask God for help (7:7–11). If we should forget our duties to our neighbors, we can remember this summary: "Do to others what you would have them do to you" (7:12).

Jesus does not mean that we should do to others whatever they want. Two immoral people could use "Do unto others" as a rationale for indulging each other's illicit desires. Jesus expects his disciples to want, for themselves and for others, what he wants for us.

Calvin thought that the Golden Rule is another way of saying that we should be just and fair toward all. So many quarrels occur because men "knowingly and willingly trample justice [toward others] under their feet," while demanding perfect justice for themselves. Wars between nations and wars between individuals both begin this way. All of us can "explain minutely and ingeniously what ought to be done" for us. We should apply the same skill and wisdom to the needs of others.[7]

Sadly, we can so fix our attention on our own needs and desires that we are hardly aware of the needs of others. The whole Bible sets the standard for what we owe others. But then, for our benefit, Jesus gives us summaries of the Law and the Prophets. So, to paraphrase slightly, Jesus says, "Do for others what your sense of justice would require others to do for you." Later, he simply says, "Love your neighbor as yourself" (Matt. 22:39). But we are quick to think first of ourselves, and thus we fail to keep the standard. Consider, for example, the game that many families play after dinner, called "Who worked hardest today and so should be excused from household chores?"

We might *wish* we could do for others what we ask for ourselves, but we know we cannot keep it up. We briefly tried an experimental form of discipline in our house. When one child caused serious harm to another, we made the offending child a "servant," bound to obey the other for perhaps an hour to do whatever the "master" wished. In this way, the theory went, we would reduce the incidence of recklessly harmful behavior. But the experiment never worked. No one could keep up the relationship for more than a couple of minutes. I suspect that nearly all of us would fail if we had to play that game.

Once again, therefore, Jesus' laws lead us to see our sin and our need for grace. We simply cannot keep his law. We cannot stop judging others for their failings. We cannot keep even the simplest summary of his teaching: "Do to others what you would have them do to you." What then shall we do? We return to the first word in our passage. We must ask God for mercy to forgive and ask him to make us new.

Then, Jesus says, it will be given to us. The Lord will give us his mercy, the forgiveness of our sins. The same Jesus who laid down all these laws also gave his life for those who would break them. He will give us his Spirit, so that we might see our neighbor with more of the eyes of Jesus, the eyes of love, and might serve that neighbor and serve our Lord.

# 18

# TWO WAYS OF LIFE

*Matthew 7:13–20*

DAVID WAS LIVING the good life. At twenty-four, he had completed two years at Yale Law School. His summer job as a legal associate paid him more than he could spend. His career promised the same, but much more.

David was a handsome man with light brown hair, intense eyes, and a fast social life. Four or five nights a week, he would hit the city's hottest restaurants and bars, splurging on lavish dinners and running up big bar tabs in a continuous quest for entertainment. Life was very good—and very empty. The parties seemed meaningless, and David wondered if he had any real friends.

He had gone to church occasionally as a child and still had an intellectual interest in the faith, though he often went months without attending church. One day he was sitting at his computer, writing a paper about Abraham Lincoln, when he realized that he knew more about Lincoln than about Jesus, even though he professed to be a Christian. He knew that Jesus was more important to him than Lincoln, yet he had never approached his faith with anything like the rigor he put into his studies.

He decided to get serious. He read landmark authors; he studied church history. He made time for church. It took a couple of years for David to overcome his secular impulses and change his freewheeling lifestyle, but change he did. David's relationship with Christ now consumes him far more than his partying ever did.[1]

205

There is a stereotype that says that people seek God when life gets rocky, when they hit a low point in life. But successful people also seek Christ when they drink from the golden cup and find that the nectar tastes the same as it does from an ordinary mug. They wonder about the meaning of life: "Am I on the right road? Have I missed a turn? Is this all there is?"

Some people are troubled by the countercultural element of Christianity.[2] Others are attracted by it. They want a philosophy that can resist contemporary ideological trends. They seek an ethic that offers an alternative to living for career, for parties, and for weekends.

## THE NARROW GATE IN CONTEXT

> Enter through the narrow gate. For wide is the gate and broad is the road that leads to destruction, and many enter through it. But small is the gate and narrow the road that leads to life, and only a few find it. (Matt. 7:13–14)

Christianity is more than a philosophy, and this passage is more than a summons to choose a road less traveled. Like the previous passage (7:1–12), this text asks Jesus' audience to hear him correctly. As that passage showed, it is quite possible to misuse Jesus' teaching. We can use it to condemn others' failures, instead of applying it to ourselves (7:1–5). We can fall into despair at our inability to obey him. Jesus gives us three points of counsel to help us hear him aright.

First, however many rules there are, the essentials are simple. We must serve God and seek his righteousness. We must love our neighbor and "do to others what you would have them do to you" (6:24, 33; 7:12). Second, when the commands seem daunting, we must ask God for help. When we seek his grace, he will grant it (7:7–11). Third, the path of discipleship is harder, but better, than drifting along with the world. We should choose the harder but better road (7:13–14).

Jesus regularly offers choices to his hearers. He delights in presenting antithetical choices between one path and another. He asks: Will you follow the letter of the law or its spirit? Will you practice righteousness to be seen by men or to be seen by God? Will you serve God or money? In Matthew 7, Jesus uses four images to describe these choices.

There are *two roads* (7:13–14), a wide road that is easy now, but leads to destruction, and a narrow road that is hard now, but leads to life. Many take the easy road, perhaps largely by accident. But a few find the hard road, which implies that they are looking. Which road will you take?

There are *two trees* (7:15–20). Good trees bear good fruit, and bad trees bear bad fruit. What fruit do you bear? What do your words and deeds reveal about your nature?

There are *two ways to call upon Jesus* (7:21–23). Some call upon his name and even prophesy and perform wonders in that name. But they do not know him and are not saved. Others call upon him as their true Lord and are saved. On the last day, when all stand before Jesus, the Judge, there will be one question. Do you know Jesus as Savior or not?

*Two builders* construct houses on *two foundations* (7:24–27). In dry weather, both look sound. But when the rain comes, the rivers rise, and the wind blows, all is revealed. A house built on sand will collapse, but a house built on rock will stand. Upon what foundation do you build?

## The Choice in Biblical Thought

Jesus says there are two gates (one narrow and one broad), two kinds of prophet (true and false), and two foundations (rock and sand). With this language, he enters a deep stream of biblical thought. Early in the history of Israel, the Lord began to tell his people that there were two ways of life. One could live in covenant with him and be blessed, or one could follow the world and be cursed.

Moses presented the choice to Israel this way: "See, I am setting before you today a blessing and a curse . . . life and prosperity, [or] death and destruction" (Deut. 11:26; 30:15). At the end of a long and faithful life serving God, Joshua challenged Israel: "Choose for yourselves this day whom you will serve." Some Israelites were interested in the pagan gods of Canaan. "But," he concluded, "as for me and my household, we will serve the LORD" (Josh. 24:15; 23:7, 16).

David opens the Psalms by telling the worshipers of Israel that they must choose a path of life and an authority for life:

Blessed is the man
    who does not walk in the counsel of the wicked
or stand in the way of sinners
    or sit in the seat of mockers.
But his delight is in the law of the LORD,
    and on his law he meditates day and night. . . .
For the LORD watches over the way of the righteous,
    but the way of the wicked will perish. (Ps. 1:1–2, 6)

There are several choices here. Will you follow the counsel of the wicked or the counsel of God? And if you choose the counsel of God, will you be serious enough to meditate on it? Will you turn it over and over in your mind to see how it applies to the issues of life? Or will you claim it as your standard one day and ignore it the next? Which path will you take: the way of the righteous or the way of sinners and scoffers? The way of life or the way of death? God's way is the better way, since it leads to eternal life. Yet the better road is also the harder road.

## THE NARROW GATE, THE HARD ROAD

Jesus was speaking to a large crowd when he said, "Enter through the narrow gate" (Matt. 7:13). Most of the people in that crowd were disciples, but only in a loose sense. They were not full-fledged Christians—indeed, there were none until the resurrection and Pentecost. Most of them were not even dedicated disciples. Jesus wanted to win them, but not by deception, so he told them the plain truth.

Jesus says his road leads to life, but before it ends, it is narrow and hard. To this day, many who are lightly committed to Christ need to hear the same word. On the broad, easy road, people do as they please. The way of Christian discipleship is hard. The gate is also narrow, restricting us in certain ways.

First, the gate is narrow because Jesus' commands are restrictive. Eight of the ten commandments begin with "You shall not." When the law forbids certain actions, it narrows our options. But the law is not the restricting principle. The character of God is the pattern for our character, and that restricts us too. God is faithful, therefore we must be faithful and keep our promises. God is generous, therefore we should be generous. God is kind, therefore we should be kind. The indulgence of bad moods that leads to meanness or cruelty simply is not an option. Disciples resist the temptation to break the law and to ignore God's character.

Second, the gate is narrow because the Bible teaches truths— doctrines—that we must believe. The Bible says that God created the world out of nothing, that Jesus is truly God and truly man, that this age will end when Jesus returns and calls mankind before him for judgment. The Bible directs us to think in these ways, not in others, and that restricts us. We cannot plausibly claim to be Christians and reject the cardinal truths of the faith.

Third, the gate is narrow because we can miss it. We miss it if we do not believe in Christ. We miss it if we deny that we are sinners, in need of a Savior. Jesus' way is hard. The word translated "hard" comes from a family of words that refers to suffering and persecution. This reminds us that Jesus' way is also narrow in the sense that it can lead to opposition. We enter the kingdom after passing through many hardships (Acts 14:22).

The other road is easy. As Jesus said, "Wide is the gate and broad is the road that leads to destruction, and many enter through it" (Matt. 7:13). Most people prefer to do whatever they please, at least in the short run. The easy road lets them do just that. They like to live the easy way:

- Getting up when they are tired of sleeping
- Eating whatever appeals to the eye and the tongue
- Fulfilling whatever promises seem convenient
- Keeping rules only if they do not interfere with their desires

The way of sin and rebellion is easier in other ways. Sin often looks attractive. The man who forgets God can ignore his rules and standards. He need not practice self-denial or exercise self-discipline unless he so chooses. Sin often seems natural, but repentance often feels unnatural.[3] We hate to admit our errors and change our ways. So sin seems easy, and the life of faith can seem hard.

The Bible describes Israel, at one particularly low ebb, this way: "Everyone did what was right in his own eyes" (Judg. 21:25 ESV), or

"Everyone did as he saw fit" (NIV). Subjective feelings and goals, unrestricted by any absolutes, ruled the day.

We are much the same today, but some new things seem right in our own eyes. We have new ways to make the path easy for ourselves. For example, we reserve the right to remain uncommitted, to be detached from everything, and to be critical of everything. By now, every American fancies himself a movie critic. We expect our friends to be critics too. We constantly ask each other for an opinion on the latest important movie. Everyone is supposed to have a comment on the cinematography, the acting, the characterization, the special effects, and perhaps the film's fidelity to the original book.

We should critically evaluate our entertainments, but many now claim the right to criticize everything. Indeed, it is much easier to criticize someone else's performance than it is to stand up and perform. Which is easier, to sing and dance, or to criticize those who sing or dance in public? Moreover, everyone seems to think that his or her opinion is just as valid as that of anyone else. Indeed, no truth claim is necessarily superior to any other, people think, because our culture now doubts that truth, in any absolute sense, exists.

The influential postmodern philosopher Richard Rorty says that truth is what our peers let us get away with. That is, there is no truth; there are simply ideas that a particular community agrees to be true. On other occasions, Rorty, like the pragmatist John Dewey, says that the truth is simply an idea that works. However Rorty defines truth, if there is no objective truth, life becomes far less demanding. One simply finds ideas that work in one's chosen community. Like-minded friends can get together and live by their chosen ideas and rules. Rorty recommends the stance of irony—not taking things too seriously. Ironists do not hope to have their doubts "settled by something larger than themselves. Their criterion for resolving doubts . . . is autonomy rather than affiliation to a power other than themselves."[4] The need to test ideas against the facts of history, science, mathematics, or Scripture disappears. Sometimes it seems that the easy road gets easier all the time. But that prompts a question: if the broad road is indeed so easy, why take the narrow road?

# WHY TAKE THE NARROW ROAD?

There are several reasons to take the narrow road. First, the easy road later becomes hard. If we get up whenever we please for a long enough period, we will probably become poor. If we eat whatever appeals to us long enough, our health will suffer. If we keep only convenient promises, eventually no one will trust us.

Second, there is great joy in facing a good challenge. Most people want the easy road. Jesus says that "many" take the easy road through the wide gate, while "few" find the hard road through the narrow gate. But the hard road appeals to people who like the right kind of challenge. They know they were destined to do more than drift along. They are willing to work hard in order to achieve worthy goals.

My family hikes in the Colorado mountains whenever we can. After we hiked at relatively lower altitudes (10,000 to 13,000 feet), a friend recommended that we tackle a 14,000-foot peak that was near our cabin. Three of us trekked to the summit. The skies were crisp and blue, and the trail was well-marked. We had plenty of food and water. No one got blisters or fell down. We met a band of docile mountain goats at 13,000 feet and met friendly climbers at every level. At the summit, we surveyed spectacular vistas. We agreed that the goats were impressive and that the trail was pretty, but overall the climb was a disappointment because the trail was too easy. We never really struggled. The trail was tame; we wanted adventure. Not everyone wants to climb mountains, of course, but when the Lord ordained that we should rule and subdue the earth for him (Gen. 1:26–28), then he also gave us an appetite for exploits.

Third, the hard path is better because it is the true path. We are attracted to the hard road because we want to know how things are. We hate the thought of living for a false faith or philosophy, even if it "works." Aristotle said, "All men by nature desire to know." The simple fact that we prefer to keep our eyes open, rather than closed, proves this, he said.[5] On the other hand, T. S. Eliot said, "Humankind cannot bear very much reality."[6] Both men are probably right. We often want to deny uncomfortable truths, but we are pleased when we know the way things really are.

Why, again, should we struggle for the hard truths of Christianity? Because, finally, the hard road leads to life. Both the easy road and the hard road lead somewhere. One day life ends. One day history will end. The hard road restricts, then it opens—to eternal life. The easy road leads to destruction. The easy road makes no demands, but it offers no rewards. The hard road makes great demands, but offers great rewards.

To do anything great, we must pay a price. Every quest eventually becomes hard. The movie *A League of Their Own* describes life in the women's baseball league of the 1940s. In that film, the team's star catcher decides to quit the team just before the league championship. "It just got too hard," she explains. The manager ignites, "Hard? It's supposed to be hard. If it wasn't hard, everyone would do it. The 'hard' is what makes it great." The manager got it right for baseball and, more importantly, for life.

## TRUE AND FALSE PROPHETS

Jesus says that there are two ways, one easy, one hard; two gates, one broad, one narrow; taken by two crowds, one large, one small; ending in two destinations, death and life.[7] He also says there are two prophets, the false and the true.

*The false prophet's message (Matt. 7:15).* Jesus mentions false prophets here because it is a hallmark of false prophets to deny that the way is hard. False prophets say "All is well" when disaster looms (e.g., 1 Kings 22:5–23). They say "Peace, peace" when there is no peace (Jer. 8:11; 23:17). False prophets let people sleep when they should arise and face dangers. True prophets wake people up (Isa. 56:10; Joel 1:5; Rev. 3:2).

A false prophet does not simply make a mistake in his teaching; everyone makes mistakes. False prophets make mistakes in the fundamentals. They misrepresent God himself. They misrepresent the gospel. They deny that we are saved by grace, through faith in Christ alone. They oppose God's message and his messengers, and they resist correction.

*The false prophet's disguise (Matt. 7:15–17).* False prophets are wolves "in sheep's clothing" (7:15). That is, they claim to be sheep, part of the flock of God. In their disguises, they troubled Israel long ago (Jer. 6; 8; Ezek. 13). They troubled the apostles (2 Cor. 11; 2 Peter 2; 1 John 4), and they have troubled the church down through the centuries. To complete their disguise, they use biblical language even while they distort its meaning. They recite creeds, but reinterpret their meaning. They also have credentials—graduate degrees and ordination certificates.

But their disguises fail if sound leaders watch both the teaching and the life of the false teachers. Jesus compares false teachers to thornbushes (Matt. 7:16). Thornbushes bear small, dark berries that resemble grapes at a distance. But if you examine them closely, you see what the berries are. So too with false prophets. We distinguish true from false by examining the fruit of their ministry and the patterns of their life. As Jesus says, "Every good tree bears good fruit, but a bad tree bears bad fruit" (7:17).

*A tree is known by its fruit (Matt. 7:18).* Many can deceive for a time, but words and deeds eventually reveal where the heart lies. Jesus says, "A good tree cannot bear bad fruit, and a bad tree cannot bear good fruit" (7:18). A prophet's fruit includes both words and deeds. True prophets teach sound doctrine and lead a holy life. False prophets may dazzle with oratorical skill and social grace, but their doctrine and their ethics are gravely flawed. We do not hunt heretics, but neither are we indifferent to doctrinal error. Some error is so grave and persistent that it can issue only from a false prophet.

*Everyone is known by his fruit (Matt. 7:19–20).* Jesus assesses false prophets in 7:15–16. In verses 17–19, he begins to speak about "every tree." In this way, Jesus takes the principle for false prophets and applies it to all people who falsely claim to belong to the Lord: "By their fruit you will recognize them" (7:20). It takes time to grow fruit, and it takes time to examine fruit. We must not be hasty; we should let the pattern of a life reveal everything in due time. It cannot be otherwise. People can pretend only for so long.

During his long reign of terror, Saddam Hussein claimed to be a bold fighter and a brilliant leader. But his deeds and words at his capture unmasked him. The "great warrior" had a loaded pistol at his side, but he chose not to fight. His "fruit" showed him to be a coward. He said, "I am willing to negotiate" at his capture, as if he was in a position to bargain. His words showed that he was vain and deluded, not brilliant.

Many tyrants never meet justice in this life. But no one evades God's justice forever. Bad trees, trees that bear no fruit, are cut down and thrown into the fire (7:19). But it is not enough to examine others. We must watch ourselves as well.

Some who attend church know that their words and deeds prove that they have not yet given their lives to Christ. In every evangelical church, there are opportunities, week by week, to come to Christ. In a confession of sin, there is opportunity to repent. In a confession of faith, anyone can join in to declare newfound faith.

There are also occasions for believers to take their flawed fruit to Jesus, whom we trust, to set things right. Worms infest a few apples even in good trees. And even good dogs get fleas. So too, even good people, the sons and daughters of God, bear some bad fruit. In worship, we celebrate the work of Jesus, who forgives our bad fruit and strengthens us, so that we might bear better fruit. To desire to bear fruit for the Lord is one element of the good, hard road. By God's grace, the Lord neither demands perfect fruit nor a perfectly straight walk on his road. If we have taken his road, if we belong to him, we will bear some good fruit and he will forgive the bad.

# 19

## THE POUNDING SURF AND THE NEON BOARDWALK

*Matthew 7:21–29*

ONE YEAR, when my children were young, we drove to the beach for a summer vacation. We arrived at the end of a long day of driving, and my wife and children fell asleep almost at once. Wide awake, I decided to walk the beach alone. Waves punished the evening sand. A wild wind buffeted the shore and whipped sea foam along the coastline. The waves poured out their roar and thunder. The faintest light remained over the ocean; I peered into the charcoal gray sky, seeking the point where waves and sky met on the horizon. But the horizon defied detection. Suddenly it seemed that there was no horizon, that the ocean went on forever. The power and vastness of the sea overwhelmed me. I felt so puny, and then I remembered that the visible ocean represents only a tiny speck of God's creation.

Enveloped by the sound and texture of the ocean, I walked silently for a long time. Away to the west, the boardwalk shone brightly, full of people, the size of mites, strolling past shops full of T-shirts and baubles, past pizza, French fries, and video games. Why had the masses chosen neon signs over a charcoal sky? Why did they choose ice cream and cigarettes over the surf's sensory explosion? Why do thousands wear out the boards, while so few patrol the beach?

Let the evening walk on the stormy beach serve as a metaphor. The shops and boardwalk represent daily life, so safe and so banal. The roaring surf and the majesty of the ocean represent God's awesome grandeur. People typically choose the boardwalk over the beach because we prefer

215

what is familiar and tame to what is strange and powerful. We like to be in control. We shy away from great forces, forces that compel awe. We prefer the distractions of pizza and video games to the contemplation of our small role in the vast cosmos.

We pose questions such as "Do I want fries or onion rings with my burger?" and "What entertainment is on the schedule for tomorrow?" But Jesus sends us to the vast ocean, not the boardwalk. He poses questions such as "What is your place in this world?"

## THE CHOICES: TWO ROADS, TWO TREES, TWO FOUNDATIONS, TWO CONFESSIONS OF JESUS

Jesus likes to present choices and to pose questions. He says there are two gates and two roads (Matt. 7:13–14). He asks, "Will you find the narrow gate and follow the hard road?" The hard road is good, for it leads to life. Or will you enter the broad gate and take the easy path? The easy road makes no demands, but it offers no rewards and leads to destruction.

Two trees bear two kinds of fruit (7:15–20). A fruitless tree deceives people who stand at a distance. Just so, a wicked person can deceive others for a time. But eventually the sum of their words and deeds reveals all. Good trees bear good fruit; bad trees bear bad fruit. Jesus asks each person, "What fruit do you bear?"

There are two ways to call upon the Lord (7:21–23). Some call upon his name and do great things in that name, but do not know him. Others call upon Jesus truly, as he is presented in the gospel.

Finally, two builders construct houses on two foundations (7:24–27). We can build on sand or on the rock. When the rains come, when the rivers rise, when the winds blow, only one house will stand. We have studied the two gates, the two roads, and the two destinations. Now we consider the two ways to call upon the Lord and the two foundations we can lay for life.

In our passage, Jesus describes a choice every hearer must make. It is easy to be fond of Jesus, even to revere him and call him Lord. But it is deadly, then and now, to claim to be a disciple while falling short of true discipleship.

216

In Jesus' day, almost everyone was willing to listen to his teaching and call him a prophet (Matt. 21:11, 46; Luke 7:16). Today, most Americans think they are Christians. As long as they are not atheists or Buddhists, as long as they go to church occasionally, as long as they think well of Jesus, they call themselves Christians.

## A FALSE PROFESSION OF FAITH AND FALSE WONDERS (7:21–23)

Jesus' warning about false claims of discipleship in this passage (Matt. 7:21–23) is connected to his warning about false prophets in the previous passage (7:15–20). There are links between the two sections. In 7:15, Jesus warns, "Watch out for false prophets." In 7:22, people say, "Lord, Lord, did we not prophesy in your name?" In 7:18–19, Jesus compares false prophets to trees that bear bad fruit and says such trees are thrown into the fire. In 7:23, Jesus also judges those who falsely profess Christ: "Away from me, you evildoers!"[1] These warnings apply to us in two ways. First, Jesus describes false prophets so that we can be watchful. Second, he warns disciples neither to succumb to their influence nor to follow in their footsteps.[2]

False prophets appear to be church leaders. They prophesy. If they "prophesy" in Jesus' name (7:22), they claim to teach God's word. Jesus says they also perform miracles and cast out demons, all "in Jesus' name." That is, they claim to perform signs in Jesus' power. We may think that Jesus is talking about situations that cannot occur. How many people prophesy and perform miracles in Jesus' name and still do not know him personally? Perhaps Jesus is setting up a hypothetical case: even if someone should prophesy and perform miracles in his name, and yet did not know him personally, he would say, "Away from me" (7:23). Their works would not deliver them.

But perhaps the discussion is not so hypothetical after all. Judas preached, performed miracles, cast out demons, and walked with Jesus for three years, but he did not know Jesus in a personal, saving way. Similarly, a number of ordained pastors or priests become believers each year. They say, "I preached and counseled and baptized in Jesus' name, but I did not know him as my Savior. I never understood the gospel, never knew Christ's love until this year."

At the beginning of the Reformation, thousands of priests converted to Christ. Martin Luther was a priest long before he grasped the gospel truth that God forgives and justifies the wicked, not the good. Before he became a famous theologian, educator, and politician, Abraham Kuyper was a pastor. He was converted by an elderly woman in his church who suspected that he was not a believer and arranged to meet with him. Sadly, many ordinary people attend church, pray, and serve the church, but do not know Jesus personally.

The confession "Lord, Lord . . ." seems to be proper. First, it is polite, for the word *lord* is respectful. Second, it is orthodox, because all believers confess that Jesus is Lord. Third, it is fervent, because the repetition "Lord, Lord" sounds emphatic and devoted. Fourth, it is public, in that it leads to prophecy and to deeds done in Jesus' name.[3]

Thus "Lord, Lord" meets all the external criteria for a good confession. Yet in this case it fails to meet the most important criterion—genuineness. There are two signs of genuineness: doing the will of the Father and knowing Jesus.

## Doing the Will of the Father (7:21)

A false profession of faith can come only from someone who calls himself a disciple. In Jesus' day, they called him Lord. Today, people still call themselves Christian without grasping what that means. In Jesus' time, *lord* could simply mean "master" or "sir." It could be a polite address to a great man. It is a perennial temptation to call Jesus "great" without trusting in him. In Jesus' day, they called him a prophet or even a "great prophet" (Luke 7:16). Today they call him a great man, a supreme moral teacher, but deny that he is more than that.

Thomas Jefferson, America's third president, admired Jesus as a great man. Yet Jefferson did not properly call Jesus Lord. In his study of Jesus, Jefferson set out to separate "diamonds from dunghills" in the Gospels, using this standard: "I am a Christian in the only sense in which he wanted anyone to be: sincerely attached to his *doctrines*, in preference to all others; ascribing to himself every *human* excellence; and believing he never claimed any other." Jefferson made his own Bible by cutting out everything that seemed irrational. He said, "I have selected . . . only those passages that seem to me authentic accounts and sayings of Jesus."

He judged all miracles to be inauthentic. Because they were not credible, he took scissors and literally cut them out of his Bible.[4]

Few people literally take scissors and mutilate their Bibles, but many call Jesus Lord without living like they mean it. Many profess faith with their lips and even produce some good deeds, but do not follow the whole counsel of Christ. In Luke 6:46, Jesus says, "Why do you call me 'Lord, Lord,' and do not do what I say?" Selective obedience—obedience to the commands we happen to like—is not genuine obedience at all; it is mere agreement. If we truly confess that Jesus is Lord, we must also be willing to bend our will to his, even if his directives seem unpleasant or foolish to us.

Most Americans see ethics from a Judeo-Christian perspective. They gladly follow biblical rules because they seem like common sense. They describe the way we do things. It is a blessing to *agree* with the word of the Lord. But agreement does not test us much. The test of loyalty, the test of our submission to the Lord, comes when his will crosses ours. We truly obey (we submit) to God whenever we obey a command that requires painful or strange actions.

Disciples strive to heed every command from Jesus (Matt. 28:20), the easy and the hard alike. As one person said, "If you want to know what the Lord is saying to the church today, read the parts of your Bible that are *not* underlined."

### Our Confession and Jesus' Confession (7:23)

So then, we can call Jesus Lord and not know him as Lord of our life. Just as important, it is possible to obey Jesus on many points and not know him personally. It is also possible to perform singular service in his name and not know him. Jesus does not say this to frighten tender or introspective disciples. Notice precisely what he says: "And then will I declare to them, 'I never knew you; depart from me, you workers of lawlessness'" (7:23 ESV). Every word counts.

*Declare* is a solemn, public, formal term. The Greek word is usually translated "confess." Some people confess, "Jesus is Lord," but Jesus confesses, "I never knew you." *Confess* is a legal term, a word from the sphere of the courtroom and judgment (cf. Matt. 10:32). Jesus confesses "to them," not "to you." He does not mean to frighten believers, but to awaken those who profess faith without having faith. He stirs up all who know *about* Jesus without knowing Jesus. Jesus aims the warning at false prophets and their followers, not at disciples.

"I never knew you." We have said that the false prophets do not know Jesus. More to the point, Jesus does not know them. This must not be taken too literally. In his deity, he knows all things. He is the judge of all the earth; he knows our every thought and deed (Matt. 25:31–46; Luke 5:22). He never has to ask, "And who might you be?" (cf. Luke 19:5). So then, "I never knew you" means "I never knew you as my child, as a member of my covenant family" (cf. Amos 3:2). Jesus says, "I am the good shepherd; I know my sheep and my sheep know me" (John 10:14). Paul says, "The Lord knows those who are his" (2 Tim. 2:19).

"Depart from me" is what Jesus, as judge, will say on the last day when he sends "evildoers" away from his presence (Matt. 7:23). From the beginning, since God banished Adam and Eve from the garden, this has been the essential punishment for rebellion. Jesus sends away "evildoers" (NIV) or "workers of lawlessness" (ESV). Since we all do evil, does Jesus send everyone away? No, he sends away evildoers who have no interest in repentance. Paul says, "Everyone who confesses the name of the Lord must turn away from wickedness" (2 Tim. 2:19; cf. Rev. 21:8). There is plenty of room in heaven for those who *were* immoral and idolaters (1 Cor. 6:9–11).

Let us pause to harvest our lesson. Notable as they are, prophecy and miracles do not possess supreme spiritual importance. In fact, spectacular deeds can call our attention away from the more pressing issues mentioned in Matthew 5–6: obedience to Jesus, sincere prayer, selfless giving to the poor, and a willingness to travel the narrow road, even if it promises hardship more than glory. Spectacular deeds do not demonstrate that a claim of faith is genuine. If they promote vanity and worldly glory, spectacles may be a curse.[5] Even if they bless others, they are guns with a strong recoil. They strike the adversary, but endanger those who wield them. At any rate, great deeds never grant entrance to the kingdom of God.

The Bible often warns that false leaders can perform wonders. But even believers can wrongly focus on them. Jesus told his disciples, "Do not rejoice that the spirits submit to you, but rejoice that your names are written in heaven" (Luke 10:20). And Paul said, "If I have the gift of prophecy and can fathom all mysteries . . . and if I have a faith that can move mountains, but have not love, I am nothing" (1 Cor. 13:2). We need to pay more attention to the heart than to prominent people and big performances. The quietest Christian may please God far more than the most public and visible church leader. Only God can fathom the works and the hearts of humanity.

We cannot overlook the alarm, the dire warnings in Matthew 7:21–23. Yet Jesus does not call his hearers to redouble their efforts, to ensure that knowledge produces action. On the contrary, he warns against vain activity. The question is: do you know Christ? How then do we know Christ, so that we "enter the kingdom of heaven" (Matt. 7:21)? Humble repentance and faith in Jesus open the door to eternal life. A man must first say, "I am a sinner." A sin is more than a mistake. Sin violates the law of God and offends him. A sinner does more than commit isolated misdeeds. To call oneself a sinner is to say, "These misdeeds are typical of me, not aberrations."

A sinner is unable to reform himself sufficiently to please God. People can change their patterns, of course. They can reform particular habits, such as smoking or cursing. But no one can lay aside all sin. We can change the way we sin. Someone who slouches may, after hearing a rebuke, change posture at once. But he will probably change from one kind of bad posture (slouching) to another (excessive rigidity). So too, sinners may change their behavior, but they never stop sinning.

Jesus is the Savior and Lord of sinners. He *can* save because he is God and has in himself the power to save. He *can* save because he is a man and bears, as a substitute for men, the punishment due to mankind. He *can* save because after he died for our sins, he rose, showing he has power over the last enemy, death. Jesus *will* save if we ask him to do so, on his terms. First, we admit our need of salvation. Second, we confess that we trust him as Savior. Third, we own him as Lord. That requires us to lay aside the old life that, like the boardwalk, seems so very safe, so very much under our control. Instead, we take the harder, riskier path. We choose the wild ocean because it is the truth. So we must choose between two paths. Jesus also says that we must choose between two foundations.

## TWO BUILDERS AND TWO FOUNDATIONS (7:24–27)

### Building on the Rock (7:24)

Jesus begins the concluding paragraph of the Sermon on the Mount by saying, "Therefore everyone who hears these words of mine and puts them into practice is like a wise man who built his house on the rock" (Matt. 7:24). The order of the words is a little different in the original Greek. In the Greek, Jesus' sentence goes this way: "Everyone therefore who hears me, these words, and does them. . . ." I am not suggesting that there is a flaw in our English translations, but the order in the Greek brings something to our attention: when we listen to the Sermon on the Mount, we do not simply hear Jesus' *words*. We hear *Jesus*.

When we speak, gaps open between our words and our person. We can lie and so deliberately misrepresent ourselves. We can change our minds, so that our past speech represents what we formerly believed, but not our current convictions. We can speak imprecisely and so accidentally misrepresent ourselves. There is a gap between the person and the words of every speaker—every speaker except Jesus.

Jesus' words perfectly express his character, his mind, his will. He never deceives, never changes his mind, never misspeaks. He never has to say, "Do as I say, not as I do." This world has all too many obese gym teachers, divorced marriage counselors, and debt-ridden financial planners. Not so with Jesus. He does what he says. He *is* what he says. Every word perfectly reflects his mind, his character, and his actions. Therefore, if we would be wise and godlike, we should listen attentively and do whatever Jesus says. His words will be a rock, a sure foundation for life.

Yet there is an odd word in Matthew 7:24. Jesus does not say that the wise man builds his house on "*a* rock." Rather, he says that the wise man builds his house on "*the* rock." What is "the rock"? Since Jesus has never mentioned rocks before, we wonder what rock he might have in mind. This is the kind of question we slip into our back pocket, where it rests until we come across the answer. Jesus answers this question much later, in Matthew 16. When Peter confesses to Jesus, "You are the Christ, the Son of the Living God" (v. 16), Jesus replies, "On this rock I will build my church" (v. 17).

### Standing Strong in the Storm (7:25–27)

Jesus says that two builders construct two houses on two foundations (Matt. 7:25–27). In dry weather, every building plan and every house looks sound. But when the rain comes, the rivers rise, and the winds blow, they reveal the quality of the work (7:25). If the catastrophes of life fall upon the solid house, it will not fall. But when troubles befall the house that rests on a flawed foundation, it will collapse.

Similarly, any creed or philosophy seems to work when life is easy. But when the storms of life beat upon us, those who build on Christ remain strong. A secular person may say, "I have faced many storms on my own and stayed strong." But what about the final storm, when life ends?

Everyone must ask, "What is the rock on which I build? Is my foundation sure?" The Bible says God is a rock, a refuge for his covenant people (Pss. 27:5; 31:2–3; 42:9; 62:1–7; 78:35; 92:15; 94:22). Jesus later says that he is the rock. He also says that the wise man "hears these words of mine and puts them into practice" (Matt. 7:24), whereas the foolish man hears them and does not put them into practice. His house collapses with a crash (7:26–27).

Why does Jesus end the Sermon on the Mount with the words "a great crash" (7:27)? This is hardly the upbeat way in which preachers typically end their sermons. But Jesus is making a point. It is not enough to study or applaud the words of Jesus. We must do what he says. Otherwise, we are in danger of hypocrisy, in danger of facing a great crash.

## The Authority of Jesus (7:28–29)

In his epilogue, Matthew comments that the crowds were amazed at Jesus' authority. "When Jesus had finished saying these things, the crowds were amazed at his teaching, because he taught as one who had authority, and not as their teachers of the law" (7:28–29). He spoke with royal assurance, with sovereign majesty. He legislated, on his own authority, the standards of life in God's kingdom. "Truly I say to you" is his distinctive statement. In Jesus' day, the rabbis constantly quoted earlier rabbis to corroborate their teachings. Today, adults quote noted experts and students validate their claims with footnotes.

Jesus challenged the old traditions that the scribes quoted. He was a legislator, not a commentator.[6] He spoke on his own authority, not the authority of others. He insisted on the supremacy of his teaching; the wise build their lives upon his word, for he is the Savior and Lord.

So we come again to the beach, to the choice. Shall we stay on the boardwalk, taking the safe and tame and predictable path? Shall we live like the masses, minimizing risks, refusing to face the wildness of this vast creation? Or shall we take the narrow road, drinking in the pounding surf and the grandeur of God and his creation? If we take that road, we never know where we are going. But we do know the one whom we follow.

# NOTES

## Chapter 1: Reading and Interpreting the Sermon on the Mount

1. W. D. Davies, *The Setting of the Sermon on the Mount* (Atlanta, GA: Scholars Press, 1989), 95.

2. For the history of its interpretation, see Robert Guelich, *The Sermon on the Mount* (Waco, TX: Word, 1982), 14–22; G. N. Stanton, "Sermon on the Mount/Plain," in *Dictionary of Jesus and the Gospels*, ed. Joel Green, Scot McKnight, and I. H. Marshall (Downers Grove, IL: InterVarsity Press, 1992), 735–44.

3. See Thomas Aquinas, *Summa Theologica*, trans. Fathers of the English Dominican Province (New York: Benziger Brothers, 1947–48), 1:1118–19.

4. Martin Luther, *Luther's Works*, vol. 21: *The Sermon on the Mount (Sermons) and the Magnificat*, ed. Jaroslav Pelikan (Saint Louis: Concordia Publishing House, 1956), 73.

5. There are, from a technical or morphological perspective, fifty imperatives, but, in addition, at least five future indicatives function as commands (5:21, 27, 33, 43, 48). Subjunctives, infinitives, and participles can also function as imperatives on rare occasion.

6. The sermon has 204 indicative verbs, 67 subjunctives, 24 infinitives, and about 25 adverbial participles. Again, five indicatives function as imperatives. Further, if a sentence has one subjunctive and one imperative, the whole probably functions as an imperative. Still, 320 of the 370 verbs are not imperatives.

7. It may seem simplistic merely to count verb forms, since meaning lies in sentences. But an effort to evaluate whether a sentence is imperatival or not faces several problems. First, Greek and English have somewhat different concepts of a sentence. Second, some sentences are technically imperatival, even though their thrust is not (e.g., 5:17), while others are not technically imperatival, though their thrust seems to be (e.g., 5:22). Third, how should we evaluate sentences that quote an Old Testament passage that has a future indicative functioning as an imperative, but which do not require obedience to the quoted statement (e.g., 5:31, 33)? Given all these uncertainties, a count of verbs is still useful, even if not especially sophisticated.

8. John Stott, *Christian Counter-Culture: The Message of the Sermon on the Mount* (Downers Grove, IL: InterVarsity Press, 1978), 29.

9. Passive phrases such as "it will be given" and "the door will be opened" are divine passives. When a verb is passive and no agent is specified, God is typically the understood agent. There are about 150 divine passives in the Gospels, with at least eight in our sermon. The Gospels use divine passives to respect a first-century Jewish custom. The Jews avoided taking God's name in vain by avoiding the name altogether. See Joachim Jeremias, *New Testament Theology* (New York: Macmillan, 1970), 10–11.

## Chapter 2: A Blessed Character

1. Wayne Joosse, "With Friends like This . . . ," *Reformed Journal*, April 1989, 9.

## Chapter 3: Character and Its Consequences

1. Aristotle, "Nicomachean Ethics," in *The Basic Works of Aristotle*, ed. Richard McKeon (New York: Random House, 1941), 952–53.

2. See Daniel Doriani, *Putting the Truth to Work* (Phillipsburg, NJ: P&R Publishing, 2001), 105–9.

3. See Richard Brookhiser, *Washington* (New York: Free Press, 1996), 121–32.

4. John Piper, *Future Grace* (Sisters, OR: Multnomah, 1995), 85–86.

5. D. A. Carson, *The Sermon on the Mount: An Evangelical Exposition of Matthew 5–7* (Grand Rapids: Baker, 1978), 55.

6. Edwin Black, *IBM and the Holocaust* (New York: Crown Publishers, 2001).

7. William R. Hawkins, "Commerce über Alles," *The Weekly Standard*, April 9, 2001.

## Chapter 4: Four Results of a Blessed Life

1. D. A. Carson, "Matthew," in *The Expositor's Bible Commentary*, vol. 8 (Grand Rapids: Zondervan, 1984), 137.

2. Mark Kurlansky, *Salt: A World History* (New York: Penguin, 2002).

## Chapter 5: Be Still, O Angry Heart

1. *The Mishnah*, trans. Herbert Danby (New York: Oxford University Press, 1933), 446 (*Aboth* 1:5, 7).

2. Helpful readings include: Leon Kass, *Life, Liberty, and the Defense of Dignity* (San Francisco: Encounter Books, 2002); Gilbert Meilaender, *Bioethics: A Primer for Christians* (Grand Rapids: Eerdmans, 2004); Stephen Lammers and Alan Verhey, eds., *On Moral Medicine: Theological Perspectives in Medical Ethics* (Grand Rapids: Eerdmans, 1998).

## Chapter 6: Be Still, O Wandering Eye

1. D. A. Carson, "Matthew," in *The Expositor's Bible Commentary*, vol. 8 (Grand Rapids: Zondervan, 1984), 151.

2. John Stott, *Christian Counter-Culture: The Message of the Sermon on the Mount* (Downers Grove, IL: InterVarsity Press, 1978), 88.

3. In the Greek of 5:27–28, the verb *moicheuō* means "to commit adultery" in the narrow sense. (The sister verb *moichaomai* and the noun *moicheia* also refer to adultery, narrowly defined.) A broader term, *porneia*, covers all sexual sin. Jesus forbids *porneia* explicitly in Matt. 15:19 and implicitly in 5:32 and 19:9.

4. See the unparalleled work by Robert Gagnon, *The Bible and Homosexual Practice: Text and Hermeneutics* (Nashville: Abingdon, 2001).

5. Lewis Smedes, *Sex for Christians: The Limits and Liberties of Sexual Living*, rev. ed. (Grand Rapids: Eerdmans, 1994), 97–116.

6. Ibid., 105–6.

7. Ibid., 110–11.

8. David Brooks, "Patio Man and the Sprawl People," *The Weekly Standard*, August 12–19, 2002, 20.

9. Stott, *Christian Counter-Culture*, 88.

10. Craig Keener, *Matthew* (Grand Rapids: Eerdmans, 1999), 187–88. Keener rightly notes that this text "indicates Jesus' belief in the bodily resurrection of the damned for torment" (n. 83).

11. *The Mishnah*, trans. Herbert Danby (New York: Oxford University Press, 1933), 321 (*Gittin* 9:10).

## Chapter 7: To Tell the Truth

1. For a sample of rabbinic regulations of oaths, see *The Mishnah*, trans. Herbert Danby (New York: Oxford University Press, 1933), 385 (*Sanhedrin* 3:2), 411–20 (*Shebuoth* 3:1–7:8).

2. Josephus, *The Wars of the Jews*, in *The Works of Josephus*, trans. William Whiston (Peabody, MA: Hendrickson, 1987), 2.135 (p. 606).

3. John Stott, *Christian Counter-Culture: The Message of the Sermon on the Mount* (Downers Grove, IL: InterVarsity Press, 1978), 101.

4. One hint that oaths are inferior is that most New Testament oaths are rash (Matt. 14:7; 23:16–18; 26:72; Acts 23:12–21).

5. Frances Goodrich and Albert Hackett, *The Diary of Anne Frank* (New York: Random House, 1956), 47.

## Chapter 8: Do Not Resist Evil

1. On Israel's penal code, see Christopher Wright, *An Eye for an Eye* (Downers Grove, IL: InterVarsity Press, 1983), 152–53, 163–73. I apply these principles to parenting in *The Life of a God-Made Man* (Wheaton, IL: Crossway, 2001), 97–99, and to restitution for theft in *Putting the Truth to Work* (Phillipsburg, NJ: P&R Publishing, 2001), 243–45.

2. The *lex talionis* also protects victims, since criminals make restitution to them, not to the state. It bars both sentimentality and wrath from the judicial arena (Deut. 13:8; 19:13; 32:35).

3. The Greek word in Gal. 2:11 is the same as in James 4:7 and 1 Peter 5:9: *anthistēmi*.

4. N. T. Wright, *Jesus and the Victory of God* (Minneapolis: Fortress Press, 1996), 290–91; Joachim Jeremias, *The Sermon on the Mount*, trans. Norman Perrin (Philadelphia: Fortress Press, 1963), 28–29.

5. Epictetus, *Discourses*, trans. W. A. Oldfather (Cambridge, MA: Harvard University Press, 1966), 4.1.79 (p. 269).

6. W. D. Davies and Dale C. Allison Jr., *A Critical and Exegetical Commentary on the Gospel According to Saint Matthew*, International Critical Commentary, 3 vols. (Edinburgh: T & T Clark, 1988–97), 1:546.

7. Timothy Keller, *Ministries of Mercy*, 2d ed. (Phillipsburg, NJ: P&R Publishing, 1997), 194–95.

## Chapter 9: Love Your Enemies

1. W. D. Davies and Dale C. Allison Jr., *A Critical and Exegetical Commentary on the Gospel According to Saint Matthew*, International Critical Commentary, 3 vols. (Edinburgh: T & T Clark, 1988–97), 1:552.

2. D. A. Carson, "Matthew," in *The Expositor's Bible Commentary*, vol. 8 (Grand Rapids: Zondervan, 1984), 158; John Stott, *Christian Counter-Culture: The Message of the Sermon on the Mount* (Downers Grove, IL: InterVarsity Press, 1978), 119.

3. Augustine, *Homilies on the Gospel of John*, trans. John Gibb, in *The Nicene and Post-Nicene Fathers*, vol. 7 (Grand Rapids: Eerdmans, 1956), 411.

4. See Daniel Doriani, *Putting the Truth to Work* (Phillipsburg, NJ: P&R Publishing, 2001), 46–47, 201–6.

5. Matthew divides mankind into two classes, the evil and the good, the righteous and the unrighteous. See also 7:13–27; 13:11–17; 22:10. Like much wisdom literature, Matthew ignores shades of gray to put readers to the test: which side are you on?

6. Alfred Plummer, *An Exegetical Commentary on the Gospel According to S. Matthew* (1910; reprint, Grand Rapids: Eerdmans, 1956), 89.

7. Some see a problem here. Matthew says Jesus reached out to tax collectors and commanded his disciples to evangelize pagans. How then can Jesus belittle them so casually? But there is no contradiction. First, Jesus is communicating to his generation. Whatever he thought of tax collectors and pagans, his original audience despised them. Second, Jesus can critique their behavior without despising their person. Third, Jesus can reach out to them as people, while disapproving of their conduct. In fact, their very weakness draws Jesus to them. Jesus came to heal the sick, not the healthy (Matt. 9:12). He both disapproves and reaches out.

8. Frederick Buechner, *The Magnificent Defeat* (New York: Harper & Row, 1966), 105.

9. See chapter 1 on imperatives in the sermon.

10. D. Martyn Lloyd-Jones, *Studies in the Sermon on the Mount*, 2 vols. (Grand Rapids: Eerdmans, 1959–60), 2:9.

## Chapter 10: Holy One or Hypocrite?

1. Jesus does not specifically charge the Pharisees with hypocrisy, but they fit the description. Prayers, alms, and fasting marked pious Jews, and the Pharisees strove to be very pious. Jesus also associates giving, praying, and fasting with the Pharisees, whom he calls hypocrites (Matt. 23). Luke also says that the desire for recognition was typical of Pharisees (Luke 14; 18).

2. D. A. Carson, *The Sermon on the Mount: An Evangelical Exposition of Matthew 5–7* (Grand Rapids: Baker, 1978), 55.

3. Henri Nouwen, *In the Name of Jesus: Reflections on Christian Leadership* (New York: Crossroad, 1989), 20.

4. Krister Stendahl, "Biblical Theology, Contemporary," in *Interpreter's Bible Dictionary*, ed. George A. Buttrick et al. (Nashville: Abingdon, 1962), 1:419–22.

5. Michael Polanyi, *Personal Knowledge* (Chicago: University of Chicago Press, 1968), 49–57.

6. John Stott, *Christian Counter-Culture: The Message of the Sermon on the Mount* (Downers Grove, IL: InterVarsity Press, 1978), 126–27.

7. C. S. Lewis, *The Weight of Glory and Other Essays* (New York: Macmillan, 1949); Stott, *Christian Counter-Culture*, 132.

8. See chapter 13 for a full discussion of fasting.

9. D. Martyn Lloyd-Jones, *Studies in the Sermon on the Mount*, 2 vols. (Grand Rapids: Eerdmans, 1959–60), 1:24–26.

## Chapter 11: The Disciple's Prayer

1. John Stott, *Christian Counter-Culture: The Message of the Sermon on the Mount* (Downers Grove, IL: InterVarsity Press, 1978), 143–45.

## Chapter 12: The Lord's Prayer: Our Petitions

1. John Stott, *Christian Counter-Culture: The Message of the Sermon on the Mount* (Downers Grove, IL: InterVarsity Press, 1978), 144.

2. John Calvin, *Commentary on a Harmony of the Evangelists, Matthew, Mark, and Luke*, trans. William Pringle, 3 vols. (reprint, Grand Rapids: Baker Book House, 1979), 1:314.

3. John Frame, *No Other God* (Phillipsburg, NJ: P&R Publishing, 2001), 161–78.

4. Stott, *Christian Counter-Culture*, 149–50.

5. I have not commented on the final phrase of the Lord's Prayer, as most Christians recite it, "For thine is the kingdom and the power and the glory forever. Amen." The sentence is omitted from most modern translations (e.g., NIV, ESV, RSV; NASB and NKJV include it) because all of the earliest and best New Testament manuscripts omit it. Virtually all scholars conclude that it is not part of Matthew's original text. See Bruce M. Metzger, *A Textual Commentary on the Greek New Testament* (London: United Bible Societies, 1971), 16–17.

## Chapter 13: Food, Fasts, and Feasts

1. The next segment follows John Piper, *A Hunger for God* (Wheaton, IL: Crossway, 1997), 14–45.

2. Ibid., 14.

3. Ibid.

4. Quoted by Richard Foster, *The Celebration of Discipline* (New York: Harper and Row, 1978), 41.

5. John Stott, *Christian Counter-Culture: The Message of the Sermon on the Mount* (Downers Grove, IL: InterVarsity Press, 1978), 71–72.

6. C. S. Lewis, *The Problem of Pain* (New York: Macmillan, 1944), 112.

7. D. Martyn Lloyd-Jones, *Studies in the Sermon on the Mount*, 2 vols. (Grand Rapids: Eerdmans, 1959–60), 2:38.

8. Let me answer a few of the most common questions for readers who want to start fasting:

*Should we drink water?* Yes. Spiritual leaders recommend normal hydration.

*How long should we fast?* A typical fast may last twenty-four hours. Some fast for several days, some for one or two meals. This is different from skipping a meal since it has a spiritual purpose.

*What about headaches?* Fasting can lead to headaches, especially for those who depend on caffeine in the morning. If so, a pain reliever is sensible.

*How do we plan fasts?* Some people find it helpful to schedule a fast, so they do not go years without practicing this discipline. Others fast on special occasions, when facing great needs or great decisions. The form of a fast matters less than the desire to focus on the Lord.

9. Foster, *The Celebration of Discipline*, 48.

10. Piper, *A Hunger for God*, 19–21.

11. Ibid., 23.

## Chapter 14: God or Mammon

1. To be precise, 2 Cor. 8:2 and 9:13 uses the cognate noun *haplotēs*, meaning "generosity" or "liberality," and James 1:5 uses the cognate adverb *haplōs*, meaning "generously."

2. The evil eye (*ponēros ophthalmos*) is a greedy or stingy disposition in Matt. 20:15; Luke 11:34; Deut. 15:9. The good eye (*agathos ophthalmos*) is a generous disposition in Deut. 28:54, 56; Prov. 23:6. The Old Testament references are to the Greek translation of the Old Testament used in Jesus' day, called the Septuagint.

3. Gordon Dahl, *Work, Play, and Worship in a Leisure-Oriented Society* (Minneapolis: Augsburg, 1972), 20, cf. 11–23.

4. R. V. G. Tasker, *The Gospel According to St. Matthew*, Tyndale New Testament Commentaries (Grand Rapids: Eerdmans, 1961), 76.

5. For a short theology of mammon, see Jacques Ellul, *Money and Power*, trans. LaVonne Neff (Downers Grove, IL: InterVarsity Press, 1984), 94–97.

6. The term *mammon* probably originates from the Aramaic *aman*, "trust." The prefix *m-* makes it a substantive: that which one trusts. It is a most suitable term for money, viewed as a rival deity. See F. Hauck, "*mamōnas*," in *Theological Dictionary of the New Testament*, vol. 4, ed. Gerhard Kittel, trans. Geoffrey W. Bromiley (Grand Rapids: Eerdmans, 1967), 388–90. See also W. D. Davies and Dale C. Allison Jr., *A Critical and Exegetical Commentary on the Gospel According to Saint Matthew*, International Critical Commentary, 3 vols. (Edinburgh: T & T Clark, 1988–97), 1:641–42.

7. Ellul, *Money and Power*, 30–31.

## Chapter 15: Not Worry but Trust

1. W. D. Davies and Dale C. Allison Jr., *A Critical and Exegetical Commentary on the Gospel According to Saint Matthew*, International Critical Commentary, 3 vols. (Edinburgh: T & T Clark, 1988–97), 1:652.

2. William S. Babcock, "*Cupiditas* and *Caritas*: The Early Augustine on Love and Fulfillment," in *Augustine Today*, ed. Richard John Neuhaus (Grand Rapids: Eerdmans, 1993), 32.

3. Davies and Allison, *Matthew*, 1:653.

4. Both "watch" (*emblepō*) and "observe" (*katamanthanō*) invite concentrated observation and deduction.

5. Cited in John Stott, *Christian Counter-Culture: The Message of the Sermon on the Mount* (Downers Grove, IL: InterVarsity Press, 1978), 167–68, to whom I owe the quotation and the larger point.

6. The translation merits several comments. (1) The Greek words for "run after" (*epizeteō*) in 6:32 and "seek" (*zeteō*) in 6:33 are etymologically related. (2) There is a well-supported textual variant in 6:33; "the kingdom of God" is probably the correct reading, not "his kingdom." (3) The verb "will be given" is a divine passive; it means "God will give." The verb might also be translated "added." (4) The NIV gratuitously adds "as well" at the end of the verse. There are no corresponding terms in the original.

## Chapter 16: "Judge Not" and the Right Use of the Law

1. P. J. O'Rourke, "The Backside of War," *Atlantic Monthly*, December 2003, 71–84.

2. Douglas Groothius, *Truth Decay: Defending Christianity Against the Challenges of Postmodernism* (Downers Grove, IL: InterVarsity Press, 2000), 20–26.

3. Leon Morris, *The Gospel According to Matthew* (Grand Rapids: Eerdmans, Eerdmans, 1992), 164.

4. Jesus sometimes used the divine passive as a concession to the sensibilities of his audience.

5. This interpretation was advanced by Thomas J. Bennett, "Matthew 7:6—A New Interpretation," *Westminster Theological Journal* 49 (1987): 371–86.

6. Morris, *Matthew*, 244.

7. John Calvin, *Commentary on a Harmony of the Evangelists, Matthew, Mark, and Luke*, trans. William Pringle, 3 vols. (reprint, Grand Rapids: Baker Book House, 1979), 1:349.

8. Prosperity theology also neglects biblical teachings about suffering and poverty. It insults Christians who suffer persecution in hostile lands. It insults all who are poor due to forces outside their control. It "explains" that their difficulties are due to weakness or unfaithfulness.

9. John A. Broadus, *Commentary on the Gospel of Matthew* (Valley Forge, PA: American Baptist Publication Society, 1886), 162.

## Chapter 17: Ask and It Will Be Given

1. Biblical poetry is not recognized by rhyme and meter, but by structured repetition and variation, as in Matt. 7:7–8 (though not printed as poetry in the NIV). See Robert Stein, *The Method and Message of Jesus* (Louisville: Westminster John Knox Press, 1994), 26–31; Joachim Jeremias, *New Testament Theology* (New York: Scribners, 1971), 14–22; James Kugel, *The Idea of Biblical Poetry* (New Haven: Yale University Press, 1981); Robert Alter, *The Art of Biblical Poetry* (New York: Basic Books, 1985).

2. As noted in the previous chapter, this statement employs a convention of Jewish speech called the divine passive.

3. Martin Luther, *Luther's Works*, vol. 21: *The Sermon on the Mount (Sermons) and the Magnificat*, ed. Jaroslav Pelikan (Saint Louis: Concordia Publishing House, 1956), 234.

4. He uses the particle *mē*, which anticipates a negative answer to a question: "Surely, no father would give his child a stone or a snake, would he?"

5. John Calvin, *Commentary on a Harmony of the Evangelists, Matthew, Mark, and Luke,* trans. William Pringle, 3 vols. (reprint, Grand Rapids: Baker Book House, 1979), 1:353.

6. If parents wonder when children can begin to attend worship and profit from it, let us propose that a child who can attend school all day can attend worship for an hour.

7. Calvin, *Commentary on a Harmony of the Evangelists,* 1:355.

## Chapter 18: Two Ways of Life

1. Colleen Carroll, *The New Faithful: Why Young Adults Are Embracing Christian Orthodoxy* (Chicago: Loyola Press, 2002), 25–27.

2. An indignant visitor once accosted me after a sermon: "How can you live in the twenty-first century and believe such things?" I replied that truth is not dependent on the calendar. She could not grasp my meaning, although she was a professor at a leading university.

3. W. D. Davies and Dale C. Allison Jr., *A Critical and Exegetical Commentary on the Gospel According to Saint Matthew,* International Critical Commentary, 3 vols. (Edinburgh: T & T Clark, 1988–97), 1:697.

4. Kevin J. Vanhoozer, *Is There a Meaning in This Text?* (Grand Rapids: Zondervan, 1998), 55–58, 100–101; Douglas Groothius, *Truth Decay* (Downers Grove, IL: InterVarsity Press, 2000), 20, 197–202; Richard Rorty, *Philosophy and the Mirror of Nature* (New York: Cambridge University Press, 1989), 176; Richard Rorty, *Contingency, Irony, and Solidarity* (New York: Cambridge University Press, 1989), 73–75, 97–99, 189.

5. Aristotle, "Metaphysics," in *The Basic Works of Aristotle,* ed. Richard McKeon (New York: Random House, 1941), 689.

6. T. S. Eliot, *Murder in the Cathedral* (New York: Harcourt, Brace & World, 1963), 69.

7. John Stott, *Christian Counter-Culture: The Message of the Sermon on the Mount* (Downers Grove, IL: InterVarsity Press, 1978), 196.

## Chapter 19: The Pounding Surf and the Neon Boardwalk

1. W. D. Davies and Dale C. Allison Jr., *A Critical and Exegetical Commentary on the Gospel According to Saint Matthew,* International Critical Commentary, 3 vols. (Edinburgh: T & T Clark, 1988–97), 1:693–94. The two passages shares six key words, including *prophet/prophesy, know, do,* and *cast/throw* in the Greek, although some do not show in English translations.

2. John Calvin, *Commentary on a Harmony of the Evangelists, Matthew, Mark, and Luke*, trans. William Pringle, 3 vols. (reprint, Grand Rapids: Baker Book House, 1979), 1:367–68.

3. John Stott, *Christian Counter-Culture: The Message of the Sermon on the Mount* (Downers Grove, IL: InterVarsity Press, 1978), 206–7.

4. Thomas Jefferson, letter to John Adams, cited in Stephen Mitchell, *The Gospel According to Jesus* (New York: Harper Perennial, 1991), 4–5.

5. Davies and Allison, *Matthew*, 1:716.

6. Stott, *Christian Counter-Culture*, 215.

# Index of Scripture

**Daniel M. Doriani** (M.Div., Ph.D., Westminster Theological Seminary; S.T.M., Yale Divinity School) is senior pastor of Central Presbyterian Church, Clayton, Missouri. He previously was dean of faculty and professor of New Testament at Covenant Theological Seminary. He is a frequent speaker at conferences and seminars, and is the author of several books, including *Getting the Message: A Plan for Interpreting and Applying the Bible*; *Putting the Truth to Work: The Theory and Practice of Biblical Application*; and *James*, in the Reformed Expository Commentary series.